TEACHING
1 SAMUEL

From text to message

ANDREW REID

SERIES EDITORS: JON GEMMELL & DAVID JACKMAN

PT RESOURCES

CHRISTIAN
FOCUS

Unless otherwise indicated all Scripture quotations are taken from *The Holy Bible, New International Version*. Copyright © 1973, 1978, 1984 by International Bible Society. Used by permission of Hodder & Stoughton Publishers, a member of the Hodder Headline Group. All rights reserved. 'NIV' is a registered trademark of International Bible Society. UK trademark number 1448790.

Scripture quotations marked ESV are from *The Holy Bible, English Standard Version*, copyright © 2001 by Crossway Bibles, a division of Good News Publishers. Used by permission. All rights reserved.

Copyright © Proclamation Trust Media 2020

ISBN: 978-1-5271-0532-4

10 9 8 7 6 5 4 3 2 1

Published in 2020
by
Christian Focus Publications Ltd.,
Geanies House, Fearn, Ross-shire,
IV20 1TW, Scotland, Great Britain
with
Proclamation Trust Resources,
Willcox House, 140-148 Borough High Street,
London, SE1 1LB, England, Great Britain.
www.proctrust.org.uk

www.christianfocus.com

Cover design by Moose77.com

Printed and bound by
Bell & Bain, Glasgow

All rights reserved. No part of this publication may be reproduced, stored in a retrieval system, or transmitted, in any form, by any means, electronic, mechanical, photocopying, recording or otherwise without the prior permission of the publisher or a license permitting restricted copying. In the U.K. such licenses are issued by the Copyright Licensing Agency, Saffron House, 6-10 Kirby Street, London, EC1 8TS www.cla.co.uk.

This is an excellent book in a great series. It will foster preaching that is firmly grounded in the text, richly theological and viewing the book as an important part of Christian scripture. It is biblical theology at its best. ... There are great insights here about why we should teach from these rich narratives. Andrew builds on his earlier commentary and a lifetime of powerful preaching to provide a major resource for the church as it gathers around the word. It contains great practical help and advice aimed at both preachers and bible study leaders. This book is pure gold, making it a 'must have' if you want to teach others how to teach God's truth from narrative.

Lindsay Wilson
Senior Lecturer in Old Testament, Ridley College,
Melbourne

I have benefitted significantly from Andrew Reid's teaching and thinking on the books on Samuel for many years – what a rich provision for preachers and bible study leaders to have this comprehensive teaching guide! The format of this series suits Andrew's approach down to the ground – he summarises the scholarship on the books with a beautifully delicate touch, moves smoothly into the vital task of breaking up the book, and backs that up with a wealth of exegetical insight, embedded seamlessly in insights for teaching. This will be an invaluable (and should be a compulsory!) companion for anyone teaching 1st Samuel... and bring on 2nd Samuel!

Gary Millar
Principal, Queensland Theological College, Queensland,
Australia

It is so good to have the fruit of Andrew Reid's study of 1 Samuel now applied to how to be preaching this Old Testament book. Here we have an experienced guide helping us study God's Word carefully: there are no pre-packaged sermons (or Bible studies), but instead you will find yourself motivated to look again at the biblical text more carefully.

Neil Watkinson
International Director, Proclamation Trust

The Scriptures urge us to delight in God's words and meditate on them. In this book we see the wonderful results of such delight and such meditation over many years. Andrew Reid generously shares his insights into the text of 1 Samuel, enriched by biblical theology, and with practical advice for preachers and Bible study leaders. Not a word is wasted, and just the right amount in information is provided. A good book for personal Bible study, as well as for those who preach and teach.

Peter Adam
Vicar Emeritus of St Jude's Carlton, Melbourne
Former Principal of Ridley College

Andrew Reid has given us an excellent resource for preaching 1 Samuel. Built on years of studying, commentary writing and preaching in a church, Andrew is supremely well qualified for this task. The book blends the fruit of serious academic study and countless gems of wisdom for expounding this important book. ... Indeed, anyone who reads Andrew's book can have little excuse for making a mess of an exposition of 1 Samuel.

Mike Raiter
Director of the Centre for Biblical Preaching
Author of several books, including *Stirrings of the Soul*

Contents

Series Preface 9

Author's Preface 11

How to use this Book 13

Part One: Introducing 1 Samuel 17

   1. Getting Our Bearings in Samuel 19
   2. Why Should We Preach and Teach Samuel? 41
   3. Planning to Preach on Samuel 53

Part Two: The Rise of Samuel and Kingship
(1 Samuel 1:1–8:22) 59

   4. The Story of Hannah
     (1 Samuel 1:1-28; 2:11) 61
   5. The Prayer of Hannah
     (1 Samuel 2:1-10) 77
   6. Samuel's Rise and Eli's Demise
     (1 Samuel 2:12-36) 93
   7. Famine and Fullness (1 Samuel 3:1-21) 109
   8. The Story of the Ark
     (Part 1: 1 Samuel 4:1–5:12) 123
   9. The Story of the Ark
     (Part 2: 1 Samuel 6:1–7:17) 145
  10. Moves Toward Monarchy
     (1 Samuel 8:1-22) 163

Part Three: The Beginning and End of Saul's
Kingship (1 Samuel 9:1–31:13) 179

11. Israel's First Human King
    (1 Samuel 9:1–11:13) 181
12. King and Covenant
    (1 Samuel 11:14–12:25) 201
13. The Reign of Saul as King
    (1 Samuel 13:1–14:52) 217
14. The Rejection of Saul as King
    (1 Samuel 15:1-35) 235
15. The Anointing of David
    (1 Samuel 16:1-23) 253
16. Seeing as God Sees
    (1 Samuel 17:1–18:5) 271
17. Saul's Alienation
    (1 Samuel 18:6–19:24) 289
18. Covenants, Fugitives, and Strange
    Bedfellows (1 Samuel 20:1–23:28) 305
19. Encounters in the Life of a Fugitive
    Anointed One (1 Samuel 24:1–26:25).. 325
20. David in Philistia (1 Samuel 27:1–31:13)... 343

Further Reading..359

For …

Mum (Wendy Reid), a godly and beloved example of simple but deep and steadfast faith in Christ in adversity and of sacrifice and generosity.

Series Preface

The book of 1 Samuel is a blockbuster. Whilst some parts of the Old Testament are sadly neglected, 1 Samuel is a staple.

The gripping narrative is dominated by big characters and they can easily eclipse what is going on in the book as a whole and the vital part it plays in the unfolding story of the Bible. Our hope is that this volume will be very useful to preachers as they seek to open up this book for their congregations in its entirety. Andrew Reid has been studying 1 Samuel for many years; his guiding hand as the pages of 1 Samuel are opened will be of great assistance.

This volume, like all in the series, is written with the preacher, Bible teacher and Bible student in mind. Part One, the introductory section, contains lots of important information to help us get a handle on the book of 1 Samuel, covering aspects like structure, place in the Biblical story, how to plan a preaching series, as well as lots of encouragements to give yourself to the task of preaching and studying 1 Samuel.

Then Part Two works through the book, giving insight into the text and the content of each preaching unit. As well as introductory material and analysis of the content of each section, there is also special attention given to biblical theology, theological themes and application – all to help the preacher get a firm grip on the passages. Each of the chapters finishes with some sermon outlines and also how you might lead a Bible study on the section. These are not there to take the hard work out of preparation but to be a helping hand as people invest their time, efforts and gifts in preparing to teach the Bible to others.

Teaching 1 Samuel brings the number of published volumes in this series to twenty-two. From the comments we hear from people involved in regular Bible teaching and preaching ministry, we are encouraged by how well this series is developing. We long for these books to help people to keep working hard at the Word in order that they might proclaim the unsearchable riches of Christ ever more clearly.

Our thanks go to Christian Focus for their continued partnership in this project. Without their faith, expertise, enthusiasm and patience, none of these books would ever make it on to the bookshelf.

Jon Gemmell &
David Jackman
Series Editors
London 2020

Author's Preface

It was the first year of my first assistant pastor position. In theological college, we had been fortunate in being set the 'succession narrative' (2 Samuel 9–20) for our Old Testament set text. I became hooked gradually but very evidently as David, the golden boy of 1 Samuel 17 –2 Samuel 5, came under the less positive exposure of the author's writing.

Then came the gift from my senior pastor, Allen Quee – I could choose and structure the sermon series that I preached to the youth at the evening services. There was no competition in my mind, it must be those tantalising passages from 2 Samuel 9 to the end of the book. While preaching I discovered the narrative-critical work of Jan Fokkelman and windows into new worlds were opened. The 'man after God's own heart' (1 Sam. 13:14) who was 'better than' Saul (1 Sam. 15:28) was indeed a *type* of our Saviour, the Lord Jesus, the Christ, but David was not perfect. He too was a descendant of Adam and Eve, made mistakes, was manipulative, had flaws as a father, and doubted God's goodness. Thus I began a lifelong love-affair with the books of Samuel which I have now preached to a variety of congregations in different contexts, written light commentaries and assorted Bible studies, as well as tirelessly trying out ideas in endless conversations with my wife, Heather.

It was therefore with enormous delight that I accepted the task from the Proclamation Trust to turn those years of fun into a book for fellow preachers and I offer it here in thankfulness to God for His Word about His Christ in 1 and 2 Samuel and in even greater thanks for 'Great David's greater Son!'[1]

I must also express my appreciation for permission from my friends at Aquila Press, who have generously allowed the use of material from *Hope for the Helpless*, my commentary on 1 and 2 Samuel in the 'Reading the Bible Today' series. 'Reading the Bible Today' is a wonderful series, rich in biblical theology and the team have been great to work with over many years in a variety of projects.

---

1. James Montgomery, 'Hail to the Lord's Anointed' in *Songs of Zion*, Longman: Longman, Hurst, Rees, Orme, and Brown, 1882, pp. 59-63.

How to use this Book

This book has clear goals. These may first be defined in relation to what it is not. Although it is based on full exegetical exploration of the text of Samuel, it is not a commentary. Although it is based on sermons actually preached, it does not seek to give you pre-packaged sermons and outlines that you can just regurgitate or make your own.

Instead, the goals of this book are:

1. To help you think through how you might preach or teach the entire book of Samuel in a way that is consistent with its purpose as a whole.

2. To understand the central aim of its individual parts within this overall purpose and to be able to preach those parts so that people might be built up in their knowledge and love of God, learn more of His ways and be encouraged to 'the obedience of faith' (Rom. 1:5; 16:26 ESV).

To help preachers and teachers understand and communicate how both (1) and (2) might be done in a way that is sensitive to God's overarching purposes in Christ.

Volume 1 (1 Samuel 1–31)

Given the length of the books of Samuel, these purposes have necessarily involved producing two volumes which belong together. The first volume is comprised of a number of parts. 'Part One: Introductory Material' introduces the book and how it should be read in a way that is consistent with its nature and origin. It also outlines the purpose and structure of the books of Samuel as well as briefly surveying technical matters such as date, authorship, and text.

Following this, we survey the challenges facing the preacher and teacher of Samuel, as well as some encouragement that we glean from the New Testament as to how and why we might overcome those challenges. There are significant and particular problems faced by those preaching Samuel; I have chosen not to address them in this chapter but as they occur in the text.

The temptation for many will be to skip over Part One. However, succumbing to this temptation should be avoided as it provides an essential orientation to the book as a whole as well as outlining the issues and shape of all that will follow.

Parts Two and Three make up the first volume of this two-volume survey of 'Teaching Samuel'. They contain separate chapters on each of the preaching units that have been identified in Part 1 that might make up a series of studies or sermons on the book.

The structure of each chapter is much the same. There is a brief introduction to the unit followed by a section called 'Listening to the Text'. This section outlines the structure and content of the unit and takes the reader through an overview of the text. This is the heart of each of these chapters and arises out of the conviction that all good biblical teaching and preaching arises out of careful and detailed listening to the text.

The second section of each chapter consists of a section called 'Listening to the Whole of Scripture'. This is where we engage in the task of biblical theology, exploring how the theology underlying this section fits into the theology of the Bible as a whole which has its centre and end in Jesus Christ.

The third section of each chapter is called 'From Text to Message'. This section looks at some of the matters faced before you actually get to considering how you will preach the passage or draw up an outline. These include the main theme and aim of the passage and some possible ways to introduce the sermon. This is also where ideas for application might be considered.

The fourth section is called 'Suggestions for Preaching'. This may differ for each section of the text under scrutiny but will often consist of outlining one or more ways in which a sermon might be constructed, mostly without actually providing an outline. The reasons for not providing an outline is to allow creativity and stifle laziness on our part, and possible boredom on the part of our hearers. Preaching is a lively interaction between the text of Scripture and a living group of people with whom the preacher is familiar. An outline that has been constructed by you for your context is likely to have more power than one you copy that I designed for my context.

The final section in each chapter is called 'Leading a Bible Study'. This will be variously structured but is generally designed to do the key elements of all group Bible study, that is, observation, interpretation, and application. It is not intended that these questions necessarily supply all the input needed for the study, but they will be indicative of the sorts of questions needed for those planning a study series. I have also tried to vary the structure in order to give relief and ideas as to how such studies might be structured.

Because these questions for leading a Bible study arise out of work done in earlier sections of the book, they will be particularly helpful for those situations where study groups are studying in tandem with the sermon series. Such a practice is to be warmly commended as it allows small groups to drive home understanding and application in a way that is consistent and coheres with the direction of the preaching. It also allows lively interaction and opportunity for exploration and discussion that is not often available in the more formal church service context.

A Final Note

Finally, as indicated at the beginning, this first volume does not have time or space to go into the details of the exegesis of the text of 1 Samuel. It is simply to give some pointers to key things which should guide the preacher and teacher. If you are seeking further explanation, I would point you toward my light and easily read commentary on the books of Samuel which is listed in the 'Further Resources' section at the end of this book.

Part One:
INTRODUCING 1 SAMUEL

1.
Getting Our Bearings in Samuel

Introduction

The books of 1 and 2 Samuel are full of the sorts of ingredients that make great movies. There are kings and queens, adventurers, prophets, insignificant people who make good, adulterers, warriors, failed parents, people with deep psychological impairment, as well as individuals going about ordinary life who find themselves inadvertently swept up into events that shape the destiny of a nation and of all humanity. We find such elements as intrigue, incest, murder and mayhem, lust and shame, children pitted against parents, women struggling with infertility, and war with all its valour and brutality.

We might find it hard wading through books such as Leviticus and Numbers, but these two books of Samuel rarely let up in their excitement and their exploration and analysis of human character. This gripping narrative engages and excites us as readers, it is a real blockbuster. The result is that these two books have rightly won a significant place deep in the memories of God's ancient

Jewish people as well as Christians. These are books that delight and inspire.

The period covered by the books of Samuel is one of enormous transition and change. At the beginning of 1 Samuel we find Israel in the position of being a loose tribal federation of largely agrarian peoples facing both internal pressure because everyone was doing 'what was right in their own eyes' (Judg. 17:6; 21:25 ESV) and also facing significant external military pressure (e.g. 1 Sam. 4–7; 11; 13–14) as well as internal religious threat (1 Sam. 1–3). However, when we arrive at the final page of 2 Samuel we find a reasonably settled monarchy under David characterised by relative internal cohesion and benefitting from external success against its oppressors.

These books, however, are not simply great stories or chronicles of the transition from the period of the judges to that of the kings. They are profoundly theological works with a deep theocentric focus. They tell the story of God the King negotiating and overseeing the future of His people in the midst of His people who are tarred with the same brush as their spiritual ancestors, Adam and Eve, and who are therefore constantly at risk of supplanting God's kingship with their own. Because these books focus on such deep theological matters, they exercise enormous influence on Christian faith. They raise issues of messiahship and the Davidic kingship. They give us some of the key titles by which we know Jesus our Lord and they form the backdrop for many New Testament themes and presentations of Jesus.

For all these reasons and more, it is very important that the books of Samuel are heard and explained in Christian pulpits and explored in Bible study groups. That said, it is also important that the task of bringing their message to God's people is undertaken with due care, so that we who do the task may have no need to be ashamed as we rightly handle the Word of truth (2 Tim. 2:15).

The focus of the pages which comprise this first part of this book is therefore multifaceted. First, we will need to briefly get our bearings in terms of some of the more technical background issues that affect interpretation of the book. Second, we will need to ponder more deeply why the effort of preaching and teaching these two books is important and worthwhile. Third, particularly in view of the size of these books, we will need to consider the best way of approaching them as potential teachers and preachers. In the subsequent parts, which will stretch into a second volume, we will work our way through the whole of 1 and 2 Samuel and suggest ways in which it might be preached and taught. At the end of each volume suggestions are made as to further resources that might be useful in undertaking this task.

What Are We Dealing With?

Name and Origin

The attachment of Samuel's name to the books of Samuel appears to be because of his prominent role in the early chapters of 1 Samuel and possibly from the fact that from early times (e.g. the Talmud) he was also considered to be the author (probably based on 1 Chron. 29:29, which talks about 'the records of Samuel the seer'), with chapters subsequent to his death considered to be the work of the prophets Nathan and Gad (see also 1 Chron. 29:29).

Like many other parts of the Old Testament, the text of Samuel itself makes no suggestions regarding authorship and it is not possible with any certainty to give a date when the books reached the form in which we have them now. That said, there are indications that various sources such as those mentioned above were used to compile the books and there is no reason why these and others (e.g. the Book of Jashar; 2 Sam. 1:18) may not have been contemporaneous to the events themselves.

No matter how these sources came together and were shaped into their final form, there are strong indications that the books as we have them are considerably shaped by the theological interests of the Torah, and the overall presentation of Israel's history that stretches from Joshua to the end of the books of Kings.

The books of Samuel were originally not two books but one. They were probably first divided into two for the practical reason of accommodating standard scroll size when the Greek-speaking Jewish community translated them into Greek.[1] Since the Greek translation of the Old Testament was the major Old Testament for Christians, it was inevitable that they followed this division even though the Jews themselves did not make the division until the fifteenth and sixteenth century.

Dividing the books where they did was probably motivated by the death of the major figure of Saul. That said, it is not an entirely helpful place, in that it not only separates the two accounts of the death of Saul, but also results in the division of David's rise to power which begins in 1 Samuel 16 but does not reach its climax until 2 Samuel 5. Nevertheless, given the logic behind it and the fact that the readers in

---

1. The resulting division was 1 and 2 Kingdoms or 1 and 2 Reigns (i.e. Samuel), followed by 3 and 4 Kingdoms/Reigns (i.e. 1 and 2 Kings which, like Samuel, was originally one book).

our congregations have received it this way, it may very well shape the way in which we break the book up into blocks for the purposes of preaching and teaching.

Literature

The books of Samuel are therefore fundamentally one book and ought to be treated this way.[2] Whatever its origin and its sources, this book was written by an author who wished to convey a particular message and to accomplish a particular purpose. In the process of doing this he draws on various sources and brings them together using a whole host of literary devices and storytelling skill through which he carefully constructed this large and entrancing work that is full of history and God but also theology, pathos, humour, and things which are both beautiful and fearful. The art and skill of this author is such that it is also rightfully recognised as a classic work of literature.

This then is the first way in which we must approach Samuel. We must read it as literature and as story. In other words, we observe its literary dimensions, catching its drama, watching out for, and being drawn in by the author's literary skill and technique. For this reason, let me encourage you if you haven't done so already, to sit down and read it all the way through. Even better, since it was undoubtedly written to be listened to rather than read or read aloud instead of reading silently, start the process of being a preacher and teacher of God's Word by listening to it read aloud in large slabs. Why not get hold of a copy

---

2. From this point on, the singular 'Samuel' will not only be used to refer to the person of Samuel but also the two books as a whole. This language is not only a convenient shorthand but also acknowledges that they were originally one work and should be considered together as this.

of it read aloud and sit down and listen to it in its entirety? This would give you a big-picture feel for it and help you to see or hear things you might not otherwise notice. This would be an invaluable aid to you as you set out to explain it to others.

In my experience, the skill of listening to, observing, and preaching from narrative literature is one which Christian preachers can find overwhelming and difficult, particularly if most of their preaching is devoted to the epistles of the New Testament. For this reason, we will spend some time thinking about interpreting and preaching or teaching from narrative at the beginning of the second volume of this work.

Jewish Canonical Scripture

If the first thing to recognise about Samuel is that it is literature, then the second is that it is Jewish canonical literature. Thinking about how the Jews put together their Bible will help us as we grapple with the significance of the books of Samuel and how we should read it.

The Hebrew Bible is made up of three major divisions, the 'Torah' (*tôrâ*), 'Prophets' (*nĕbî'îm*) and 'Writings' (*kĕtûbîm*), otherwise known as the 'Tanak'.[3] The 'Prophets' can be subdivided into the 'Former Prophets' consisting of Joshua, Judges, Samuel, and Kings, while the 'Latter Prophets' is made up of Isaiah, Jeremiah, Ezekiel, and the twelve minor prophets.

Setting Samuel among the prophetic books in the Hebrew Bible is significant and demonstrates something that is not as evident in the way in which the Christian canon is organised. Clearly the compilers of the Hebrew

---

3. 'Tanak' is an acronym formed by taking the first letter of each named division of the Hebrew Bible (T-N-K).

canon wanted us to catch on that Samuel is to be considered somehow 'prophetic' rather than simply 'historical'. This can be seen clearly in Samuel where there is significant stress on the place of prophets and also on the need for the people of God (and particularly the king) to submit to the prophetic Word if they are to enjoy the LORD's blessing in the land. Furthermore, setting Samuel and the other books of the Former Prophets among the prophetic books indicates that they are to be read as 'prophetic' or even 'theological' history. While they are historical, they are not simply historical but theologically-interpreted history.

Understanding the Jewish canon, therefore, helps us to understand how we should read these books. First, the Torah lays the theological framework for all that follows, and the prophetic books should be read in the light of that framework, a process that will be overseen and interpreted through the guardians of it, the prophets.

Secondly, these books should not be primarily viewed as historical chronicles that are interested in relating history for history's sake but rather as accounts of the history of Israel given from a prophetic perspective or point of view.

Understanding these books in this way might also explain such things as the gaps that occur in places, the fact that some events are only mentioned in a cursory manner while others are given in great detail and also how there is sometimes a focus on aspects of personal life that might not be important in something like a chronicle. After all, Torah is not only concerned with theology but also with morality and the outworking of faith in God in the everyday.

The point is that all the prophetic works, whether in the Former or Latter Prophets, were regarded by the

Jewish compilers of the Hebrew Bible as accounts of God speaking. In the Former Prophets the stress is on God speaking through the events of history and God's response to Israel's obedience to Torah (or lack of it!). The stress in the Latter Prophets is more on the future as the prophets speak to both warn Israel of the consequences of disobedience to Torah and call them back to obedience. The combined stress on both God's actions and His Word through the prophets indicates that the God who was at work in both, is the God revealed in the Torah.

There is more to say here that has arisen out of biblical scholarship in the first half of the twentieth century.[4] Martin Noth proposed a link between the book of Deuteronomy and the books which followed it, maintaining that Deuteronomy through to the end of Kings was a unified work (called the 'Deuteronomistic History') which demonstrated how the theology of Deuteronomy shaped and critiqued the history of Israel.

While many aspects of Noth's theory have been rejected by conservative scholars, there is no reason for doubting what seems obvious among much of the prophets, that is, that Israel's history in the land stands under the judgment of the theology outlined to the nation of Israel in Deuteronomy as they were about to enter the land. However, it must also be said that even if the books which follow stand under the shadow of such theology, this does not mean that each of the individual works could not have their own particular interests, focus, and style.

---

4. Martin Noth, *The Deuteronomistic History* (JSOTSup 15; Sheffield: JSOT, 1981), a translation of Part 1 of *Uberlieferungageschichtliche Studien*, second edition (1957).

What does this mean for us as we read Samuel and seek to interpret it faithfully? First, we should read the individual books as they present themselves, self-contained works with their own distinctive literary style and purpose. Second, we should read them in the light of the Torah as a whole and particularly the book of Deuteronomy, which outlines how life was to be lived in the land in which Israel found itself. Third, we should not read these books as simple history but as theologically or prophetically interpreted history which is informed by the theology given to God's prophet Moses and his successors that God would raise up (Deut. 18:14-22).

Before moving on to consider the setting of Samuel in Christian canonical scripture, it is helpful to remember the larger context. The book of Deuteronomy had left the reader somewhat in suspense. We had heard of God's promise to Abraham and of God remembering His covenant to Abraham and rescuing His people in Exodus. The Sinai covenant had been enacted and then reiterated on the plains of Moab on the boundary of the promised land.

As readers of the earlier stories in the Torah, we know that the people have been in a similar position before. The last time was in the book of Numbers, and the result was failure and forty years of wilderness-wandering. The question posed is, therefore, whether those who follow after entry into the land will be any better than those who preceded them. Will they trust the Lord to bring about His Word and fight for them? Will they follow his instructions in war? Will they be overwhelmed and cowed by the significant populations within the land? Will they obey the law that Moses had outlined for them? Will their existence in the land be marked by obedience and blessing or by disobedience and the prospect of the terrifying curses outlined in both Deuteronomy and Leviticus? Moreover, if and when they enter the land, will they be able to settle down to a stable existence and be able to manage the land and properly govern themselves?

If these are the questions posed before entry into the land, the other end of the Former Prophets supplies us with answers. At the end of the books of Kings God's people and their kings have demonstrated that they are made of the same stuff as their parents and Adam and Eve before them. The people of Israel and the kings they beseeched God for have largely proved to be flagrant rebels, with a very small number of notable exceptions, and God has enacted the curses of the covenant outlined in the Torah.

The Former Prophets, therefore, end with the fall of Jerusalem to the Babylonians and their king becoming a lackey of the king of Babylon in his court (2 Kings 25:27-30). If the Former Prophets began with the question of Israel's future in the land, it ends by posing the question of Israel's future now that the land has been forfeited because of sin. This is the larger theological context which we need to bear in mind as we approach the books of Samuel. This is the larger story of which Samuel is a part and understanding this will help us apprehend the detail and give it its proper perspective.

Christian Canonical Scripture

As Christians, we understandably take into account how our Jewish spiritual forebears understood Samuel. However, we also consider that the true fulfilment of those Scriptures is found in the One to whom they bear witness,

Jesus the Messiah/Christ (John 5:39-40). In Him all the promises of God have their 'yes' and 'amen' (2 Cor. 1:20).

This fulfilment of the Old Testament in Jesus is particularly evident in the case of Samuel, although not in a way that is immediately evident. Samuel is quoted relatively sparsely in the New Testament when compared to such books as the Psalms and Isaiah. Nevertheless, it is clear that many of the concepts developed in Isaiah and Psalms and then taken up in the New Testament have their genesis in the books of Samuel. For example, the concept of kingship is a primary concern of Samuel as is the covenant made with David by God (2 Sam. 7; 23:1-7). God as King and His appointment of David and his successors is taken up extensively within the Psalter (e.g. Ps. 2; 18; 89; 110; 118; 145) and many of the Psalms are inextricably linked to David and his life situation (e.g. in the first book of Psalms—Psalms 1–42—only a few do not have David's name in the heading). The Psalms are, therefore, regularly used by Jesus and the New Testament authors in relation to the identity, destiny, and role of Jesus (e.g. Ps. 2; 22; 110; 118).

If we are Christians, we therefore see that what God does in Jesus and in His church is a continuation and fulfilment of His activity witnessed in the Old Testament. We must therefore read the Old in its own right and see it pointing forward to Jesus and fulfilled in Him. We must also see that there is continuity between the ancient Jewish people of God and us, God's Christian people. Reading Samuel as a Christian is therefore a multifaceted task and one which we will explore in a little depth in the next chapter and then pursue throughout our examination and interpretation of Samuel.

The Word of God

Finally, when we come to read Samuel, we should acknowledge that what we are reading, interpreting, and proclaiming is the Word of God. No matter which human was responsible for Samuel in its final form, as Christians we believe that this human was so borne along by the Holy Spirit that God Himself was speaking (2 Pet. 1:21). As the human author recounted history, told the story, and put forward the things of God to us, he did so under the sovereign hand of God, so that his writing was what God intended and so he conveyed the God-intended message.

The implication for us as readers is that we are to listen for God's revelation of Himself through the human author. We are to hear God speak to us about Himself, us and the rest of humanity as well as His purposes in His world. Moreover, even though we cannot put aside our own presuppositions or background, as far as we are able, we are to hear the Word of God to us as the original author presents it and intended it.

A Word About Biblical Theology

A discipline that takes seriously these various perspectives on the text of the Bible is that known as biblical theology. Unfortunately, ever since the term 'biblical theology' was first coined, it has been argued about and defined differently. In fact, the term 'biblical theology' has some affinities with the term 'football' in the sense that it has now come to have a broad range of meaning which tends to vary among Christians according to where they live or the family (in the case of biblical theology, the *theological* family) in which they have been reared. For this reason, it would be helpful to define what is meant here.

The first thing to say is that biblical theology is a distinctively Christian discipline, formed by Christian presuppositions. Chief among those presuppositions is the Christian's open and declared faith in Jesus and God's Christ and the One who is the fulfiller and centre of God's plans and purposes (Eph. 1:2-10).

The second thing arises out of the first, and that is that biblical theology takes seriously what we outlined above, that is, that Christians view seriously the fact that their Scriptures contain two Testaments that have a theological unity. Biblical theology is, therefore, of necessity 'whole-Bible' biblical theology.[5]

Third, because we are convinced that God's purposes in the Old Testament witness to Jesus Christ and find their fulfilment in Him, we recognise that it is impossible for us to completely throw off this Christian and New Testament presupposition when we read the Old Testament.

Nevertheless, this doesn't mean that we read the Old Testament into the New. Rather, we allow it to speak for itself, or have its own voice so that it may truly point to Christ and so that we may truly apprehend Christ as the Old Testament presents Him.

At its best, biblical theology takes into account the different perspectives we have acknowledged above, and it functions at a theological level to see how God's purposes and plans flow through His whole revelation of Himself in the Old Testament, the person and work of Christ, and the New Testament. As we work through Samuel

---
5. Donald A. Carson, 'Systematic Theology and Biblical Theology,' ed. T. Desmond Alexander and Brian S Rosner, *NDBT* (Leicester: Inter-Varsity Press, 2000), pp. 89-104.

and think about how we should teach it to, and preach it among Christian congregations, we will constantly be doing this very rich exercise. If we do it well, then we will be feeding our people with riches and also teaching them to read the Bible thoroughly, Christianly, and well for themselves.

The Purpose of Samuel

There are multiple themes and directions within the books of Samuel and it is always somewhat risky to try and reduce them to one purpose. However, looking at the beginning and end of the book can be helpful in orienting us toward what the author is seeking to communicate within the work as a whole.

In a helpful work, Bill Dumbrell has pointed out that an examination of the beginning and end of the books of Samuel can help us in this way, as can the larger context in which they are set.[6] In the Former Prophets, the book of Judges is situated immediately before Samuel and it recounts God's remarkable preservation of His people despite their apostasy and religious degeneration. They rejected God's kingship by doing what was right in their own eyes and evil in God's eyes (e.g. Judg. 2:11; 3:7, 12; 4:1; 6:1; cf. 17:6; 21:25).

Immediately after Samuel we have the narrative of 1 and 2 Kings, which takes us from the high point of Israel's political history—the reign of Solomon—through to the extinction of political monarchy at the hands of the Babylonians in 586 B.C.

---

6. William J. Dumbrell, 'The Content And Significance Of The Books Of Samuel: Their Place And Purpose Within The Former Prophets', JETS 33/1 (1990), pp. 49-62.

Within Samuel itself we see a transition from God's kingship debased at the corrupt shrine in Shiloh overseen by Eli and his sons to the purchase of the temple site by David from Araunah and the prospect of there being a permanent site in Jerusalem where God can be rightly worshipped as King (2 Sam. 24). In between these two events we see the development of human kingship and at seminal moments in the story we are shown how it can exist without threatening God's kingship. Chief among those moments are the poems of Hannah and David (1 Sam 2:1-10; 2 Sam 22; 23:1-7) and the giving of the promise to David in 2 Samuel 7.

The books of Samuel therefore tell us (1) that God can establish the kingship of David and integrate it into His covenant relationship with His people without threatening His own kingship; (2) how Israel and her kings might live in a way that gives God His right place in their lives; and (3) that in view of the sinful nature of humans the future of God's people can never rest on any human king but on the sovereign God alone.

The Shape of Samuel

One of the difficulties of thinking about preaching on Samuel is breaking up the book into appropriate sections. The fundamental problem is that there are significant overlaps that make choices difficult.

Chapters 1 to 7 are relatively straightforward in that they describe Israel's situation prior to the introduction of kingship. However, that then raises the question as to whether chapter 8, which concerns the request for a king, belongs with the chapters that precede it or the chapters which follow. The best way is probably to view it as a hinge (or even 'interlocking') chapter between the chapters leading up to the request for a king and the chapters which describe how kingship develops (see diagram below).[7]

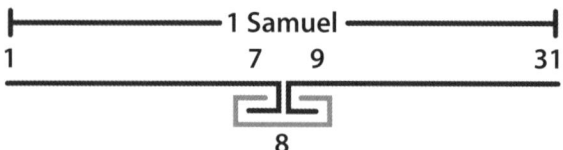

Having said this, if we were forced to place a break structurally, then it would seem to best place the break after chapter 8. This preserves it as a climax to those chapters and an ultimate sinful act that finishes the era of the judges while introducing the concept of kingship. It also separates the rise of Saul from the broader introduction to kingship. Against this is the observation that chapters 1–7 begin and end by connecting Samuel's family with Ramah (e.g. 1:1, 3, 19; 2:11; 7:17) and with a process of going 'from year to year' to various places (1:3, 7; 7:17).

This same dilemma is faced as we continue on through the book. If we look at the other end of Samuel, we find that there are at least two clear sections. There are signs within the text that 2 Samuel 21–24 is a tightly integrated section that gives a sort of theological reflection on kingship. Moreover, 2 Samuel 9–20 is largely concerned with trouble within the house of David and the succession to the throne.

These observations, therefore, leave us with a section running from 1 Samuel 15 when God announces that Saul's kingship will end (15:23) and the kingdom will be

---

7. Of course, this dilemma could be avoided in the way that David Tsumura does, that is, by having chapter 8 stand on its own; David Toshio Tsumura, *The First Book of Samuel* (NICOT; Grand Rapids: Eerdmans, 2007), pp. 73-75.

given to another 'better than' him (15:28). This one who is better is identified and anointed in the same chapter by Samuel in Chapter 16. However, the actual king whose kingship is doomed and the king in prospect overlap for fifteen chapters. The whole period between 1 Samuel 16 and 2 Samuel 5 presents David in a very positive light. The kingship comes to him from the hand of God and not from his own actions. However, in 2 Samuel 1–4, David is not king over all Israel and so there is a transition period until what God had clearly intended comes about in 2 Samuel 5:1-5 and David is anointed king over all Israel.

From this point on, the focus falls upon David as his position is consolidated by both himself and God. As we will see, he is not entirely without blemish in this period and there are signs of decline. Nevertheless, his reign is crowned by the blessing of God in 2 Samuel 7. At the end of chapter 8 there is a list of officers in David's court (2 Sam. 8:15–18), which mirrors the list of his sons in 2 Samuel 5:13–16.[8] This device ties together chapters 5–8, and provides a portrait of a king who can accomplish what Israel wanted to do. In 2 Samuel 9–20 David's frailty becomes far more evident both in his own personal life and in the life of his family, showing some of the realities of human kingship, although even here there are signs of greatness.

With this overview, we can see that again there are transition moments. 1 Samuel 15 represents one such moment as God indicates a prospective end of one king's reign and the prospective reign of another king. However, as with chapter 8, it appears that chapter 15 really belongs with

---

8. And also the list of officials at the end of the history of David's court (2 Sam. 20:23-26).

the chapters that preceded it. At the other end, 2 Samuel 1 presents David as victor and Saul as vanquished. However, David is not yet king and so this chapter is again one that interlocks the previous chapters with the future ones.

The next interlocking passage would appear to be 2 Samuel 5:1–5, which really culminates the process that has been going on since 1 Samuel 16 and points toward the future. God's anointing is now ratified as God and people together acknowledge David as king. This is crowned by the acquisition of Jerusalem, the city of David (2 Sam. 5:6-16), the bringing up of the ark to Jerusalem (2 Sam. 6), the promise of God to David's house (2 Sam. 7), and the military successes that Israel had wanted kingship to accomplish (2 Sam. 5:17-25; 8:1-18).

We might therefore diagrammatically summarise one analysis of the book as below and then break up the book into units that not only summarise the book, but which also work in terms of sections that might form the basis for preaching and teaching units.[9]

|———————1 Samuel———————|—————2 Samuel—————|
1   7 9   31 2   4 5:6 8 9   20 21 24
      ⊐⊏   ⊐⊏   ⊐⊏ ⊐⊏
       8   15   2 Sam 1 5:1-5

1 Samuel 1:1–8:22   The rise of Samuel and kingship
   1:1–2:11   The story of Hannah
   2:1-10   The prayer of Hannah
   2:12-36   Samuel's rise and Eli's demise
   3:1–4:1a   Famine and fullness
   4:1b–7:17   The story of the ark
   8:1-22   The transition to monarchy

---

9. The written structural breakup of the book outlined below come from Andrew Reid, *1 & 2 Samuel : Hope for the Helpless* (Reading the Bible Today; Sydney: Aquila Press, 2008), pp. 266-267.

Part One: Introducing 1 Samuel

1 Samuel 9:1–15:35	**The beginning and end of Saul's kingship**
9:1–15:35	The story of Saul
9:1–11:13	The appointment and confirmation of Saul as King
11:14–12:25	Kingship and covenant
13:1–15:35	The reign of Saul as King
13:1-23	Saul and the Philistines
14:1-52	Saul and Jonathan
15:1-35	The rejection of Saul
1 Samuel 16:1–20:42	**The transition to David**
16:1–18:4	The appointment and confirmation of David
16:1-13	The anointing of David
16:14-23	Yahweh, David, and Saul
17:1-54	David and Goliath
18:1-5	Saul, Jonathan, and David
18:6–20:42	David in Saul's court
18:6–19:24	Saul's alienation
20:1-42	The covenant between David and Jonathan
1 Samuel 21:1–31:13	**David the fugitive**
21:1–22:23	Ahimelech and the priests of Nob
23:1–26:25	Encounters in the life of a fugitive anointee
27:1–30:31	David in Philistia
31:1-13	The deaths of Saul and Jonathan
2 Samuel 1:1–5:5	**The struggle to come to the kingdom**
1:1-27	Learning of and lamenting the deaths of Saul and Jonathan
2:1-11	David: King over Judah
2:12–5:5	The transition from Saul
5:1-5	David: King over all Israel

2 Samuel 5:6–8:18	**David the great: Consolidation of king and kingdom**
5:6-25	Success and prosperity in the city of David
6:1-23	Journey's end for the ark of the covenant
7:1-29	A house for David
8:1-18	David's military successes
2 Samuel 9:1–20:26	**David the not so great**
9:1-13	Remembering Jonathan
10:1-19	Military success again
11:1–12:31	David and the house of Uriah
13:1–20:26	David: Family and throne
13:1–14:33	The rape of Tamar and its consequences
15:1–19:43	Absalom's rebellion
20:1-26	Sheba's rebellion
2 Samuel 21–24	**Theological reflections on kingship**
21:1-22; 23:8–24:25	The blessings and curses of Israel's kings
22:1–23:7	Reflections on the life of David, God's king

Date and Authorship

There is no indication within the books of Samuel or within the rest of the Old Testament as to the identity of their author. As indicated earlier, we know that there were sources of various sorts and there is some evidence within Samuel that whoever put together the final form of Samuel used already existing material such as narratives concerning the ark and the story of the succession to David, along with various songs and poems (for example, 1 Sam. 2:1-10; 2 Sam. 22; 23:1-7). The one explicit reference to such sources in Samuel is to the Book of Jashar (2 Sam. 1:18). References to other sources are made in Kings and Chronicles although we do not know whether they were used in Samuel (1 Chron. 27:24; 29:29).

Whoever was responsible for the final form of the book appears to want it to be read as a unified story that tells of the transition from the period of the judges to an established monarchy under the headship of David. The author used whatever sources were available to him for this purpose and it is entirely possible that there may have been a history of compilation prior to his giving the work final form. However, most of this history is beyond our grasp and the best way forward is to deal with the final form as it has come to us. This final form seems to be part of a history that stretches from Joshua through to the end of 2 Kings and which has similar theological interests that flow across all these parts.

The Text of Samuel

Most modern English translations of the Old Testament rely upon what is called the 'Masoretic Text' (MT), which is based on a family of Hebrew manuscripts that were carefully preserved by a group of Jewish scholars called 'Masoretes'. The Masoretes were the successors to the scribes. The most complete version of their text that we have can be dated to about A.D. 1000.

Unfortunately, of all the texts that they laboured so hard to preserve, it appears as though the text of 1 and 2 Samuel suffered the most in transmission. In the original Hebrew, this shows itself in a number of different ways. Some passages are very difficult to read (see the NIV, ESV and NRSV on 1 Samuel 13:1), others appear to have sections omitted and others seem to have suffered from errors in transcribing.

In the face of such difficulties, various scholars turn to different textual sources other than the MT and put their priority in different places. Occasionally in our English translation you can see some of the debate pop up (e.g. compare 1 Sam. 10:25–11:1 in various English translations).

Having noted the difficulties, we should say that most of the textual difficulties do not significantly affect the larger meaning of the book. However, where differences do occur, the best way forward is to treat each variation on a case-by-case basis. Practically, this largely means going with the text that is reflected in the NIV84, which has been chosen as our base text in this book and we will assume that the translators have made good decisions on our behalf. Occasionally I may alert you to difficulties or differences that I think you should be aware of or where my interpretation is based on a different choice than that made by the translators of the NIV84.

2.
Why Should We Preach and Teach Samuel?

The Challenges Facing the Preacher and Teacher of Samuel

While the books of Samuel are full of excitement, profound theology, and hold wonderful potential for preaching and teaching, the person who decides to do so is faced with formidable obstacles.

First, these are greatly loved books and contain some of the most familiar of Old Testament stories even for modern Christians who are increasingly unfamiliar with the Old Testament. Because they are loved and reasonably familiar, they often have attached to them some well-worn interpretations or patterns of interpretation which the preacher may need to challenge. This process of challenging interpretations that have been important to people and to their spiritual development or that were given to them by beloved teachers and mentors, is often fraught with difficulty.

Second, the books of Samuel are largely narrative and many interpreters (and preachers!) do not really know how to handle narrative. They are unsure how it is to be interpreted in its own right and they are uncertain about how it applies to a twenty-first-century audience that is so far removed from it in time, culture, and social context. Moreover, they are sometimes wary of what they perceive as incorrect or fringe means of interpretation but do not know what the alternative might be.

Third, contemporary Christian interpreters often feel that the religious gap between them and any Old Testament text is too significant. After all, they are Christians and they live in a Christian culture that often feels or acts as though the Old Testament is either non-Christian or pre-Christian and therefore has no real relevance or can only be relevant with significant modification or adaption.

The first and the third problems we have already spoken about. The second will be addressed as we work through the text of 1 Samuel and then with a special introductory chapter in our second volume. However, in the meantime, it will be helpful for us to see what sort of encouragement we can receive from the New Testament as to how to approach this task of rightly handling the Word of God found in Samuel.

Encouragement from the New Testament
Quotations and Allusions
The first encouragement from Jesus and the New Testament authors comes by way of quotations and allusions. By way of definition, a quotation might be defined as 'a direct citation of an Old Testament passage that is clearly recognizable by its clear and unique verbal parallelism', while an allusion could be understood as 'a brief expression consciously intended by an author to be dependent on an

Old Testament passage.'[1] The former are more direct while the latter are indirect references. Moreover, the former are easier to identify than the latter. Hays, who provides one of the best criteria for discerning allusion, also proposes a third and distinct category, 'echoes'.[2] Here we will confine ourselves to quotations and allusions.

While direct quotations from Samuel are relatively sparse in the New Testament (e.g. 12:22 in Rom. 11:2; 13:14 in Acts 13:22; 2 Sam. 7:8 in 2 Cor. 6:18; 2 Sam. 7:14 in Heb. 1:5; and 2 Sam. 22:50 in Rom. 15:9), allusions and language deriving from Samuel are not. Even the very first verse of the New Testament has an example as it speaks of 'A record of Jesus Christ the son of David, the son of Abraham' (Matt. 1:1). The terminology of 'Christ' and 'son of David' both have their roots in the language and thought of Samuel.

But perhaps most significant groupings of allusions and apparent dependencies upon the books of Samuel are gathered around the birth narrative on Luke's Gospel. In Luke 1:15, we are told that John the Baptist will, like Samuel, 'never take wine or other fermented drink' (cf. 1:11 LXX, reflected in the NRSV). Zechariah 'returning home' from worship in the temple and then Elizabeth conceiving (Luke 1:23-24). These connections are built

---

1. Gregory K. Beale, *Handbook on the New Testament Use of the Old Testament: Exegesis and Interpretation* (Grand Rapids: Baker, 2012), pp. 29, 31.

2. Richard B. Hays, *Echoes of Scripture in the Letters of Paul* (New Haven: Yale University Press, 1989), pp. 29-32; *The Conversion of the Imagination: Paul as Interpreter of Israel's Scripture* (Grand Rapids: Eerdmans, 2005), pp. 34-44.

upon when Mary echoes The Prayer of Hannah in the Magnificat in Luke 1:46-55.

Even though many other passages undoubtedly underlie Luke 1:32-33, the language and conceptual world are clearly dominated by 2 Samuel 7. Jesus will be of Davidic descent (2 Sam. 7:12), shall be great (2 Sam. 7:9), have the throne of David (7:13), be the Son of the most high (2 Sam. 7:14; see also Luke 1:35), and rule over an eternal kingdom (2 Sam. 7:14). As we saw earlier, although these ideas may be refracted through later Old Testament passages such as Psalm 89, their roots lie within Samuel. The role of Jesus is explained in the light of Samuel, something that continues to dominate the whole of the Lukan birth narrative.

Even the link between Jesus and the Holy Spirit has links that go back to Samuel. For example, only two kings in Israel's history have a particular pattern associated with their appointment and rule. Both Saul and David are chosen by God Himself (9:16; 10:24; 16:1), are anointed by God's prophet (9; 16:3), are endowed with the Spirit (10–11; 16:13), and are publicly affirmed in mighty acts of deliverance (1 Sam. 11; 17). This pattern setting out God's choice, involvement, and empowering of His king is repeated only again with Jesus. Jesus a descendant of David chosen by God (Matt. 12:15-21) who is brought to God's prophet, anointed, and filled with the Spirit (Matt. 3:13-17) and who then goes on to perform mighty acts of deliverance for the people of God (Matt. 4:23-25; 12:22-29).

These observations are but a small snapshot of what appears throughout the New Testament and they offer us a powerful encouragement for preaching through Samuel. These quotations and allusions demonstrate that if we really want to understand Jesus and help our people understand

Jesus then we will want to go back to Samuel. As Jesus indicates, such Scriptures will testify to Him that people might come to have life through Him (John 5:39-40).

Luke 24

Luke 24 is often cited in relation to preaching from the Old Testament, and rightly so. However, it is not always rightly understood. The particular verses are set within a discussion by Jesus with some disciples on the road to Emmaus and are focused on verses 25-27 wherein a number of things are said.

First, the disciples are described by Jesus as 'foolish' and 'slow of heart', indicating that Jesus considered that the reality of what had happened to Him should not have been unexpected to them given 'all that the prophets have spoken!'

Second, in verse 26 Jesus asks the rhetorical question which will set the stage for His revelation to them in verse 27. The question concerns the necessity which Jesus indicates is evident from the prophets, that the Christ would suffer and then be exalted ('enter his glory'; v. 26).

Third, Jesus gives to the disciples present the perspective of 'all the Scriptures' concerning Himself. The combination of 'beginning with Moses and all the Prophets' with 'all the Scriptures' implies comprehensiveness, that is, that 'he went through the entire Scripture, front to back'.[3]

Verse 27 needs to be understood in this context. Jesus is giving the disciples enlightenment from Scripture about the things concerning Himself. There does not appear to be any sense here that every verse or even every passage

---

3. Darrell L. Bock, *Luke* (vol. 2: 9:51–24:53; Baker Exegetical Commentary on the New Testament 3B; Grand Rapids: Baker, 1994), 1917.

points toward Jesus. Rather, it is that the (Hebrew) Scriptures in every part contain Scriptures that speak about the Messiah and His suffering, resurrection, and entering into His glory.

However, the picture is not yet complete and so we need to look at verses 44-46 as well. In between the 'slowness of heart' in verse 25 and verses 44-46, Luke uses a number of key descriptions which demonstrate how he wants us to understand this narrative. In verse 31 the eyes of the disciples are *opened*, and they *recognise* Jesus. In verse 32 they describe how their hearts had been burning within as He *opened* the Scriptures to them. These references provide a link to verse 45 where Jesus is among the larger group of disciples and *opens* their *minds* so that they can *understand* the Scriptures. In other words, He repeats the pattern seen with the two disciples in the central narrative.

The background to this 'opening' is found in the Old Testament itself. Since the sin of the golden calf, after which God spoke about the people being 'stiff-necked' (Exod. 32:9; 33:3, 5; 34:9), the Scriptures often talk about a fundamental problem affecting the heart and sensibility of God's people (e.g. Ps. 95; Isa. 6:9-10; 48:4; Ezek. 2:3-5). This is picked up in the New Testament in such places as the disciples' reactions in the Gospels, Romans 11, 2 Corinthians 3, and also here. Such hardness of heart demonstrates itself in an inability to understand God's purposes as outlined in the Old Testament Scriptures. However, as this passage demonstrates, association with Jesus, faith in Him, and education by Him reverses this. Those taught by Jesus become people who *recognise*, whose eyes and minds *are opened*, and whose hearts are warmed by what they find in those Scriptures.

With this larger picture in mind, the detail of verses 44 to 46 can be explored. In verse 44, Jesus refers back to His own words earlier concerning His own destiny as outlined in Scripture (such as those found in 9:22, 44; 17:25; 18:31-32; 22:37). He remarks that just as it was *necessary* for Him to suffer (24:26), so it was *necessary* that everything written about Him in the Scriptures be fulfilled. He then outlines what it is that He sees to be prophesied in those Scriptures. The key elements are clear: a suffering Messiah, resurrection, and mission consisting of proclamation in His name throughout the world.

The implication of the teaching of Jesus here is that from now on the Old Testament Scriptures must be read in reference to Him, just as He Himself had read them. Similarly, there can be no doubt that Jesus considers that the whole of the Scriptures are in some sense about Him. Hence, following on from this, it may be appropriate to say that Jesus considers that the whole of the Old Testament is speaking about Him or even that He is the subject of the whole of the Old Testament. What the Scriptures testify to has been realised in Him and that to know Him is to know and understand their purpose and direction.

The key to understanding the plot and purpose of the Old Testament is, therefore, to see it in the light of who Jesus is, but particularly in what He has done through His death.[4] This stirs us up in our preaching of Samuel and gives us both a reason and a rationale as we go about it. First, we should preach it because it will speak of Jesus and will direct us toward Him and His suffering. Second, we

---

4. Note the references to the necessity of the Messiah suffering that frame these two key references.

will be aware as we do so that we shouldn't force passages to speak of Him that don't. However, we will constantly expect and keep our eyes open for those which do contain the things 'concerning him'.

2 Timothy 3:14-17

The third element from the New Testament that should encourage and guide us in preaching from the Old Testament is 2 Timothy 3:14-17. Again, there are few things to note that will help us understand these verses.

The terms 'holy Scriptures' (v. 15) and 'all Scripture' appear to be talking about the same thing—the Old Testament Scriptures—although the latter term probably has the sense of 'every (text of) Scripture'.[5]

Verse 15 indicates that these Old Testament Scriptures instruct in the way of salvation and that without knowledge of Christ and faith in Him those Scriptures will be misunderstood.

Verse 16 indicates that these Scriptures have their source in God, being so much His words that it is as though God Himself were speaking them with His own breath.

The statement by Paul about the inspiration of Scripture is made on the way to stating that, having their source in God, they are 'useful'.

The four words or phrases describing the usefulness of Scripture in verse 16 are in broad design chiastic. The first and the last ('teaching' and 'training in righteousness') have to do with education and the second and third ('rebuking' and 'correcting') have to do with identifying and addressing sin. The sense of the four when combined is that Scripture's

---

5. Philip H. Towner, *The Letters to Timothy and Titus* (NICNT; Grand Rapids: Eerdmans, 2006), p. 587.

usefulness has to do with positively educating both in terms of doctrine and behaviour as well as correcting aberrant doctrine and behaviour. In the language of verse 17, Timothy and all Christians can therefore find in the Old Testament Scriptures everything that will fully outfit them for good works.

The encouragement for us as readers, interpreters, teachers, and preachers of the Old Testament is, therefore, that (1) the Old Testament Scriptures *as a whole* are able to make people wise for salvation through faith in the Messiah Jesus (v. 15) but that they are also (2) useful for keeping people straight in terms of doctrine and godliness and (3) for helping pastor-teachers such as Timothy and ourselves to keep their people straight in the same.

So, as we preach and teach from Samuel we will not be embarrassed to point people to Christ and make doctrinal and ethical applications from it. Such is entirely in accord with the purpose for which God caused it to be written as explained by Paul here. It is also entirely in line with what we see both Jesus and the writers of the New Testament doing.

1 Corinthians 10:1–14 and James

There are many more encouragements we might take from the New Testament. However, because through abuse it has become fashionable in some circles to play down the exemplary use of the Old Testament, it will be helpful for us to look briefly at 1 Corinthians 10:1-14 and James 5 and the encouragement they offer for us as we set out to preach and teach Samuel.

In 1 Corinthians 10 Paul is instructing the somewhat over spiritually confident Corinthians. In doing so, he focuses on one story from the Old Testament which has echoes of their own situation; the wilderness wanderings. There, in very concrete form, the Corinthians could recognise themselves and their own circumstances. Paul indicates that God's attitudes and actions should teach them, rebuke them, correct them, and train them in righteousness. His acts of judgment in the past point towards His attitude now where His people are sinning in similar ways. God judged the worship of idols then. He judged fornication and testing and grumbling then, and He will do so now.

Clearly Paul is not averse to using the Old Testament as a record of God's dealings with His people that provides us with concrete positive and negative examples of what it means to live before God (see particularly verse 6).[6]

As for illustrative or exemplary use of the OT, the book of James uses a number of Old Testament figures as examples of various attitudes and actions, some illustrative and others to be modelled. Such include Rahab, Abraham, 'the prophets who spoke in the name of the Lord', Elijah, and Job (James 2:14-26; 5:10-11, 17-18). When James does this, he is not using these figures Christologically or even in a redemptive-historically oriented manner. For example, Job, along with 'the prophets of the Lord' (James 5:10), is explicitly labelled as an 'example' that should spur others on to imitation. We find similar things elsewhere in the New Testament where examples from the Old are given of both a negative and positive sort (e.g. Heb. 11; Jude 7-11).

This encouragement from the New Testament can guide our preaching and teaching from Samuel. It will

---

6. For a further explanation of this passage in relation to preaching from the Old Testament, see Adrian Reynolds, *Teaching Numbers: From Text to Message* (PT Resources; Fearn, U.K.: Christian Focus, 2013), pp. 41-43.

not be unusual for us to see things in the lives of Samuel that we might rightly urge our people to either follow or shun. Because of the sometimes ambiguous nature of Hebrew narrative it may not always be easy for us to rightly ascertain when God thinks a particular behaviour is right or wrong, to be followed or to be shunned. Nevertheless, we should not be closed to such application as a possibility.

For Joy

The final reason for preaching Samuel—and much of the rest of Scripture—gravitates around joy. There is no doubt that sometimes bearing the Word of God weighs heavily on the preacher and teacher of God's people. Some of this weight can be seen in the Old Testament prophets, such as Jeremiah (e.g. Jer. 11:18-20; 12:1-6; 15:10-21, 17:14-18; 18:18-23; 20:7-13), in scribes such as Ezra (Ezra 9), and in New Testament apostles such as Paul (note the double reference to tears in Paul's address to the Ephesian elders in Acts 20:17-38). Nevertheless, it is clear that joy and gladness can also characterise bearing the Word of God, making it clear to others, and seeing their lives transformed. For this reason, the writer of Hebrews can talk about pastoring the people of God as not being burdensome but appropriately accompanied by joy (Heb. 13:17; cf. 1 Pet. 5:2-3).

The note of joy is understandable in relation to pastoring the people of God in any capacity. After all, it is the Word of God which is God's agent of bringing the person of Jesus to the lives of people. Preaching the Word of God in the power of the Spirit of God is being where God is and doing what God is doing. It is therefore rightly filled with joy. Surely there can be little more rewarding and fulfilling task than this!

Perhaps a personal example would not be out of place here. Some years ago in ministry, I became aware that I was unwell, and that public ministry might be part of the cause. I took a year out of ministry to sort myself out and also to work out what ministry would look like in the future for me. For a year, I declined all invitations to preach except for a couple of invitations that occurred early in that year. After the year, I was involved in planting a church and therefore I was to be back preaching. I can still recall the first time I stood up to preach. I began to speak and before long I found myself becoming overwhelmed with emotion. I understood that deep underneath I had feared that because of illness I might never be in this position again and I had desperately missed the joy of being a pastor of God's people ministering the Word of God to them and watching them be transformed by it. It was not something I returned to reluctantly, but gladly and willingly.

Of course, there is another aspect of joy in this and it is hinted at in the writer of Psalm 119. He often speaks of delight and wonder in relation to the Word of God (e.g. Ps. 119:18, 24, 35, 47-48). What a privilege and joy it is then to be able to dig deeper into God's Word and marvel at His ways.

So, why preach Samuel? Because it is the Word of God. It is a wonderful part of the Word of God full of excitement, interest, and delight. It is also a part of the Word of God that speaks fully of the Christ who is to come and whom we have come to know. It is rich in biblical theology and therefore rich in God's purposes in His world through His Son. It is also bursting with in-depth analysis of people like us and those to whom we minister. It is therefore incredibly helpful pastorally and theologically as I watch God deal with people like us.

3.
Planning to Preach on Samuel

The books of Samuel are very long books (55 chapters in all, including some very long chapters).

So, how do we go about preaching them?

A Series of One or Two

A few years ago, I came across a book that I wished I'd thought of first. Mark Dever had worked his way through the whole of the Bible preaching one sermon on every book.[1] He did cheat a little at times and Samuel was one example (i.e. two sermons for all of 1 and 2 Samuel).

The idea of preaching every book of the Bible in one sermon is, however, quite brilliant and a great idea.[2] Such an approach might work well for an introduction or a conclusion to a series on the whole of the two books. The

---

1. Mark Dever, *The Message of the New Testament: Promises Kept* (Wheaton: Crossway, 2005); *The Message of the Old Testament: Promises Made* (Wheaton: Crossway, 2006).

2. Moreover, Dever has done 1 Samuel well, although I am much less convinced of his coverage of 2 Samuel.

latter would probably be better in that it would allow the preacher to have worked through the whole book in detail before trying to summarise it.

A 'Big Picture' Series

A second potential idea for preaching Samuel is to preach a 'Big Picture' series where you go through the whole book in its major sections. Although this is not quite as daunting or demanding as a series of one on all of Samuel, or two on all of Samuel, it nevertheless requires significant skill, because some of the same abilities are required. One still needs a thorough knowledge of both books, an ability to preach large sections of narrative, and also an ability to summarise succinctly the main theme in a way that is not only understandable, but also able to be applied in a way that is true to the text, whilst remaining distinctively Christian.

A breakup of the text of Samuel that would allow such a series might be as follows:

> *1 Samuel 1–3: Shiloh and Samuel*
>
> *1 Samuel 4–8: The Ark Narrative*
>
> *1 Samuel 9–15: God and Saul*
>
> *1 Samuel 16:1–18:4: David's Rise*
>
> *1 Samuel 18:5–31:13: The Demise of Saul*
>
> *2 Samuel 1:1–5:5: The Struggle to Come to the Kingdom*
>
> *2 Samuel 5:6–8:18: David the Great*
>
> *2 Samuel 9:1–20:26: David the Not So Great*
>
> *2 Samuel 21–24: A Theological Reflection on Kingship*

A Group of Series

The third way is to take clearly demarcated sections of Samuel and to preach or teach your way through the whole book using those sections. This is my preferred method for a number of reasons, not least that it allows you to preach a variety of genres and across Testaments in a given year. It also allows your congregation to have a break from the unrelenting length of Samuel.

My personal approach is to aim for somewhere between eight and twelve weeks on one book of the Bible; perhaps splitting into two sections of four to eight weeks is ideal. I think that this can be accomplished with relative ease with Samuel in a way that does not necessitate a breaking up of key sections of the book. Although it is not necessarily essential, my view would be that each section might be separated by either seasonal series (e.g. Christmas or Easter) or other series. This simply breaks up the series and gives hearers some variety.

Here is my suggested outline for a series of sermons that gradually work through Samuel over a number of years. The series below could probably be done in three or three and a half years and could be matched by small group Bible studies on the same sections.

Series 1: The Rise of Samuel and Kingship (1 Samuel 1:1–8:22)

The Story of Hannah (1 Sam. 1:1-28; 2:11)
The Prayer of Hannah (1 Sam. 2:1-10)
Samuel's Rise and Eli's Demise (1 Sam. 2:12–4:1)
The Story of the Ark (Part 1: 1 Sam. 4:1–5:12)
The Story of the Ark (Part 2: 1 Sam. 6:1–7:17)

The Transition to Monarchy (1 Sam. 8:1-22)

Series 2: The Rise and Fall of Saul (1 Samuel 9:1–15:35)

Chosen, Appointed, and Confirmed (1 Sam. 9:1–11:13)

Kingship and Covenant (1 Sam. 11:14–12:25)

Saul and the Philistines (1 Sam. 13:1-23)

The Reign of Saul as King (Part 1: 1 Sam. 14:1-23)

The Reign of Saul as King (Part 2: 1 Sam. 14:23–14:52)

The Rejection of Saul as King (1 Sam. 15:1-35)

Series 3: David's Rise and Saul's Demise (1 Samuel 16:1–26:25)

The Anointing of David (1 Sam. 16:1-23)

Seeing as God Sees (1 Sam. 17:1–18:5)

Saul's Alienation (1 Samuel 18:6–19:24)

Covenants, Fugitives, and Strange Bedfellows (1 Sam. 20:1–22:23)

Encounters in the Life of a Fugitive anointee (1 Sam. 23:1–26:25)

David in Philistia (1 Sam. 27:1–31:13)

Series 4: The Struggle to Come to the Kingdom (2 Samuel 1:1–5:5)

[Possibly start this series with a single sermon on 1 Samuel]

Learning of and Lamenting Death (2 Sam. 1:1-27)

The Transition from Saul (2 Sam. 2:1–5:5)

Piety and Pragmatism (2 Sam. 5:6-25)

Series 5: David the Great (2 Samuel 5:6–8:18)

Success and Prosperity in the City of David
(2 Sam. 5:6–6:23)

God's House or David's House? (2 Sam. 7:1-29)

Davidic Covenant and Aftermath (2 Sam. 7:1–8:18)

Remembering Jonathan (2 Sam. 9:1-13)

Series 6: David the Not So Great (2 Samuel 9:1–20:26)

When Kings Go Off to War … not!
(2 Sam. 10:1–12:31)

Eating Sour Grapes (2 Sam. 13:1–14:38)

Power and Presence in Weakness
(2 Sam. 15:1–19:8a)

Return and Rebellion Again (2 Sam. 19:8b–20:25)

Cripples, Cunning, and Kings (2 Sam. 9; 16:1-4;
19:24-30)

Series 7: Theological Reflections on Kingship (2 Samuel 21:1–24:25)

The Blessings of Israel's Kings (2 Samuel 21:1-22;
23:8–24:25)

Poetry and Reflections on David, God's King
(2 Sam. 22:1–23:7)

God or Satan? (2 Sam. 24:1-25)

Epilogue (Ps. 145)

One Long Series

Of course, another possibility is that you take a full year to work your way through the whole of the book. In the breakup that I've suggested of approximately thirty-five sermons, this would allow for breaks for Christmas and Easter and the various other activities that inevitably happen in a year.

The approach that I've taken in the chapters which follow allows for the breakup outlined above but makes no decision about whether this might be done over one year or over a series of years.

Some Other Possible Approaches

One way of looking at Samuel which I've toyed with but never actually done is to approach Samuel via the psalms.

Many of the psalms have headings that locate them in some part of David's life (although it is not always possible to definitively locate them in the narrative of Samuel). Perhaps the section of Samuel could be preached on one week, followed by the psalm that is situated in that context. The difficulty with such an approach is that it is not really that helpful for giving a congregation a feel for Samuel as a whole. However, it might be a good approach for preaching on a selection of psalms.

Another approach that suffers from the same problem is one which attempts a 'Life of David' approach. The risk is that the context in which David's life is set is not considered as it might be and therefore the concepts raised in the whole are not adequately pursued.

Part Two:

THE RISE OF SAMUEL AND KINGSHIP

(1 Samuel 1:1–8:22)

4.
The Story of Hannah
(1 Samuel 1:1-28; 2:11)

Within the Old Testament there are some intriguing and strategically placed references to women. For example, after the scene of the book of Exodus is set, the main characters are largely nameless until verse 10 of chapter 2, when Moses is named by Pharaoh's daughter. In these same twenty-four verses, five women act as rescuers or deliverers of God's people, therefore pre-empting God's acts of deliverance in the book. Two of those women are named – Shiprah and Puah and are therefore singled out for either being like God or for siding with God.

In the books that record the history of God's people in the land (Joshua to Kings), the first and the last prophets named are women – Deborah in Judges 4–5 and Huldah in 2 Kings 22:14.

Similarly striking is the introduction to the books of Samuel. In the Hebrew Bible the verse that immediately precedes 1 Samuel 1, Judges 21:25, literally says, 'In those days there was no king in Israel. Everyone did what was right in his own eyes' (ESV). Such background sets the scene for 1 Samuel 1 which opens with the mention of a man but focuses on a woman whose actions and words set the scene for the whole of Samuel. Her actions and her words will, in many ways, set the standard by which those who follow will be measured and weighed.

In teaching Samuel and preaching from it, this chapter and a half are therefore very important for God's people to understand. For this reason, one chapter will be spent looking at the story of Hannah and another examining her prayer.

Listening to the Text
Context and Structure
The whole section from 1 Samuel 1:1–2:11 is structured around five geographical references. The first, middle and last concern the family of Elkanah at their hometown of Ramah. The second and fourth focus on the same family at the city of Shiloh where the ark of the Covenant is situated at this particular time in history. There is a repeating pattern that is found in what happens at Shiloh that involves a problem, action, interaction with Eli and response in worship.

The following structure illustrates how the whole functions.

A	1:1-3	The family of Elkanah at Ramah (Hannah childless)
B	1:4-18	The family at Shiloh
(i)	1:4-8	The problem introduced: Hannah without child
(ii)	1:9-11	Hannah acts on her own and proposes solution: 'You *give* me a son' 'I will *give* him to you'

	(iii)	1:12-18	Hannah and Eli: Opposition and resolution
	(iv)	1:19a	Worship
A	1:19b-20		Return to Ramah (Hannah with child – resolution 1)
B	1:21–2:10		The family at Shiloh
	(i)	1:21-23	The problem introduced: Hannah does not give the child back to God
	(ii)	1:24	Hannah acts on her own and takes her son with sacrifices and gifts
	(iii)	1:25-28a	Hannah and Eli: Hannah *gives* child (resolution)
	(iv)	1:28b	Worship
	(v)	2:1-10	The prayer of Hannah of exaltation and reversals
A	2:11		The family of Elkanah at Ramah (Hannah without child; God has child – resolution 2)[1]

One further item which bears the story along is the reference to 'giving', unfortunately not obvious in most English translations. Its importance will be seen as we move through the content of the passage below and will need explanation in the context of preaching and teaching.

Once Samuel the child is situated in Shiloh in 1 Samuel 2:12, Ramah is largely left behind except for occasional visits throughout Samuel, mostly linked with Samuel himself (e.g. 1 Samuel 7:17; 8:4; 15:34; 16:13; 25:1). The focus shifts to Shiloh where it remains until the ark is captured by the Philistines in 1 Samuel 4; it then moved to Kiriath Jearim in 1 Samuel 7:1–2, where it will remain

---

1. Reid, *1 & 2 Samuel*, pp. 2-3.

until Jerusalem is conquered by David in 2 Samuel 5 and the ark is then moved there in 2 Samuel 6.

Content

The family of Elkanah at Ramah (1:1–3)

The context of the book and this particular passage is set by its place in the Hebrew canon where the last verses of Judges summarise the context as being one where there was no king and everyone did what was right in their own eyes (Judg. 17:6; 21:25). This connection is strengthened by the wording of the introduction to Elkanah ('There was a certain man from…') which echoes the introduction to Samson in Judges 13:2.

While the setting and the identification of Elkanah are important, the focus of this section is the childless state of Hannah in contrast to the fertility of his second wife, Peninnah, a fact that is stressed chiastically in verse 12 (Hannah … Peninnah … Peninnah had children … Hannah had no children). In the original Hebrew, this is emphasised by the addition of 'the name of the *first* was' and 'the name of the *second* was' before the names of the two women.

If verse 1 sets the historical context and verse 2 identifies the problem that will be the focus of the larger passage, then verse 4 sets the religious context and places this family in it. At this time, the centre of religious focus is Shiloh, where the ark is situated (rather than Bethel as it had been at the end of Judges; Judg. 20:24-28) and is under the oversight of a priestly family consisting of a father, Eli, and his two sons, Hophni and Phinehas. Eli alone features in this passage but the sons of Eli will be the foil against which Samuel is compared in the ensuing story.

Part Two: The Rise of Samuel and Kingship

The family of Elkanah at Shiloh (1:4–19a)

In this section, the problem of Hannah's childlessness moves to centre stage and is heightened not only by the religious setting but also by some unusual emphasis (for a Hebrew storyteller) on the level of mental anguish being experienced by Hannah (e.g. vv. 8, 10, 11, 16).

The reasons for this level of stress are multiple and outlined by our writer. First, where in other places in Scripture barrenness is simply stated without reason (e.g. Gen. 11:30; 29:31; Luke 1:7), here Hannah's barrenness is twice said to originate with God (vv. 5 and 6). God is the source of her trouble and therefore in some sense the source of her stress.

The second source is the persecution of Peninnah (v. 6), who is here called a 'rival'. The sense is that she would greatly provoke Hannah to the point of bringing her very low.

The third source appears to be her husband. Although we know that he loves her (v. 5), his words in verse 8 have a somewhat accusative feel to them. Three times he says, 'Why … you …?' before a final, 'Am I not more to you than ten sons?' (ESV).

The last source of stress, which is not stated but which would undoubtedly be understood by the original hearers, is social expectation. Hannah's world was one where a woman's status and influence were often tied to her ability to produce children for her husband and an inability to do so caused grief.

It was somewhat inevitable that family gatherings in the presence of God, her husband, and her rival, along with the reminders of her situation would push Hannah's stress to high levels. The text makes this apparent by telling us that on such occasions she cannot even eat (v. 7), despite the fact that her husband showers her with extra food (v. 5).

In the narrative, there is a distinct turn which occurs at verse 9. Up until this point Hannah has been described as one who is the victim of others. Actions are largely taken against her and words are directed at her. In verse 9, she takes decisive action herself (in Hebrew, the verb for rising is the first word in the sentence).

In the remainder of verse 9 the narrator intervenes to let us know that Eli is nearby but then the focus falls on Hannah's grief again in verse 10 and then her vow in verse 11. The language of that vow is very important for understanding the rest of her story. There are a number of important words that may need to be explained to hearers. First, the verb 'to remember' is important in Hebrew and has the sense of determining to act upon something. An example can be seen at the critical juncture of the flood story in Genesis where God 'remembers' Noah and the animals in the ark. Such remembering is tied with His action to send a wind to cause the waters to recede (Gen. 8:1). So, when Hannah asks God to remember, she is asking Him to act.

Second, the language of remembering also has reference back to the book of Exodus, where God's apparent silence in Exodus 2 is shattered by the words of the narrator who says that He 'heard' the groaning of His people, 'remembered' His covenant with Abraham, Isaac, and Jacob, 'saw', and 'knew' (Exod. 2:23-25 ESV). These words, and the request to 'look upon' and 'remember' simply echo what we have observed already, that Hannah's situation is somehow linked to, or representative of, Israel's own situation.

Third, she gives definite shape to the action she is seeking. The critical words are captured in the NIV84 translation where she talks of reciprocal giving: 'if you *give* ... then I will *give* him to the Lord' (v. 11). The rest of this passage will repeatedly pick up the word 'give'. First, we will see whether God will indeed remember and 'give'. Then we will wait to see whether Hannah will live up to her promise and 'give'. This will provide some of the narrative tension and relief for the rest of the story.

The first example of the word 'give' being taken up is found in verse 17. In verses 12 to 16 there is an interaction between Hannah and the representative of God, Eli the priest. This interaction closes with Eli pronouncing a blessing and saying '… and may the God of Israel grant (literally 'give') you what you have asked of him.' One can imagine that Hannah would have taken this word from God's representative as some encouragement that He would regard her request positively. Certainly, she leaves able to eat and with her face no longer downcast (v. 18).

The family of Elkanah back at Ramah (1:19-20)
There are a series of rapid-fire verbs in verses 19-20 that indicate that God is not slow in answering Hannah's request. Only one of those verbs has God as its subject—'the LORD remembered'—echoing The Prayer of Hannah from verse 11 and resulting in His 'giving' as Hannah had requested, and Eli had wished on her.

The family of Elkanah back at Shiloh again (1:21–2:10)
In verse 21, Elkanah and his family return to Shiloh again. When they were last there, the problem that needed a solution or resolution was that of Hannah's childlessness. Now the problem is that she has a child whom she promised to 'give' back to God. However, she is not at Shiloh with the family (v. 22), which would be the proper time and location for her to do this.

Verses 21-23 have some difficulties that may possibly need to be addressed when teaching or preaching. First, there is the reference in verse 21 to Elkanah fulfilling *his* vow. This possibly indicates that he has confirmed and taken on Hannah's vow in accord with Numbers 30:10-15, even though he had the right to disallow it. The second has to do with the meaning of Elkanah's words, 'only may the Lord make good his word.' If Numbers 30 provides the background, then this presumably means that Elkanah thinks that her decision to 'give' is God's will and is therefore urging her not to stand in the way of that will being fulfilled, that is, Samuel being given back to the Lord.

If we were original readers, we would probably have thought of weaning as taking two or three years, and so, as we heard in the second half of verse 23, we would have wondered if Hannah really was going to 'give' the boy. However, just as Hannah initiated action toward God in the first visit to Shiloh, so she does here, culminating in her echoing the vow of verse 11 as she speaks of how she prayed for the child and the Lord 'gave' her what she asked. In resolution to the problem raised in verse 21, she will now dedicate him to the Lord (the word 'give' in the NIV84 is not the same one that has been used earlier).

The final close of the story, indicating without doubt that Hannah has 'given' the boy, comes in 2:11, where we are told that Elkanah goes home (and the next chapter indicates he does so with Hannah), and Samuel remains to minister before the Lord. It is apparent that although she now has a child, Hannah can live without having him present and the grief that gave rise to the story has been resolved.

Theological Themes

The Bible is a book of theology and stories are used to carry that theology. In these sections throughout the book, my personal patterns in preaching will be used and the theological themes which are apparent within the passage will be addressed.

The narrative section of this portion of Scripture can be seen as one which concentrates on the helpless situation of one person, Hannah. This situation is symptomatic of the position confronting Israel during this time. During this period of the judges, they are somewhat helpless as a result of the anarchy and mayhem within their borders and increasing foreign threats outside. These two themes will come together in this book. Samuel is both the answer to Hannah's prayer as well as the person who will bring religious stability and oversee the introduction of kingship.

Hannah's story, when confronted by her own childlessness and that of an external oppressor, also models what the people of God should do, that is, turn to Him as one who loves helping those who turn to Him, dependently for help, and rescue.

Listening to the Whole of Scripture

Looking Back

As we look back in the Bible, we find that the things we see here about God and His people are often found. On the one hand, Adam and Eve's striking out for independence resulted in judgment. On the other, when Israel found herself in deep distress in Egypt, they cried out to God whose response was to hear, remember, look and take notice (Exod. 2:23-25). In the time of the Judges, independence causes them to worship other gods and brings them distress. However, calling upon

God causes Him to respond in mercy and to send a judge to deliver them and give them victory over their enemies (Judg. 3:1-11).

Looking Forward
As we look forward from here through the rest of the Bible we see similar themes repeated time and again. An example would be in Daniel's decision to be faithful and to call upon God for help and God's response in Daniel 2. However, the book of Daniel also demonstrates that our call for help may not always be answered in this life (hence Dan. 12:1-3). However, the New Testament also testifies to the same things about God. For example, when we consider the human situation when faced with the helplessness of sin portrayed in Romans 1–3 or Ephesians 2, we read that God sees our need and announces to us the great news that when we were still powerless and helpless, Christ died for us to reconcile us to God (Rom. 5:6, 8, 10).

Throughout Scripture then, there is a dominant theme about God which we see here in 1 Samuel 1. God loves it when people are in helpless situations, because then they are ready to cast themselves upon Him in dependence. Living dependently before God is how to be, and how God wants us to be.

From Text to Message
A passage like this one needs careful and sensitive preaching and teaching. Although it is not the primary purpose of the narrative, it raises the issues of infertility and other forms of suffering which people will want addressed. Undoubtedly, there will also be people the preacher and teacher is ministering to who are or have experienced infertility and its after-effects. It is important that to such

people we avoid giving trite promises. At the same time, we need to be sympathetic and urge them to bring their situation to God as Hannah did. We also need to let them know that God may or may not answer as He did here. The way to preserve this tension is to preach the thrust of the passage and not so much the details. We need to convey who God is and what He is like as the source of help.

As we have seen, the theological message is fundamentally not about our situation but about God's character – One who loves helping the helpless and who is therefore their one true hope. This passage, therefore, urges us to remember this by focusing on His help displayed by the cross and to turn the dependence exercised there by our Lord into a way of life before God. Such living should be characterised by trust in His goodness and His desire to give all good gifts to His children (Matt. 12:7-12), particularly those pertaining to salvation.

That said, it is important that we don't assume too much or read too much into this passage. When taken in the context of the whole Bible, this passage does not promise that God will always do what He did with Hannah, but it does display a God who listens, whose nature is to remember the trouble of His people and One who meets helplessness with help and powerlessness with rescue. He wants us to run to Him as Hannah did, knowing because of the cross that He is the God that Hannah found Him to be.

Suggestions for Preaching

In thinking about preaching on this passage, there are a number of particular issues to consider. First, it will possibly be the opening sermon in a series either short or long. This means it has to perform a number of functions.

Second, as noted above, the narrative proper includes a poetic section and it is clear that both narrative and prayer/poetry belong together. However, the prayer says more than the narrative itself says. Moreover, the issues raised by the poem are significant in their own right. This is the fundamental reason behind the rather artificial decision to separate the two.

Sermon 1

One way of introducing the sermon would be to raise the question of helplessness directly from the beginning. This could be done by way of story or example. Listeners could be drawn in by being asked what their characteristic response to helplessness is. This would then provide the opportunity to paint the picture of Israel's helpless state at the time of the judges. The point could then be made that in many ways Hannah epitomises Israel's own helplessness and her response might help Israel and us know how to respond to such situations.

Subsequently, the preacher would want to go through the passage, explaining it as they went. The main sections should be shaped by the passage itself and they are:

1. Introducing Hannah and her family (1:1-3)
2. The family at Shiloh for the first time (1:4-19a)
3. Return to Ramah (1:19b-20)
4. The family at Shiloh again (1:21–2:10)
5. Return to Ramah (1:27b–2:1a, 10)

In the concluding section, three fundamental points might be made:

- God is a God who is sovereign.
- He is a helper of the helpless by nature. This is seen throughout Scripture but most fully in the person and work of Christ.

- The appropriate response to our helpless state—whether it is spiritual or physical—is to go to God. Examples from life would be helpful here.

Sermon 2

This second sermon is an outline of one of my own. My goal was not only to preach from this passage but also to introduce the books of Samuel and the coming series. The introduction began by talking about my childhood in Papua New Guinea where we did not have a television but were taught a love of reading. I introduced my favourite novel and told the people by re-reading the first paragraph and the last page or two, I could recapture the whole book. This allowed me to say that in books of Scripture beginnings and endings often tell us much about the book and that Samuel is like this and therefore we needed to listen carefully. We were going to learn deep and fundamental things about God in this sermon and the next, that would unlock some secrets of the books of Samuel and some deep secrets of the Christian life.

After this introduction, I worked through the narrative as outlined above. The goal was to retell the story but highlight items of significant importance that may not have been noticed. I made sure that I didn't get bogged down in explanation but maintained the tension and tempo of the original. From experience, I have learnt that short and pithy sentences help this.

In the final section of the sermon, I moved the hearers through three stages under the headings below.

1. What is the real message here?
    This had the goal of helping people recognise what theologically undergirds the story and how it helps people approach God and live before Him.

2. The God who is sovereign
   Here I showed the hearers what is surprising about this story, that is, that on the surface there does not appear to be a national crisis in Israel, just the personal crisis of this barren woman. Nevertheless, as Samuel unfolds, we will find that there was a national crisis in Israel and Hannah's life was used to prepare a prophet who could guide His people through this crisis. His action in closing her womb (1 Sam. 1:5 and 6) was sovereignly directed towards addressing the nation's need as well as Hannah's.

3. Helper of the helpless
   Under this heading, I demonstrated that other parts of the Bible show that God loves helping the helpless and that dependence upon Him was God's intention for us as is demonstrated in the cross.

4. Responding to this God
   This is the application section, where people are urged to respond to God by putting aside their independence and turning dependently and prayerfully to Him as Hannah did. She, therefore, becomes for them a model of faithful dependence.

Leading a Bible Study

The focus in this Bible study will be the story of Hannah and not the details of the poem. You will need to tell members of the study that this is what you are doing and that you will return to the poem next time you meet.

Introduce the issues

Nearly all of us have at some time lived with situations where we feel as though life is out of control or out of the reach of God. Share some examples with one another. How have you felt about God at these times? How have you reacted to Him?

Part Two: The Rise of Samuel and Kingship

Study the passage

1. Read through the story in whole and name the places where the action occurs. Is there any pattern to what happens at each location? What is it?
2. Draw a diagram that captures the dynamics of Elkanah's family life as presented in verses 1 to 8.
3. List the words and references that describe the inner emotional state of Hannah and its outward expression in verses 1 to 20. Who or what has caused her to be in that state?
4. Hebrew narrative often uses a plot pattern that goes something like this:
    - Setting
    - Test or challenge
    - Protagonist's response
    - Divine counter-response and consequences
    - Closure
5. Do you think that this pattern fits with 1 Samuel 1:1-28 & 2:11? Put verse numbers with the various elements of the pattern if you think that they are there.
6. What are the critical or central verses in the story? Why?

Think it through

1. Where else in Scripture do we find people acting toward God in the same way as Hannah? How does God respond? What do we learn about God from this?
2. What else do we learn about God from this passage?
3. Read Romans 5:1-11. How is our situation as Christians similar to that of Hannah? How is God's response to that situation similar to and different from how we see Him act here?

Live it out

Return to those situations you envisaged at the start of this study. Having learnt what you have from 1 Samuel 1:1-28 and 2:11, how do you think God would have you respond to those situations in future? What could you put in place now that would help you respond this way?

5.
The Prayer of Hannah
(1 Samuel 2:1-10)

In various places in the Old Testament a narrative report of an incident is linked to a poetic and often more theologically reflective account. The most famous of these are the crossing of the Red Sea and the vanquishing of Pharaoh in Exodus 14–15 and the story of Deborah and Barak's rout of Sisera and his army in Judges 4–5. Other examples might include David's sections of Samuel which are the basis for Davidic psalms in the book of Psalms (e.g. Ps. 3 and 2 Sam. 15–16; Ps. 18 and 1 Sam. 18–31; Ps. 51 and 2 Sam. 11–12; Ps. 52 and 1 Sam. 21–22).

The poetic form of Hannah's prayer is probably indicative that just like these other examples, it was a prayer that was sung and can therefore also be labelled a song. As we shall see, it could also appropriately be called a prophecy.

An often neglected example of this pattern is the passage here in 1 Samuel 1:1–2:12. When the account of Hannah's story is matched with her poem, the two lay the theological grounding of much of the narrative that follows. In fact, it is probably not an understatement to say that if you can understand this story and poem along with the final four chapters in 2 Samuel (which also have poems), then you will have a firm grounding for grasping the central message of the whole of Samuel. This would be further enhanced with an understanding of the other poems that are strategically placed throughout (i.e. 1 Sam. 2:1-10; 18:7; 2 Sam. 1:19-27; 3:33-34; 22:1-51; 23:1-7).

The importance of this poem for understanding the whole book and grounding it theologically is the reason why the best strategy for preaching and teaching the whole section is to allow a separate study for the poem of 1 Samuel 2:1-10.

Listening to the Text

Context and Structure

We have already examined the immediate context of this passage at some length. However, it is helpful to build on what has been said in the introduction of this chapter; it is formative for what follows. In other words, we will have cause as the narrative continues to look at particular actions of the characters in the context of the theology of this prayer. Additionally, we will need to consider the impact of the fact that the poem of 2 Samuel 22 picks up some of the language of this prayer.

The structure of the poem is straightforward and can be summarised in the following way.

2:1-2		**In praise of the incomparable God**
	2:1	He alone gives true strength
	2:2	He is beyond comparison
2:3-8		**In praise of the God of reversals**
	2:3	Don't resort to false self-strength (characterised by boasting)

2:4-5	For reversals happen
2:6-8	And the LORD, the creator, is the source of such reversals
2:9-10	**In praise of God the judge**
2:9-10a	God the judge rewards the faithful and punishes the wicked
2:10b	This creator judge will give true strength to His king[1]

Content

In the structure above, I have tried to make clear some of the themes of the various sections. Nevertheless, they should be spelt out here so that we can understand the way the poem both echoes Hannah's experience and also outlines a theological perspective which will help us properly assess some of the narrative that follows.

In praise of the incomparable God (2:1–2)

The repeated use of personal pronouns (e.g. 'my', 'I') in this section indicate just how Hannah's prayer arises from her personal situation. This is reinforced by her mention of 'enemies', a clear allusion to her persecutor and rival Peninnah.

The reference to 'horn' is a symbol of strength, often military (see also v. 10). This is probably due to its use both offensively and defensively among animals of various sorts (e.g. Deut. 33:17; 1 Kings 22:11). Therefore to raise a horn is to display strength, vitality, power and honour (e.g. 2:10; Ps. 89:17; 112:9; 132:17), while to cut off the horn is to render them harmless and helpless (e.g. Lam. 2:3; Jer. 48:25; for both together see Ps. 75:10).

---

1. Reid, *Samuel*, pp. 12.

Despite the use of personal pronouns at the beginning, this is followed by a shift from herself to the Lord in the last line of verse 1 and Hannah is completely absent in verse 2, indicating that the true focus of this section is the Lord. Her rejoicing is a rejoicing not so much in her exaltation over her enemy, but in the glory of the Lord.

The aspect of God's nature that she rejoices in is also apparent in the language she uses in verse 2. The threefold repetition of 'There is no one like/beside…' emphasises His incomparability. Such links between rejoicing in deliverance from enemies, the exaltation of God's people, and the incomparability of God, are also seen in the exodus deliverance that is celebrated in song in Exodus 15 (especially vv. 1-11). We have already noticed previously how Hannah's prayer taps into themes from Exodus.

In a similar vein, we should observe the language of salvation that occurs both within the introduction to the Song of the Sea and Hannah's prayer (Exod. 15:1-2 and verses 1-2 here). Similarly, the language of 'salvation' in verse 2 echoes Exodus 15:1-2. Hannah's situation and Israel's are somewhat echoed. Tantalised, we might wonder if God's actions in giving her a son are also part of His means of rescuing His people.

In praise of the God of reversals (2:3-8)

The development of the prayer so far has been from personal rejoicing, to exaltation over enemies, to confession of the incomparability of the Lord. In verse 3 Hannah speaks to those hearing her. It is as though she is telling them that if God is all that she has said He is, then they should be careful of not exalting themselves against Him and, presumably, against those who take shelter in Him.

Such exaltation before an incomparable God who knows and who weighs deeds is surely a risky course of action.

The rest of this section moves away from speaking of God but probably flows out of verse 3. Hannah picks up the reversals noted in her own experience echoed in verse 1 and speaks of other reversals where those in positions of power are taken down and those in positions of weakness are lifted up. Some appear to have allusions to her own situation (e.g. the barren one now having a full complement of children; v. 5).

The inversions noted in verses 4 and 5 are then sourced in verses 6 and 7. Again, just as the experience of Hannah directs her to the Lord in verse 1, so human experience of reversal is sourced in the Lord here. Again, Hannah knows that the Lord is the source of such power inversions as she has herself experienced it.

The latter part of verse 8 provides a theological justification for the Lord's ability to do this. He is the Creator and as such He is able to subject all creation to His will. The Lord who established the world is able to turn it to His purposes at His will. If this is so, He is able to upturn humans in their pride and exalt the humble.

In praise of God the judge (2:9-10)

We already know from Hannah's earlier comments in verse 3 that God knows and weighs deeds. In verse 9, that principle is applied to two particular groups. First, there are 'his faithful ones' (ESV) (which possibly has the sense of the ones who are beneficiaries of God's steadfast love and are therefore in relationship with Him), whose feet will be guarded by the God who showers steadfast love upon His people. Then there are the rest, who are the 'the wicked.'

They will share the lot of all who are not in relationship with God. They 'will be silenced in darkness.' The reason given for the first two lines of verse 9 is supplied in the last line of verse 9, 'for not by might shall a man prevail' (ESV).[2] In other words, relationship with God determines human future not human might.

In verse 10 all of this is drawn together, and Hannah's prayer becomes fully prophetic. The words 'king' and 'anointed' (i.e. 'messiah') in lines three and four indicate that kingship is in view in the second half of the verse. It is probable that the whole verse is directed toward Israel's kings, who don't as yet exist but have been in prospect since God's pronouncement to Abraham in Genesis 17:6, 16.

In this verse Hannah indicates how kings and kingship will function. Just as all humanity had been described in terms of two fates, so it will be with kings. Where they set themselves against God (i.e. they are 'adversaries of the LORD'), there will be the judgment of God (lines 1 and 2). Presumably, where they are godly, He will 'give strength to his king and exalt the horn of his anointed' just as He had exalted Hannah's horn as she depended upon Him.

This risk for kingship is reliance on human might. Hannah in her weakness had nowhere to go but to God. So the kings of Israel are to not trust in might but flee to God, and depend upon Him (cf. Ps. 146:3-7).

Theological Themes
This prayer is so theologically rich that there is a risk of picking up each detail and avoiding the central thrust.

---

2. Preserving the 'for' here better matches the connective 'for/because' in the original language.

As so often in Scripture, a principal guide may come from noting the beginning and the end. Hannah's point appears to be that God strengthened her position (i.e. lifted her horn) among her persecutors, in her family, and in her social context when she humbled herself and let the Lord be God. Since this is His character, kings should take note and expect that arrogance will be met by being brought down while humility will be met by exaltation.

Hannah's opening verses, the middle of the prayer, and the conclusion indicate that the status of all humans, and particularly kings, is dependent upon God's actions and not on might or anything else.

In order to quickly indicate how foundational these matters are, we might reflect upon some of the events that follow. In the rest of chapter 2 we will meet the sons of Eli the priest who have oversight over sacrifices at Shiloh. They are the wicked who have no respect for God, and their father Eli refuses to discipline them. On the basis of the theology espoused in this prayer, we might expect judgment for both Eli and his sons, which is indeed promised (1 Sam. 2:27-36) and later fulfilled.

Throughout chapter 2 and 3, Eli's family is contrasted with Samuel and his mother, Hannah. Samuel grows in stature and favour with the Lord and with people, and Hannah's allegiance to God and her dependence upon Him is met with her bearing three sons and two daughters (2:21).

Later in chapter 4, Israel will be arrogant and superstitious regarding the ark and will be defeated at the hands of the Philistines. In contrast to this, David who is dependent upon the Lord is lifted up and is remarkably successful.

These are but a few examples of how the story of Hannah and the theological reflection offered in her psalm are followed through in the ensuing narrative within Samuel. In particular, we will see its importance in relation to the kings of Israel, not only in Samuel, but also in the narrative of Kings to follow.

The second theological observation about the prayer is the focus on the Lord. He is mentioned by His special name, the Lord (Yhwh), nine times and His actions in His world dominate and are comprehensive. All human existence is subject to Him and will be crowned with glory or shame according to how humans treat Him.

Listening to the Whole of Scripture

Looking Back

Again, in this section we will see how Hannah's prayer builds on the theology of the Bible up until this point and then how it flows through the rest of Scripture. We could, of course, start in the garden of Eden where fullness was promised for obedience and punishment for disobedience. Sure enough, Adam and Eve exalted themselves over God and this was met by punishment and being brought low.

The first half of the book of Exodus begins with God's people humiliated before an arrogant king who sets himself defiantly against God. In the tussle that ensues, that king is brought down and God's people are exalted. Later, these same people will exalt themselves against God in the sin of the golden calf (Exodus 32–33), which will bring God's humbling of them.

The book of Judges contains a cycle of sin and repentance which illustrates this point often. At the same time, it demonstrates a spiralling of humans 'doing what was right in their own eyes' and therefore being brought low by God's appointment of foreign aggressors to harass and enslave them and also allow them to reap the consequences of their own sin. The story of Hannah is the story of one person who goes against the trend and demonstrates how Israel as a whole should act.

Looking Forward

The examples above of 'looking back' theologically are only a few of what you might observe prior to 1 Samuel 1–2. Similarly, those which follow are only a sample as well.

As indicated earlier, the story of the kings of Israel which follows in 1 and 2 Kings is largely governed by the theology of this story and prayer. Think of the refrains that occur throughout those books either commending or decrying those leaders. Think also of how the dominant refrain of 'X did evil in the eyes of the Lord' (e.g. 1 Kings 11:6; 15:26, 34; 16:25; 22:52; 2 Kings 21:2, 20; 23:32, 37) will inevitably mean that both Northern and Southern kingdoms will be judged by God (2 Kings 17:7-23; 2 Kings 24:19-20).

Within the wisdom books, Proverbs will almost turn the theology of Hannah's song into a formula (e.g. Prov. 12:3). The books of Job and Ecclesiastes, along with psalms like Psalm 73, will interact with Hannah's theological premise by positing that God's ways should not be overly simplified and that there may be complicating factors that cause God's apparent actions to be misunderstood.

In Luke's Gospel, Hannah's prayer operates as a prototype for the Magnificat (Luke 1:46-55), which theologically indicates that God's ways have not changed. He is mindful of the humble, extends mercy to those who fear Him, scatters the proud, brings down rulers, but lifts up the humble and helps His servant Israel, remembering to be merciful to His people.

Jesus is the model of true humility in that He lives life before God in utter dependence and without sin. He is God's Christ and acts as Hannah had prophesied that a king should act. However, His life was not crowned with exaltation but with the dishonour of death on a cross.

Just as the writers of wisdom literature indicated, there may be complicating factors that might cause God's ways to be misunderstood. In this case, it was that the righteous Jesus died for the sake of the unrighteous (1 Pet. 3:18) in order to bring us to God. However, the theology of Hannah's song did not fail. God raised His Son and seated Him at His right hand. Moreover, at the end of time He will exalt the horn of His Messiah when every knee will bow in heaven and on earth and under the earth, and every tongue confess that Jesus Christ is Lord to the glory of God the Father (Phil. 2:5–12).[3]

From Text to Message

One of the great dangers in preaching narrative is that we take things that appear on the surface of the text and use them as the basis for our preaching. A much better approach is to ask ourselves what theology is 'under the surface' of the text, that is, what forms the foundational thought-world of the text that can be apprehended from the text itself. We can then work on how this theology fits

---

3. Paul's exploration in Phil. 2:1-12 of the humility and exaltation of Christ, matched with his urging of humility in his hearers, contains a great example of the fulfilment of the theology and purpose of Hannah's story and prayer.

into God's purposes in the world, which have their focus and end in Christ, and communicate these to the people we are nurturing in the Word. This will make for much richer preaching and teaching and will help our people understand how to interpret and apply Scripture.

Suggestions for Preaching

Sermon 1

This passage opens up a significant opportunity to give people an insight into the way God works in His world and how this way finds its fulfilment in Christ. It also provides a good opportunity for a cutting edge in terms of urging people to live lives of humble dependence upon God.

Ways Into the Passage

There could be a number of ways into the passage. One might be to speak of the miracle of childbirth and how even today it can never be guaranteed and should always be the grounds for praise. There might be examples from the preacher's own pastoral ministry that, with permission, might be used. This way in would not necessarily tap into the final application or even raise questions for our people, but would enable them to get into the spirit of the prayer/song that will be the focus of attention for the sermon.

Another way in might be to raise the question of who we regard to be great. Is it the successful? Those exalted by humans? The prayer could then be interacted with on the basis of people's preconceptions about greatness and humility. Even another way in might be to speak about the place of humility in the contemporary world. Prior to Christianity, it was largely shunned. Christianity made it a virtue but in the contemporary world it is increasingly no longer considered a virtue.

Moving Through the Text

Once we have engaged the attention of our hearers and given them a reason to engage with the text, the most straightforward way is to remind them of the background in Hannah's experience and then move through the text explaining its structure and theology.

It is important that people understand the structure and content of the song and therefore the best way is to work through the three sections we observed earlier. You might choose to both illustrate and apply each section as you go.

Explaining its purpose

Even if you do choose to illustrate and apply each section above, it is important that we help our people grasp why the song is here and help them understand how it sets the theological grounding for kingship and also for understanding Christ. The central thrust ought to be that humility will be met by God with exaltation and exaltation will be met by humbling.

Giving some examples of this throughout Samuel may be helpful in helping people see the importance of the prayer theologically.

Fulfilment in Christ

Particularly with this passage, our ultimate goal is to drive our people to see that Jesus is God's king, His anointed/Messiah/Christ and that He fulfils this prophecy as none other has (not even David).

Application

Having said that, this passage finds its fulfilment in Christ does not exhaust it. We should then see that the example of Christ in terms of His humility should drive us to live similarly. We might also say that as it was with Christ, this may not always result in exaltation now, but will eventually, if only in the life to come.

Sermon 2

The sort of sermon given above should be the normal diet of our congregations. However, at times there are needs for addressing particular topics from a passage. In my view, the song of Hannah provides a wonderful example of the nature of Christian music and might helpfully be used to teach God's people about good music.

- Music is a great gift from God in helping us respond to God and to grapple with God.
- Christian song may rise out of experience and reflect experience, even as Hannah's did.
- However, it should be integrated with truth about God and its focus should be God, His works, and the way He works in the world. Good Christian music should help people interact with truth about God, even as Hannah's song does.
- There are two dangers with Christian music:
  1. We get our theology right in our music but neglect the fact that song is designed to help us engage with theology (perhaps give examples). Give examples of how we might stray into this error. It often results in song that is abstract and impersonal, lacking in engagement. You might illustrate this by saying that music like this is like a man who loves his wife but never buys her flowers, embraces her, or makes love with her.
  2. We use music to engage people emotionally and experientially but forget about the importance of truth

and theology (provide examples). An illustration that fits with the previous one used above might be to say that music used in this manner is like a man who woos a woman with flowers and romance although he is simply after sex. There is a pretence of relationship but there is no substance or truth in that relationship.

Of course, in using the passage for this purpose it is still important that we work through the text. These points should arise from the text.

Leading a Bible Study

Introduce the issues

Get people to think about corporate prayer or their own personal prayers. What sort of things are prayed for? Where does the focus lie?

Study the passage

1. Read through the passage and see if you can break it into main sections according to themes. Give each of the sections a title.
2. How does the passage link to Hannah's experience and where does it do this?
3. Who is the focus of the passage?
4. What is the link between the second half of verse 8 and what is said before? How does the second half of verse 8 fit with what follows?
5. Which verse captures the 'main point' of the prayer? What are your reasons for thinking this?

Think it through

1. What do you think is the main point of this prayer? What does it tell us about God, the world, ourselves, and God's way of working in His world?

Part Two: The Rise of Samuel and Kingship

2. The word 'anointed' is the Hebrew word for 'Messiah' (= 'Christ'). Why do you think that Hannah concludes with this statement about kingship?
3. If you were to write a charter for kings based on this prayer, what would it be (in less than twenty words)?
4. If you were to measure the kings of Israel on the basis of this charter, how would they do?
5. If you were to measure Jesus on the basis of this charter, how would He do? What in His life and ministry illustrates this?

Live it out

1. Read Philippians 2:1–12.
2. What echoes of Hannah's song do you hear in verses 5-12?
3. What common application could be made about living before God on the basis of 1 Samuel 2:1-10 and Philippians 2:1-12?

6.
Samuel's Rise and Eli's Demise (1 Samuel 2:12-36)

Introduction
With this section of Samuel, we begin to move outward from one family to include another significant family with whom Hannah and her son will be contrasted. From there the focus will begin to move to all Israel.

It is not unimaginable that a Bible study might more than adequately cover the whole of 1 Samuel 2:12–4:1a (I have done this myself). However, the approach that I have taken in preaching has been to separate 1 Samuel 2:12-36 and 1 Samuel 3:1-21. The two reasons are (1) that the issues raised are best dealt with separately and (2) that the remainder of chapter 2 continues to have some links with Hannah and her prayer while Samuel comes into his own, distinct from his mother in chapter 3 and the focus begins to fall on all Israel.

Listening to the Text

Context and Structure
Ramah was the hometown of Samuel and his family and, as we have already observed, references to it in 1 Sam.

1:1–2:11 and 7:15-17 set the larger context of this passage. 1 Sam. 2:11, therefore, performs a double function. On the one hand, the mention of Ramah closes the previous section. At the same time it introduces the notion of Samuel ministering before the LORD under the supervision of Eli, a theme that will run through until a similar note in 1 Samuel 3:1. In this sense, the same pattern already seen of interlocking various narratives is performed by verse 11. The mention of Ramah looks back while the reference to Samuel's ministry before the LORD looks forward to the next section which will conclude with 3:1 (again interlocking with the next section that will continue through until 4:1 by mentioning the absence/presence of the Word of the LORD). Diagrammatically, these four chapters might, therefore, be represented as follows.

In the particular section that is our immediate focus, there is a further breakup caused by the summary statement in verse 26 that describes Samuel's growth in stature and favour with the LORD and with people (thereby dividing the section into two parts: 2:12-26 and 2:27-36). The first part is prefaced by a reference to Samuel (2:11), ends with Samuel (2:26) and finds its centre in the focus on Samuel and his parents (2:18-21). On either side of this there lies the story of Eli's sons (2:12-17) and Eli's interactions with them (2:22-25).

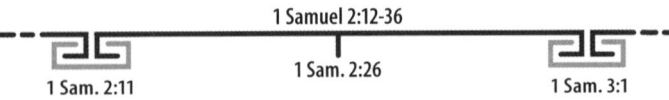

Part Two: The Rise of Samuel and Kingship 95

The second part of this section arises out of the action of Eli's sons and Eli's inaction in the first part and is taken up with the prophetic denunciation against Eli and his family by the 'man of God' (2:27-36).

As a whole, this passage forms a transition between the focus on one family and even one person within that family to its interactions with another family – the house of Eli. Allied with this are four other elements: (1) the diminishing role of Hannah while Samuel's role increases; (2) Hannah's eventual disappearing from the story while her son moves into increasing prominence; (3) the house of Eli beginning to slip from prominence while Samuel rises; and (4) the focus shifting to Israel as a whole (e.g. 3:1; 4:1). As Brueggemann has noted, critical within the whole of 1 Samuel 2:11–3:1 are the references to Samuel's growth.[1] Each of these verses also link him with the Lord. By the end of chapter 3 and the beginning of chapter 4 he is an adult and a prophet whose word comes to all Israel (3:20–4:1).

Content

The sons of Eli (2:12-17)

The first words of verse 12 are stark in their contrast to those of verse 11. Literally it reads, 'Now the sons of Eli were sons of Belial.' Although the meaning of 'Belial' is debated, it probably has the sense of utter destructiveness or worthlessness. When coupled with 'sons of' and that they 'did not have regard for/know the Lord' the overall picture painted is one in which they are unrestrained thugs. In the original language the rhyming of 'Belial' and 'Eli' captures the sense that although these young men are the

---

1. Walter Brueggemann, *First and Second Samuel* (Louisville, KY: John Knox Press, 1990), p. 22.

physical sons of Eli, they are psychologically or morally the sons of Belial – young men cut loose from any constraints either divine or paternal.

Against the backdrop of the portrayal of godly Hannah and Eli's haste to condemn her as a daughter of Belial, the contrast is profound. Hannah is godly but condemned as wicked. Eli is quick to judge others and connect them with Belial but, as we will see, is somewhat ignorant of the sins of his own sons and condemned for his laxity in relation to them. Fortunately, we are not dependent upon Eli for accurate judgment, but the LORD whom these men do not know (2:12).

While the law did allow priests and their families certain benefits and privileges (e.g. verse 28; cf. Lev. 7:28-38; Deut. 18:1-8), what these men do far exceeds their rights as priests. The narrator ensures that we know the wickedness that is being committed by including two notes: (1) an account of their forcefulness in action in verse 16 and (2) his own comment in verse 17 (such comments are not at all common in Samuel; cf. 2 Sam. 11:27).

Even without the narrator's intervention into the narrative, Hannah has already given us enough to know what God's view might be on this. Exaltation will be met by bringing down, those full will find themselves hired out for food, the wicked will be silenced and those who oppose the LORD will be shattered.

Samuel and his parents (2:18-21)

The picture in verses 18-21 strongly contrasts with that of the preceding and succeeding verses. First, the sons are entirely absent, and Eli appears to be the only contact that Samuel's family have with priests apart from their son, who wears the mark of a priest, the ephod.

Second, the marks of God's blessing and knowledge of this family are full. Eli blesses the family and prays for more children (in contrast to Eli who has wicked sons which he will lose) and God's grace is evident through Hannah giving birth.

Third, where Eli's sons do not know the Lord, Elkanah and Hannah's son 'grew up in the presence of the Lord' (v. 21).

The sons of Eli and their father (2:22-26)

The data we have about Eli so far have been somewhat mixed. However, in this section, things are clearly not so positive.

The context is that Eli is very old (v. 22), which might explain his apparent distance from what is happening in the daily activities at the sanctuary at Shiloh and his reliance on hearing from others. However, the constant reference to 'hearing' is important and provides a good summary of both the knowledge of Eli and the activity of his sons.

- Eli *heard* about *everything* his sons were doing (v. 22) and that they had added a sexual sin to their activities at the sanctuary.
- He tells his sons that he *hears* from *all* the people (v. 23).
- He acknowledges that the *report* (a noun related to the verb to *hear*) is not good that he *hears* spreading among the people (v. 24).
- He then warns his sons of theological truth that they should take heed of: direct sin against God Himself is a very risky venture (v. 25).
- Finally, the narrator tells us that Eli's sons did not *listen/ hear* (same word as used earlier) Eli's rebuke or warning

(v. 25). He also tells us that the truth of verse 25 has resulted in God's command to put them to death.

The point made in verse 25 is probably that the sin is being done in the very place designed by God for atonement and so is a direct affront to God showing disdain for His means of providing for sin.

It is clear that the portrayal of Eli given here is not complimentary. While he has all the information, he does not directly rebuke his sons and neither does he act to remove them (as he has intimated that God would do). His rather limited response to the sins of his sons will issue in the rebuke from God in the passage which follows. However, as if to highlight the sins of the sons, we are given a contrast in Samuel who grows in stature and in favour with both the LORD and men (cf. Luke 2:40, 52).

The man of God and the LORD's Word (2:27-36)

The judgment promised by the narrator in verse 25 is made public to Eli in verses 27-36. Some key things to note are:

First, the speech is directed to Eli, not his sons. In other words, Eli is held responsible for the actions of his sons.

Second, the speech of the man of God is a prophetic denunciation very similar in thrust and length to that which is delivered to David in 2 Samuel 12.

- It is announced as something that 'the LORD says' (v. 27; cf. 2 Sam. 12:7).
- The backdrop of the judgment announced is the grace of God in revelation, choice, and the benefits of office (vv. 27-28; cf. 2 Sam. 12:7-8).
- The response has been one of scorn towards God's generosity, failing to give Him the appropriate response and instead, acting in his own favour and that of his

family (v. 29; cf. 2 Sam. 12:9). Significantly, the 'you' who scorns in verse 29 is plural and the reference to 'fattening yourselves' is also plural.

- There will be a judgment that matches the sin. In Eli's case this will be God's disdain of Eli's family as a result of Eli's despising or failing to honour God in relation to his family (v. 30; cf. 2 Sam 12:10). In the case of his sons, their gluttony will be met by poverty and hunger (36).

Intriguingly, while in Eli's case a previous promise by God is turned back because of sin (v. 30; cf. Exod. 29:9; Num. 25:12-13), this will not be so with David's sin (for the promise, see 2 Sam. 7:13).

The judgment pronounced upon Eli's house is a promise to decimate his family and end their ministry within Israel, the sign of which will be the death of both sons on one day. Moreover, the scorning of the gift of priesthood will result in it being replaced and given to someone better (just as Saul's kingship will be; 15:28). In this case, there appears to be a double fulfilment or even more. Given the context, the immediate replacement appears to be Samuel. However, in the larger context of kingship, it will be seen in the replacement of Eli's descendant, Abiathar, with Zadok in 1 Kings 2:35. In an even larger context, the replacement is undoubtedly Jesus (Heb. 2:17), who will combine all roles that are prominent in the books of Samuel (i.e. priest, prophet, and king).

Theological themes

Human and divine

The first two chapters are an intriguing mix of human and divine action. The first group of humans we meet is the family of Elkanah. Elkanah himself appears to be a deeply religious man who wants the best for his family. Peninnah is a persecutor of the disadvantaged Hannah. Hannah is clearly the heroine of chapter 1 as she models dependency upon God, the fulfilment of vows, and godly motherhood toward her dedicated son. Lastly, there is Samuel of whom we are not told much in terms of his own actions, although we are aware that God is at work through him and that he ministers with divine and human favour.

The second family is that of Eli. His sons are thugs and he himself is mostly led by others such as Hannah and his sons. He is an aged and failing father and an unworthy priest.

The portrayal of these people here in Scripture is of people like those you would meet anywhere in the Bible and in the world. There are both good and bad among them, but all in all, they are very human and act with all the normal human motives.

In relation to God's activity here, there are a number of items to observe.

- God is responsible for the closing of Hannah's womb (1:5).
- He is involved in the sons of Eli not listening to their father, 'for it was the Lord's will to put them to death' (2:25).
- Although not explicitly said, the constant linking of Samuel's growth with the LORD, along with the fact that it is the LORD who remembers Hannah and gives her a child, directs us to see the source of life and growth in Him.
- It is God's decisive action that sends a man of God to Eli and causes him to speak His Word.

These references of God's action are indications that God has a programme and a purpose. He wants Samuel in place. Moreover, Hannah's poem gives larger shape to His purpose – He wants a godly king in place. Furthermore, the prophecy of the man of God also indicates that He also wants a godly priest.

The overall picture is therefore of God, active in history, pushing towards His larger purposes for His people and in His world, and working towards this through ordinary people in ordinary families.

The implications are profound, telling us that God is at work ruling His world, even in this apparently unrestrained period of the judges. This will be important to realise as the books of Samuel unfold and describe the often high-handed actions of humans. It is this observation that will give us as readers hope and security. God can and will work in, through and over human action to accomplish His purposes.

Types of Christ

As indicated earlier, Samuel lays the groundwork for much of the terminology used in relation to Jesus. As Samuel is contrasted here as noble priest in relation to the existing corrupt priesthood he clearly prepares for Jesus, a point which is made clear by the echoing of 1 Samuel 2:26 in Luke 2:52. In the chapter which follows he will function as a prophet, speaking the Word of God to the existing priesthood even as Jesus will in His ministry. Later, we will see David who shapes the kingship of Jesus. However, the books of Samuel will show all of them as flawed, indicating that we should look to another yet to come, whom we know to be Jesus, true prophet, priest, and king.

Listening to the Whole of Scripture

Looking Back

This theological theme of divine sovereignty and human responsibility as God's purposes are pursued, is one that occurs repeatedly in Samuel and regularly in narrative literature within the Old Testament. The scene is set for us in the opening pages of Scripture as they portray God creating the world purposefully while humans act defiantly by supposing that they are a better judge of what is right and wrong for them. The end result is ejection from the garden. Yet even here we see God at work forging His purpose as He speaks of a 'seed' or offspring who will crush the head of the serpent and whose heel the serpent will strike (Gen. 3:15). This notion of seed will be pursued throughout Genesis, often being complicatedly pursued amidst significant human sin (not least, the actions of Judah and Tamar in Genesis 38).

Elsewhere in Genesis we find the 'heroes' of Scripture to be frail and yet used by God. For example, in Genesis 12:1-3, Abraham is given three great promises of land, children, and blessing. However, before the chapter ends all three promises are put in jeopardy as he leaves the land, seeks shelter in Egypt, lies about his wife, and ends up being a curse to Pharaoh's household rather than a blessing (Gen. 12:10-20). Despite this, God acts on his behalf, blessing his sojourn in Egypt and protecting the promises by inflicting serious diseases on Pharaoh's household.

Similarly, Moses the murderer is used by God to rescue His people in Exodus. Some significant scoundrels are taken up into God's purposes within the book of Judges and even the most heinous sin of the golden calf (Exod. 32) is used by God to reveal Himself and His nature in a way that will form the Old Testament's view of God in a way that little else does to the same extent.

Looking Forward
As we look forward in history this mix of divine sovereignty and human responsibility reaches its climax at the cross, where humans (and God's people at that) sin with a high hand and yet salvation is wrought by God (see Peter's speech in Acts 2:22-24).

From Text to Message

These larger theological perspectives can help us as we think about preaching this passage. The world portrayed is a world common to us and our people. It is a world where God has His desires and purposes for His world and for us. It is a world where people might line themselves up with His will, live in defiance of it, or try to mix and match. This passage shows us God working in the world according to His will and even with sinful people. It, therefore, opens up the possibility for helping people think through how God's sovereignty works in the midst of human activity and how such things are even bound up with what happens in Christ.

As indicated in our previous passage, these are profoundly theological matters and it will help our people greatly if we teach them these things. It will help give perspective on God's ways, on His purposes in Christ, and on their own lives as they seek to live as God's people. For the Christian leader this will inevitably cause him to highlight Christ. However, the New Testament does not stop there but moves on to tell us the implications for how we should live before Him and the Father, in the power of the Spirit. We should do likewise.

Suggestions for Preaching

While the text does address the question of the leadership of Israel here (i.e. Eli's failed leadership and a replacement coming), it does so by exploring God's sovereign rule over His people and both godly and ungodly responses to God and His rule. In preaching, I therefore suggest that we reflect the same balance. Such will reveal God and Christ to our people and help them analyse their own lives before God.

Ways Into the Text

My way into the text by way of introduction was to do something that is quite rare in my own preaching, to give them a glimpse into the hopes and aspirations of my own Christian life. I spoke first of all about my hopes in life in general and then in terms of being a Christian. I reminded them of a picture of the godly person painted in the New Testament and then observed that I fall far short and end up hoping for something better. I then said to them that if they felt themselves asking these same questions or having the same feelings then the passage today could offer helpful insights.

Moving Through the Text

In the next section of the sermon, I reminded them of what had happened in the preceding passage both in terms of the story of Hannah, and her theological reflection given in her prayer. I said that these theological reflections would help us interpret what we find in the passage for this sermon.

I then outlined two alternative stories which I called 'Samuel: The Son of Hannah' and 'The Sons of Eli'. At the end of the second story I highlighted that the prophecy concerning the replacement of Eli was eventually fulfilled in Christ who replaces all other human priests.

In the third section of the sermon, which I called 'Two Levels of Activity', I reflected on what we saw of human activity in the passage (Hannah's family versus Eli's family) and what we saw of divine activity. I observed that God will, and has, accomplished His purposes despite human sinfulness.

My final section had the title 'Implications' and it had three sections: (1) For the books of Samuel, (2) What can we say? and (3) What can we do?

In (1) I observed that the books of Samuel are introduced this way to make a theological point: That as the readers read on they will see humans act with a high hand. However, they should know from the start that God is in control and will bring about His purposes. It is this that should give hope to the ancient readers and us.

In (2), I said that we should therefore be careful about where we put our hope. If we trust humans, then we will end up in hopelessness because humans are sinful. However, if we trust in God then we will see the sorts of things that we see happen in this passage. Eventually, if we have lined ourselves up with God's purposes, hope will become reality.

In (3), I said that we should be people of faith knowing that all the promises of God have their 'yes' and 'amen' in Jesus Christ (2 Cor. 1:20). We should also act on our faith as Hannah does, prayerfully dependent upon our gracious and loving Father who wants all good things for

His children. Such hope should also be expressed in (a) the everyday small actions that we see Hannah do, (b) the small acts of repentance when we see our own sinfulness, or (c) the encouragement of each other to be people of hope and action.

Leading a Bible Study

Introducing the study

Begin the study by getting people to discuss what they remember of the previous study and recalling what was significant for them.

Read the whole passage out loud.

Passage 1: 1 Samuel 2:12-26

Get people on their own or with one or two others to examine Eli's sons and Samuel and answer the questions (encourage them to concentrate on 2:11-26 and 3:1).

Person/Group	What are they like?	Their attitude to God?	Summary Statement or verse
Eli's sons			
Samuel			

How does Eli respond to his sons in these same verses? What does he 'do' and what does he 'not do'?

Passage 2: 1 Samuel 2:27–3:1

With the same people/group, ask people to answer the following questions.

How does God respond to Eli's sons (1 Samuel 2:30-34; cf. 3:11-14)?

How does God respond to Eli?
How does God respond to Samuel (1 Sam. 2:35–3:1)?

Large group discussion: Putting things together
Draw people back into the larger group and get their feedback from their answer to the observation questions.

As a group discuss what you've learnt from this passage about:

- What God despises
- What God values

Pray
Share prayer points with each other. If possible, share prayer points related to the things that you've learnt from the passage and areas in which you need help.

Pray together.

7.
Famine and Fullness
(1 Samuel 3:1-21)

It was the first time that I preached on John 4 and the woman at the well. I thought that I dealt well with the text and exposed the meaning of it to the congregation in a way that was faithful to its content and also applied it well. However, my wife Heather—a normally gentle, positive and friendly critic—was not so sure. So we began to talk it through together. As we did, it became obvious that a significant issue for her was that my interpretation had threatened and even contradicted an interpretation and application that was dear and significant to her in the history of her walk with God.

There are similar risks attached to preaching 1 Samuel 3, a chapter beloved of preachers. It has a boy or young man, a call narrative, intrigue, suspense, and drama. There is therefore much in it that has been used in a local church context particularly in relation to the call to ministry. Moreover, there is much in it that can and has been abused by preachers, but which has also formed the lives of congregation members. This means that we need to be particularly careful in preparing to preach on this treasured chapter. We may need to be particularly gentle in the manner in which we expose the meaning and its application.

Listening to the Text

Context and Structure

When we looked at 1 Samuel 2:12-36, we observed that there are significant links between that passage and this one. For example, we noticed that the words about Samuel ministering before the Lord under Eli form boundaries around that section (2:11 and 3:1) and that 2:26 forms a break within the section. Other links between the chapters include:

- The note that the sons of Eli 'did not know the Lord' (2:12 ESV) and that Samuel 'did not yet know the Lord' (3:7)
- That both sections have a prophetic Word that is directed at Eli (by the man of God in 2:27-36 and then Samuel in 3:11-18)

Despite these links, there is also disjunction between the two sections. For example, the focus now moves completely away from Hannah and also the household of Eli and falls on to Samuel. Prior to this passage, Samuel has been a minor figure or one who is on the periphery of the stories of other people (even though we have had the sense that he has potential to move to the fore). In this passage that sense now becomes reality as Samuel will become a dominant, although sometimes haunting figure in the narrative.

That sense that we have had of Samuel's potential can be seen in the references to (1) his service of the Lord and (2) his growth. These references are summarised in the following table:

Part Two: The Rise of Samuel and Kingship

2:11	And the boy		he was	one serving	the Lord	before				the priest
2:18	And	Samuel		served		before	the Lord			
3:1	And the boy	Samuel		served			the Lord	before	Eli	

These verses indicate that at the beginning, Samuel's service is a service of the Lord (2:11; 2:18; 3:1), under the supervision of Eli (2:11; 3:1). However, all that changes as the story goes on. While Eli is called 'priest' at the beginning (2:11), that description is gone at the end (3:1), perhaps as a result of the revelations that happen within chapter 2. Furthermore, in chapter 3 we see a shift in how Samuel is presented. The shift is away from his being identified as the 'boy' (Heb. *na'ar*) to his becoming a 'prophet' (Heb. *nābî*). A fundamental change has happened, and this is supported by the references to his growth that occur at critical points through the story (2:21; 2:26; 3:19).[1] Like the references to serving noted above, these are all linked with the Lord. As we will see in our passage, as the result of the Lord's intervention a fundamental change occurs in Israel. A famine of the Word of the Lord has been replaced by a fullness of that Word coming to Israel at the hand of the Lord, through the prophet Samuel revealing the Lord's Word to His people.

The structure of the passage itself is straightforward.

---

1. Drawing on a discussion by Jan P. Fokkelman, *Narrative Art and Poetry in the Books of Samuel: A Full Interpretation Based on Stylistic and Structural Analyses. Volume IV: Vow and Desire (1 Sam. 1-12)*, Studia Semitica Neerlandica (Assen: Van Gorcum, 1993), chapter 3, pp. 156-193.

3:1-3   Problem: Dire days of silence and famine
3:4-10 The call of God's prophet
3:11-14 The prophetic Word given to Samuel
3:15-18 God's prophet speaks God's Word
3:19-21 Resolution: Breaking the famine

Content

Setting and Problem: Dire days of silence and famine (3:1-3)
As observed above, 'The boy ministered before the Lord' recalls Samuel as he is presented in the previous chapters and links the reader to them. However, as we have observed the author is using key verses to bind together the sections of his work, so too verse 1 prefaces the rest of the chapter. We know that Eli stands under the judgment of God for his lack of appropriate oversight of his sons and perhaps his poor leadership. This is part of the reason why there is a problem: 'the word of the Lord was rare' and 'there were not many visions' (v. 1). In any case, by the end of the chapter something will have happened to reverse the oversight between Eli and Samuel as Eli places himself under the prophetic Word delivered by this 'boy' turned 'prophet of the Lord'. So the purpose of the passage gravitates around the Word of the Lord and the agent for its delivery. The heart of the passage is the prophetic Word given to Samuel by the Lord (3:11-14).

The first three verses also contain words that gravitate around the concepts of sight, light, and insight ('visions', 'eyes', 'see', 'lamp'). These are days characterised by a failed leader, no Word from God, no vision, and no reputable successor who might meet the need. The book of Deuteronomy, which gives the theology that undergirds the former and latter prophets who speak about Israel's life in the land, tell us that just as humans need food for physical sustenance, so they need the Word of God for spiritual sustenance and enlightenment as to how to live before God (Deut. 8:3; cf. Ps. 119:105). These are very dark days for Israel.

In these opening verses the only glimmer of hope appears to be the fact that the lamp of God had not gone out. The lamp referred to burned throughout the night (Exod. 27:20-21; Lev. 24:1-4) and so on one level we are simply being told that it was still night-time. However, given the other references to sight, light, and scarcity, perhaps the lamp not being out hints that God has not yet left His people alone. Such a reading may be confirmed by the end of the chapter where not only have the roles of Eli and Samuel been reversed, but God has 'revealed' Himself to Samuel through His Word and Samuel's word came to all Israel.

The call of God's prophet (3:4-10)

As we have seen, central to the whole of 3:1–4:1 is the theme of 'the word of Lord'. This phrase occurs three times (3:1, 7 and 21). In the central occurrence in verse 7 we are told of a problem in relation to that Word coming to Israel: 'Samuel did not yet know the Lord'. To deliver the Word of the Lord to the people this problem must be solved. This is what happens in these verses as God's future prophet learns to hear God speaking. As the second half of verse 7 indicates, the reason that Samuel does not yet know the Lord is that 'the word of the Lord had not yet been revealed to him.' Knowledge of God and of His Word can only come from God revealing Himself in His Word. To hear that Word and personally engage with it in obedience is evidence that you have come to know the God who speaks it. Hosea captures this when he says that there in 'no knowledge of God in the land' (Hosea 4:1 ESV), by which he means that what is known of God is not reflected in the lives of His people (hence Hosea 4:2).

Strictly speaking, although we have used the language of 'call' in the heading to this section, we do not see all the normal characteristics of a prophetic call narrative such as we see with Moses (Exod. 3:1–4:17), Isaiah (Isa. 6:1-13), Ezekiel (Ezek. 1:1–3:11) and Jeremiah (Jer. 1:4-10). There is no conventional call, appointment, or sending. Samuel is not even told to tell Eli the content of what God has told him. Nevertheless, this chapter appears to serve in place of such. After it, God gives His Word (11–14), God's prophet then delivers that Word (15–18) and the problem of a famine of the Word of the Lord is resolved, as a veritable flood of that Word ensues (3:19–4:1a).

The prophetic Word given to Samuel (3:11-14)

At the beginning of the chapter there is a link between the Word of the Lord and visions. Perhaps that is what is happening in verse 10 where we are told that the Lord came and stood there and spoke. Samuel is experiencing a vision as well as hearing a Word.

The Word given is the longest in the chapter. It is not specifically directed at Eli but that is not surprising given that Eli has already heard similar material directly from the man of God in 2:27-36. It is a Word that will make the ears of everyone tingle (cf. 2 Kings 21:12; Jer. 19:3). As in chapter 2, Eli is not accused of doing wrong but of failing to 'restrain' the wrong of his sons (v. 13). The punishment is harsh in that it has effect forever and cannot be atoned for ritually by sacrifice or offering (v. 14), despite the promise of God that his house and his father's house would minister before the LORD forever (2:30).

God's prophet speaks God's Word (3:15-18)

The picture painted in verses 15-18 gives a somewhat idealised portrait of the presentation and reception of the Word of God. The recipient asks for full disclosure. The prophet offers it without hiding anything and the recipient receives it without objection or resistance (a striking contrast to many of the kings of Israel who will later be addressed by the prophets, although not David in 2 Sam. 12).

Resolution: Breaking the famine and silence (3:19-21)

These final verses contain both the resolution of the situation posed in the first section and the climax of the narrative that began there. Samuel who now knows the LORD continues to grow. The LORD is with him. None of his words fall to the ground. He is no longer an unrecognised boy but a recognised prophet of the LORD. The LORD continues to appear at Shiloh and reveal Himself to Samuel through His Word. The famine of the Word of the LORD is over. As the first verse of the next chapter will go on to say, Samuel's word, which is the Word revealed by the LORD to him, 'came to all Israel.'[2]

Theological Themes

The strongest theological theme within this passage is obviously that of the Word of God. It begins this section and ends it. The material in between shows how it is to be

---

2. The NIV keeps 4:1 with the previous chapter where other versions have it beginning the next chapter. Recently, for reasons that will be explained in our next chapter, I've become persuaded that it should be seen as introduction to the next section.

received and how the bearers of it should bring it. However, subsidiary to that is the concept of what it is to know God. In the section that follows we will concentrate on these two themes.

Listening to the Whole of Scripture

Looking Back

Given the dominance of the concept of the Word of God, it will be helpful for us to think about what we learn theologically about this in what has come before this passage. Most importantly, Genesis 1 presents God as a speaking God. Ten times during the summary of the first six days of creation we hear the words 'And God said...' (1:3, 6, 9, 11, 14, 20, 24, 26, 28, 29). His Word shapes the existence of the first humans in chapters 2 and 3 and it is His Word that drives the history of His people in the formation of the covenant with Abraham (e.g. Gen. 12:1-3; 15:1-21; 17:1-27).

The Word of God also shapes the existence of God's people who have been redeemed by Him in the Exodus. He gives them ten to live by (Exod. 20:1–17) and tells them that they should live by every Word that comes from His mouth (Deut. 8:3). Without the Word of God, all people are in dire spiritual straits. This is what is pictured in 1 Samuel 3. It is the end of the period of the judges when everyone has done what is right in their own eyes and the sons of Eli are a typical example of what that looks like.

Looking Forward

As we look forward through Scripture, Amos gives us a portrait of what life might be like without the Word of God. He speaks of God's judgment on His people and identifies a catastrophic situation, that is, when He sends a famine throughout the land, not of food or water but of hearing the words of the Lord.

In the New Testament we see that one thing has not changed, humans are still to be shaped and nourished and to live by the Word of God, and Jesus is determined to do that. When He is tempted as Adam and Eve were, He resists and returns full of the Spirit instead of cursed (Luke 4:1-14).

But the New Testament goes further. It tells us that Jesus *is* the Word of God (John 1:1-18) and the full revelation of God (John 1:18). The writer of Hebrews tells us that God's greatest Word to the world is Jesus Christ. In Jesus Christ, God reveals Himself in a way that is unlike any previous revelation and superior to any previous revelation (Heb. 1:1-3). As a result, no one can come to know God except through Him and as the result of personal revelation (Matt. 11:28).

From Text to Message

It is obvious from what we have already seen that moving from text to message here, is going to be quite difficult if we are going to treat the original passage faithfully and also show how it witnesses to Jesus Christ and fits into God's purposes in Him. One of the best ways ahead in my view would be to move forward in the following manner.

First, we need to make clear to people that because of Jesus the world is no longer in a state of famine of the Word of God. As is seen in Hebrews 1:1–3, God has spoken a clear and definitive Word in His Son.

Second, we can also say that there is nevertheless some common ground between us and Samuel. Knowing God is more than knowing information about God. It requires personal revelation from God. We need the Spirit's work.

Third, we need to think hard about application. The risk is that we repeat the errors of those who move straight from Samuel in the dark days of the judges when the Word of God is scarce, to us as Christians who have a plethora of sources for the written Word of God but even greater than that, knowledge of Jesus who is the ultimate Word of God.

Suggestions for Preaching

Ways Into the Text

In thinking about preaching this passage, I pondered carefully about its central point and purpose, that is, the risk of God's people being in a state of famine. I thought, therefore, about trying to highlight the seriousness of famine and what it could do. As a result, I looked for grim stories of famines and in the end found that the great Irish famine of 1844 was one of the most extensively documented historical famines. I began by telling the story of that famine from the records and demonstrated the huge social impact it had had. I said that famines affect the core of human existence. I then made the point that the Bible at various times used the authors of the Bible to talk of spiritual famines, and read out to them the Amos passage mentioned above. I then moved from that to 1 Samuel and said that although the language of famine is not used, there is a real sense in which God's people are spiritually in famine in these first chapters.

John Woodhouse begins slightly differently but ends up in a similar place. He starts with a provocative, 'Sometimes God is silent' and then talks about how we often take things for granted. This leads him to Amos and the horror of being without the Word of God.[3]

Moving Through the Text

After the introduction, I turned straight to the text and systematically worked my way through it following the divisions of the passage outlined above. Because I am a natural storyteller, I retold the story while explaining the exegetical issues within it. This preserves the drama of the text and helps bring people with me. However, if you are not a good storyteller then I suggest that you might follow the main sections of the heading but explain, illustrate, and apply the sections (if there are natural applications that arise out of the parts).

When I got to the call of Samuel, I talked more broadly about the importance of knowing God and observed that knowing God can come only by God revealing Himself. I also noted that although it is not stated in the text, what God does is an act of great grace and mercy. I then observed that this is our desperate need because of sin, but that in Christ we see God fulfilling our deepest need out of grace and mercy. He does this by speaking His Word who is Jesus (quoting John 1:14-18).

Applying the Text

My last major section after the introduction (with the heading 'Drought and Famine') and the section working through the text, had the heading 'Our situation'. I began that section by noting that the situation of contemporary Christians is very different from that of the Israelites. We

---

3. John Woodhouse and R. Kent Hughes, *1 Samuel: Looking for a Leader*, Preaching the Word (Wheaton, Ill: Crossway Books, 2008), p. 73.

have Jesus Christ, God's living Word. We, therefore, have to be careful in simply transforming what we see in this passage into our own context. I then said that I thought that I could identify some truths that arise from this passage and our own situation and explained them. The truths were …

No longer in famine
- God has fully and finally dealt with the issue of famines of the Word of God (referring to Hebrews 1:1-3).

Still needing revelation
- The Bible is clear that knowing God needs God's assistance. He has put the information about Jesus in the public domain but people still need God to be at work in them if they are to know Jesus (Matt. 11:27). Christians therefore pray, asking God to be at work when the gospel truth about Jesus is proclaimed.
- We contemporary Christians have the Word of God incarnate and the written Word of God that points us toward Him. However, that Word needs proclamation and that is the role of the people of God.

The risk of self-imposed famine
- We Christians have all the riches of God's living Word, Jesus. We have an enormous wealth of resources to find out more about Him. However, it is possible for us to create a self-imposed famine through neglect. We must, therefore, make His Word the centre of our lives as individuals and congregations.

Leading a Bible Study

Reading aloud

Although not mentioned in previous studies, it is a good idea to read the Bible out loud in the group, encouraging

Part Two: The Rise of Samuel and Kingship

the readers to think hard about where to put emphasis and the like. This arises from the fact that (1) Scripture was designed to be read aloud and heard rather than privately read and (2) to read well requires some interpretation.

Introduction
The leader might summarise the background, particularly focussing on the judgment on Eli's sons in the previous chapter. Also speak about how God's people are designed to live by every Word that proceeds from the mouth of God (Deut. 8:3).

Read 1 Samuel 3:1-21 out loud in the group.

Focussing on 1 Samuel 3:1-10

Observation

- What actually happens in verses 1-10?
- What things strike you as strange or difficult? Or what questions do they raise?
- Remember that last week we compared and contrasted Samuel with Eli's sons. There is another difference here. Complete the sentences below.

The contrast between Eli's sons and Samuel is sharp.

Eli's sons refuse to ………….. to the ………….. of their father (1 Sam. 2:25).

However, Samuel ………….. to the word of …………. (v. 10).

Thinking about verse 7
In 1 Samuel 2:26, we read that Samuel was growing in stature and favour. However, how is he still incomplete as God's person? What else does he need?

How will this need be fulfilled? What needs to happen?

Interpretation

Where does true knowledge of God come from?

How is this like our coming to know God in Jesus? (Read and reflect on Matthew 11:25-27).

Focussing in on 1 Samuel 3:11-18

Observation

Imagine that verses 10 to 18 give us the picture of a true prophet at work (i.e. Samuel is the prophet and Eli is the person to whom God sends him).

Write down the 'personal profile' or characteristics of a prophet.

Interpretation

So far in Samuel, Eli hasn't had very good press. In what ways does he redeem himself here? How does he model a godly person?

Focusing in on 1 Samuel 3:19-21

Observation

How is the situation in 1 Samuel 3:1 reversed by these verses? List some of the things in verse 1 that are reversed in these verses.

Putting things together

Discuss as a group how we might apply this passage as (a) individuals and (b) a church or small group.

Share prayer points with each other. If possible, share prayer points related to the things that you've learnt from the passage and areas in which you need help.

Pray together.

8.
The Story of the Ark
(Part 1: 1 Samuel 4:1–5:12)

Introduction

There is great delight to be found for the preacher in 1 Samuel 4–7. For even if these chapters address serious matters, they do so with both humour and pathos. Consequently, they inherently have rich possibilities for points of contact and engagement with a diversity of listeners. However, the same elements can also put the preacher at risk of abusing or misusing the text. We therefore must be careful as we approach the task.

The first thing to be aware of is the ark of the covenant, around which the story gravitates. The ark is first mentioned when God instructs Moses to build the sanctuary in Exod. 25:8-22. It housed the 'ten words' (Exod. 34:28; cf. 1 Kings 8:9) or 'the testimony' which amounted to the legal document of the covenant (hence the names 'ark of testimony' as in Exod. 25:22 or 'ark of the covenant' as in 1 Sam. 4:4). The cover was called 'the atonement seat' and on the Day of Atonement the Lord promised that He would appear over it (Lev. 16:2). The ark was therefore apparently viewed as a physical representation of the footstool of the Lord's throne (1 Chron. 28:2; Pss. 99:5; 132:7-8) and the symbol of His presence among His people and His relationship with them. Hence, lifting up the ark was tantamount to declaring God's presence among His people and His being *for* them and *against* their enemies (Num. 10:35).

A second and related focus of these chapters falls on Israel at war. Twice already in Samuel we have heard God referred to as the Lord Almighty (1:3, 11). Other translations use the term 'Lord of hosts', which captures the idea present in the Hebrew of armies, either human or divine or perhaps even both. In 1 Samuel 4:4 both the ark and this manner of referring to God are explicitly linked as we hear that men bring back 'the ark of *the covenant* of the Lord *Almighty*'. Such language raises the issue of whether God does indeed dwell among His people and what that means in relation to the threat to the land posed by our third important element – the Philistines, a foreign aggressive nation highlighted in this chapter and a focus throughout much of Samuel.

The Philistines were part of a group of Sea Peoples who began to appear in the eastern Mediterranean some time before this, with the Philistines in particular being mentioned in relation to Caphtor (which probably refers to Crete; see Amos 9:7; Jer. 47:4). They invaded Syria, Palestine and Egypt and, although defeated by the Egyptians, were allowed by them to settle on the southern coastal plain of Palestine.[1] Their own records speak of

---

1. The first Biblical reference to the Philistines is found in Genesis 10:13-14 which might be translated 'Mizraim fathered Ludim, Anamim, Lehabim, Naphtuhim, Pathrusim, Casluhim (from whom/where the Philistines

them in relation to three key cities of Askelon, Ashdod and Gaza, although the Biblical record also mentions Gath and Ekron, which together with the other three make up the Philistine pentapolis, each of which may have had local leadership (Josh. 13:3; Judg. 3:3). Other cities with Philistine associations are Ziklag and Timna (1 Sam. 27:5). Dieties particularly associated with the Philistines include Dagon (1 Sam. 5; 1 Chron. 10:10), Baal-Zebub/Baal-Zebul and Ashtoreth/Ashtaroth (1 Sam. 31:8-13).[2]

The Philistines were technologically advanced in that they could forge iron, an ability apparently jealously guarded (1 Sam. 10:5; 13:23–14:16; 2 Sam. 23:13-17) and while they are recorded as a thorn in Israel's side during the time of the judges (e.g. Judg. 3:1-3; 13-16), in the time of Samuel they appear to have their eyes on expansion into the hill country where Israel lived.[3] The necessity to galvanise Israel against this common enemy (and perhaps others) appears to lie behind the desire for a king in 1 Samuel 8 (e.g. vv. 19-20).

Chapters 4–7 therefore represent a significant change of focus. We move quickly, if not sharply from Shiloh, family life, and a focus on Samuel as an established prophet bringing

---

came) and Caphtorim'. While we don't know who the Casluhim are, it is entirely possible that as the Pathrusim and Naphtuhim are Egyptian, so are the Casluhim, in which case it is being said that the Philistines came to Egypt by way of Crete (i.e. linked with the Caphtorim, see references above to Amos 9:7 and Jer. 47:4); so Victor P. Hamilton, *The Book of Genesis, Chapters 1–17*, NICOT (Grand Rapids: Eerdmans, 1990), pp. 340-341.

2. Much of the material in this paragraph is indebted to Trude Dothan, 'What We Know About the Philistines,' *BAR* 8.4 (1982): pp. 20-44.

3. Note the references to Philistine outposts in 1 Sam. 13-14.

God's Word to a very different situation indeed. Samuel largely disappears and the focus falls on the nation confronted by Philistine aggression and questions as to whether God is indeed amongst His people and, if so, on what terms and by what means? It is therefore important to observe the import of these chapters given the events of chapters 1–3.

One further matter for these chapters is the absence of Samuel, which may simply serve to indicate that Israel as a whole, like many of the kings who will follow, apparently does not value the Lord's abundant provision of the prophetic Word. If they did, then surely they would seek it from the prophet Samuel whom He has just provided. Furthermore, these chapters also demonstrate the ongoing failure of Eli's house and the execution of the promised judgment upon it, along with the eventual rise and establishment of Samuel in leadership (1 Sam. 7:2-17).

Listening to the Text

Context and Structure

Such observations about the abundance of God's Word but Israel's apparent disregard for it may indicate that 1 Samuel 4:1a performs a similar function to other passages we have observed before, in the sense that it both looks back and looks forward, or forms a link between what has gone before and what is coming.[4] In other words, rather than simply concluding the previous section, the first half of the verse also introduces the next section (while clearly picking

---

4. Tsumura suggests that the clause here is a 'an example of a "transitional technique" presenting the SETTING for the following event, linking a new episode with the previous episode', David Toshio Tsumura, *The First Book of Samuel*, NICOT (Grand Rapids: Eerdmans, 2007), p. 187.

up the theme of the LORD having revealed Himself to Samuel through His Word).[5] This could be captured by translating the verse: 'When the word of Samuel came to all Israel, the Israelites went out to fight against the Philistines.'[6]

Our structural diagram might therefore be adjusted as follows.

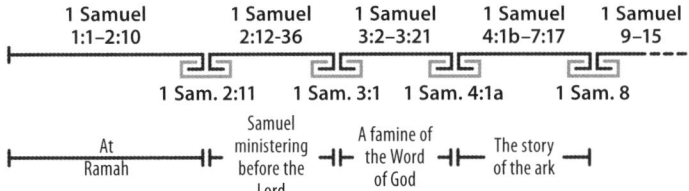

Chapter 4 and chapter 5 fall into distinct units much as they are broken up in our English Bibles. In chapter 4 there are four clear sections, which could be put under the title of 'The Ark in Israel':

1-5   An Israelite perspective
6-9   A Philistine perspective
10-11   A report of the battle
12-22   Back at Shiloh: The death of Eli (12-18) and the birth of Ichabod (19-22)

In chapter 5, there are two clear sections, which could be put under the title 'The Ark in Philistine territory':

1-5   The ark and Dagon
6-11   The ark and the Philistines

---

5. Frank A. Spina, 'A Prophet's "Pregnant Pause": Samuel's Silence in the Ark Narrative (1 Sam. 4:1–7:2),' *Horizons in Biblical Theology* 13.1 (1991): pp. 59-73.

6. Following a suggestion by Andrew E. Steinmann, *1 Samuel*, Concordia Commentary (St. Louis, Missouri: Concordia Publishing House, 2016), pp. 118-119.

Content

A geographical perspective

For the visually oriented, it is helpful to give a 'big picture' of where things happen. One way to do this is to supply a map either by way of a sermon outline, a data projector slide or even an insert in the church bulletin. The key thing is for such maps to be clear and not overly detailed.

The following map covers all the major movements of the ark outlined in these chapters in 1 Samuel. Later, in 2 Samuel 6:11-16 the ark will be moved to Jerusalem by David.

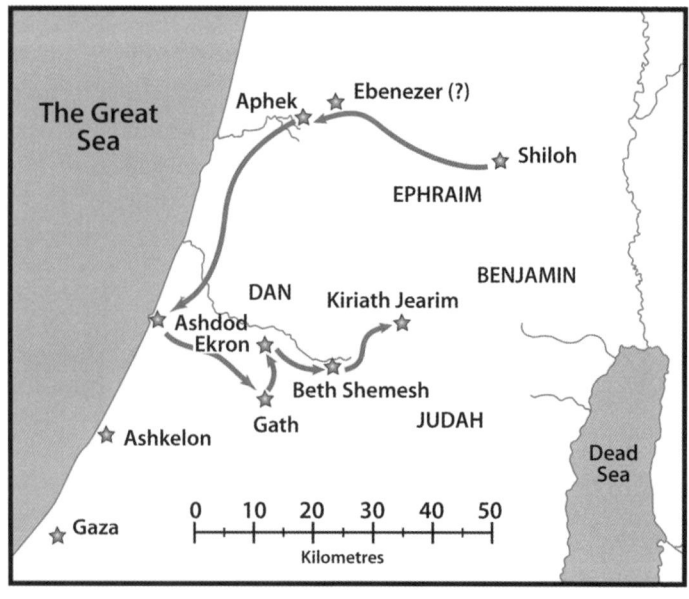

The ark in Israel (4:1-11)

An Israelite perspective (4:1-5)

These verses record Israel situated at Ebenezer with the Philistines at Aphek. The ensuing battle seems to have taken place somewhere in between; Israel was defeated.

The elders conclude (1) that the LORD is responsible and (2) that the presence of the ark will result in certain success (v. 3). Against the background of verse 1 which stresses the abundance of the Word of God, this conclusion sounds decidedly superstitious and somewhat manipulative of God.

A Philistine perspective (4:6-9)

Here the perspective changes and the narrator gives us a glimpse of the emotional state and theological reflections of the Philistines. Their first response is fear (v. 7), apparently driven by their knowledge of the past actions of the LORD (although their information seems a little confused, such as 'plagues in the desert' rather than in Egypt in v. 8) and the potential for slavery. Such fear drives them to a second response: action and resolve (v. 9).

A report of the battle (4:10-11)

In verses 10-11 the narrator leaves the camps of the combatant armies and simply tells us the result. With the ark present, Israel's losses are seven or eight times larger than previously. Moreover, the ark is captured and Eli's sons die.

The purpose of this section is multifaceted. First, it demonstrates what we already anticipated: (a) Israel's need for fresh leadership; (b) the fulfilment of the previously promised judgment; (c) the ongoing failure of Eli's family as they misuse the ark, just as they had mistreated God, the things of God, and the people of God in chapter 2; and (d) the failure of Israel to consult with God's prophet (just as Saul will later fail to submit to the prophetic Word). Second, it leads us to conclude that the LORD is still overseeing what happens in His land with His people (as concluded by the elders in v. 3).

Back at Shiloh (4:12-22)

- News to Shiloh (4:12-13)

The second half of chapter 4 shifts from the battlefield to the reception of the news in Shiloh. There are three people or groups who receive the news: (1) the people of Shiloh (v. 12-13), (2) Eli (vv. 14-18) and (3) Eli's daughter-in-law (vv. 19-22).[7] The ark is still the focus of all three episodes, Eli too is integrally bound up with each one. Here we find this blind old man ironically 'watching' out of fear for the ark. Once the man of Benjamin arrives and announces the defeat in Shiloh, 'all the city cried out at the news.'

- News to Eli (4:14-18)

In this second Shiloh episode Eli hears the news of the ark that he seems to fear, although the hearer holds off the news as a crushing end ('Israel fled … army suffered heavy losses … sons are dead … the ark of God has been captured'; v. 17). Critically, our author does not make explicit connections between these events and the prophecies of the man of God back in chapter 2 but instead focuses on the fact that it is the mention of the ark that causes Eli's fall and death. In the original Hebrew the adjective for 'heavy' (*kaved*) in verse 18 is made up of the same three consonants that make up the word for 'glory' (*kavod*), which has the sense of 'heaviness' or 'weightiness'. Moreover, this same word is often used in association with the ark. This wordplay will be carried forward into the next episode.

- News to Eli's Daughter-in-law (4:19-22)

In the first verse of the third episode, we encounter Eli's daughter-in-law, the wife of Phinehas who goes

---

7. Fokkelman, *Vow and Desire*, p. 12.

into premature labour with complications that result in her beginning to die in childbirth. Those attending her proclaimed what they considered might be a comfort to her – news of the birth of a son. The author then gives this nameless woman the final words in this story as she names her son 'Ichabod' (*i-kavod*), which probably literally means 'Where is Glory?' (with 'Glory' acting as a circumlocution for the Lord). She then offers the explanation that 'The glory/Glory (*kavod*) has departed from Israel, for the ark of God has been captured.' This explanation itself contains another possible wordplay because 'has departed' literally means 'has been exiled' and therefore the whole sentence can have the sense of 'The glory/Glory from Israel has gone into exile'. One outworking of this might then be that the interpreter finds the final form of Samuel to be exilic or post-exilic which might lead to interpreting the whole of Samuel from this particular perspective. The alternative, taken within these two volumes and outlined in the Introduction, is to interpret the document in the light that it constantly and openly appears to interact with the book of Deuteronomy.

Our author preserves in this woman's words, that while she *has* rightly seen that God's glory has departed, she is mistaken in considering that this is because the ark has been captured. Rather, the ark has been captured since God's glory has departed from Israel because His sanctuary has been defiled, His Word not respected, and His glory has been reduced to mindless superstition and mechanistic understanding.

It is at this point that it is worth noting one of the downsides of having taken chapters 4 and 5 together. Chapter 4 ends with great grief, picked up in the fivefold repetition of the loss of the ark and the final link with the word 'exile' (4:11, 17, 19, 21, 22).

This is one of the most tragic moments in Israel's history and clearly points forward to another tragedy to come, the exile. Moreover, its surprise and shock are surely a foretaste of that which would come to the followers of Jesus in His shocking death. Our chapter choice, therefore, deprives us of dealing with this as much as we might (although one option might be to break the sermon into two). Were you to divide the chapters at the end of chapter 4, that would then open up the possibility of dealing with the shock victory of the Lord in chapter 5 and the parallels in the Gospel narratives (victory over evil, vindication, etc.).

The ark in Philistine territory (5:1-12)

The ark and Dagon (5:1-5)

There are a number of things that should inform the interpretation of these verses.

- It is most likely that Dagon (pronounced dah-GOHN) is a fertility god, possibly a grain god (the name derives from a West Semitic word for grain).

- The title of the ark changes according to circumstances within the story. When it is being passively acted upon it is 'the ark of God' (1, 2, 10 x 2). When it is referred to, by or in relation to the Philistines it is 'the ark of the God of Israel' (7, 8 x 3, 10, 11). When it is a symbol of God's activity against Dagon it is 'the ark of the Lord', perhaps alluding to the 'Lord of hosts' waging war (3, 4).

- Representations of the power and superiority of conquering nations and their deities often appear to be present when symbols of their gods or people are displayed publicly. This is also seen when the symbols of other gods are placed before or beneath their deities and their rulers emphasising superiority (e.g. Daniel 1:1-2; 5:1-4; perhaps 2 Kings 25:27-30).

- The cutting off of body parts and/or their public display was a well-known treatment for defeated enemies (cf. 1 Sam. 31:9-10).
- The picture of Dagon fallen prostrate and beheaded before the symbolic presence of the LORD does double duty. First, it displays the apparently victorious god assuming a position of worship before the supposedly vanquished One. Second, it prefigures the military representative of the Philistines who will also fall prostrate and headless before God's future representative ruler and shepherd (1 Sam. 17:51). That incident, like this one, will proclaim that there is a God in Israel, and that He, the LORD, is superior in that He saves and that the battle is His (1 Sam. 17:46-47).

The ark and the Philistines (5:6-12)

Where verses 1-5 focused on the ark as the representation of the LORD's presence humbling the *deity* of the Philistines, verses 6-12 focus on the humbling the *Philistine people* (in the absence of the LORD's people). Again, there are some key things to notice:

- The language of hands seen in 1-5 remains and seems to bind both parts of the narrative together. Where Dagon has no hand, the hand of the LORD is very active.
- There have been various attempts to identify the plague (haemorrhoids, syphilis, etc.). Whatever the affliction, it is clearly uncomfortable and perhaps humorous. Moreover, the Philistines had already made links between their situation and that in Egypt in the previous chapter, and here it is repeated: God humiliates foreign gods and brings plagues against those who oppress His people.

- The result of the trouble is that the ark is treated like an undiffused bomb and by the time it arrives at the third city—Ekron—they realise that drastic action is required (cf. vv. 10-12).

Theological Themes

A difficulty encountered in reading the books of Samuel is that our narrator is often silent, not explicitly stating his views. Nevertheless, as the story is told he makes his presence felt through what is included and in statements made. One particularly significant element is his relating of the activity of 'the Lord's hand'.

The word 'hand' or its plural in our chapters is revealing. First, the Philistines use it in speaking about the might of the God of Israel (4:8) and His actions against them (5:7). Second, it is used by the narrator in relation to (a) Dagon, who loses his head and hands before the ark (5:4) and (b) the Lord's powerful activity against the Philistines (5:6, 9 and 11).[8] Noticeably, while the hand of the Lord is active, Israel and her representatives are silent and inactive. The overall picture is theologically clear: Dagon is rendered handless before the Lord whom both the Philistines and the narrator acknowledge has a powerful hand that acts on behalf of His people and without their aid (note that Dagon needs his worshippers to carry him, the Lord does not). He is well able to render handless His enemies through the action of His powerful hand. These references to hands, therefore, clearly bear theology and would appear to be worth pursuing more broadly within Scripture both before and after our passages.

---

8. The Hebrew text also has another mention of 'hand' in 4:18 but it is not significant in relation to the other references within the two chapters. Moreover, it has an alternate reading in the Hebrew text.

Listening to the Whole of Scripture

Given the language of hands and the way that our writer appears to be playing with it, perhaps a survey of the rest of the Old Testament might reveal other places that interact with this idea. Such a survey reveals that there are various groupings of passages in the Old Testament where the hand of the LORD is mentioned in association with idolatry, false worship, or the LORD interacting with false gods. These include the plague narratives and the rescue from the sea in Exodus 6–15, this passage in Samuel, and Isaiah 40–66.[9]

Looking Back

In looking back to the earlier situation in the book of Exodus, we notice the context set in the first chapter where God and Pharaoh appear almost as rival powers. God's purpose which flows through His people is threatened by Pharaoh. As the LORD makes clear to Moses in their first encounter, His goal will be to 'come down to rescue' His people 'from the hand of the Egyptians and to bring them up out of that land into a good and spacious land' (3:8). However, He knows that this will not be possible unless 'a mighty hand compels him' (i.e. Pharaoh; 3:19). In anticipation, God promises, 'I will stretch out my hand and strike the Egyptians with all the wonders that I will perform among them' and that 'after that, he will let you go' (3:20). The real deity therefore is the one who has a hand that can do what its owner wills and thereby accomplish His purposes.

---

9. There are also a number of references to the hand of the LORD in Ezekiel but they are somewhat different, largely referring to the hand of the LORD coming upon Ezekiel personally.

This perspective explains the strength of the 'hand' language that follows until Pharaoh is diminished and God has rescued His people (note the comment about the two opposing hands in the final song of victory: Pharaoh's in 15:9 and the reference to the Lord's hand bringing His people into the land in 15:17). A true God is One who can do His will for His people with the strength of His powerful hand (for a full set of relevant references to hands of the Lord and Pharaoh, see 5:21; 6:1 [x 2]; 7:4, 5; 9:3, 15; 10:12, 21, 22; 13:3; 9, 14, 16; 14:16, 21, 26–27, 30, 31 [lit. 'Israel saw the great hand that the Lord used...']).

Looking Forward

The similarities between Egypt and the situation in our passage in Samuel are obvious. In Egypt, the Lord's people are held captive outside Israel as the ark is in 1 Samuel 4–5 and there is something of a contest between Him and the local powers (and perhaps their deities). Similarly, as we look forward in Scripture, the mention of hands and idolatry in Isaiah 40–66 is quite striking. The situation to which Isaiah 40–66 is addressed is that of Israel in exile where they are described as being somewhat overwhelmed by the power of their captors and perhaps worried that the Lord was powerless (hence the consolation of chapter 40).

One way in which overwhelmed and oppressed people have historically learnt to deal with their situation or even to assert self-confidence is to diminish the source of oppression or its power with laughter or mockery. This can be observed in sport, in school, and even in religion. Moreover, it appears occasionally in the Bible. Such can be found in Isaiah 44. The context is set in verses 6-8 where the Lord asserts His supremacy. Then, from verse

Part Two: The Rise of Samuel and Kingship

9 through to 17 there is a story of an idolater at work. Isaiah mocks the idolater using the image of an ironsmith who crafts an idol with great effort, cutting down great trees that he might even have nurtured for the purpose. He then makes a fire out of part of it and cooks his meal over it. However, he also crafts another part of it into an idol that he then bows down to and worships, seeking salvation from its hand. His point appears to be the ridiculous logic of the whole action. Again, we see the note of mockery that is present in 1 Samuel 4–5 but perhaps also in Exodus.

When the LORD returns to the topic of idolatry in Isaiah 46, He notes a few key characteristics about idols: (a) they need to be carried by others, either human or animals in the service of humans (46:1-2); (b) the real God is different from idols in that He bears His people whereas idols are crafted by humans and need to be carried by them (46:6-7). They are not independent and cannot do anything of or for themselves (46:7). They are so unlike Him.

This note of mockery intertwined by very serious theology is not uncommon in the Bible. It is seen in the portrayal of repeatedly named people with repeatedly named musical instruments dancing around a grotesque image set up by Nebuchadnezzar on the plain of Dura (Dan. 3). It is one way of handling reality and this is probably part of what is going on in 1 Samuel 4–5 as well.

However, as we look ahead, we are also directed toward the truths presented in Christ in the New Testament. The book of Romans indicates that all humans are essentially idolaters who have replaced what is known about God by the inventions of their own foolish imaginations (Rom. 1:18-32). As idolaters—Gentile or Jew alike—they will be judged (Romans 2:9-20). However, the great news is that God has not left us without recourse. Rather, He has shown His love for us and given us a way out of our idolatry through the sacrificial and atoning death of His Son (Rom. 3:16-21). While we were weak and unworthy sinners, Christ died for us (Rom. 5:1-11). He is the end of the stupidity of idolatry.

From Text to Message

It is clear that the big idea of the passage we have been looking at is that there is one true God and that in the face of His power and sovereignty, all alternatives look ludicrous.

Some of the principal points we should concentrate on that would build good and helpful sermons are the following.

- In their rejection of the Word of God freely available in the prophet of the Lord, Israel, like all humans, looked for substitutes. One way we do this is to try and tame God or attempt to manipulate Him. Israel tried both but both inevitably failed.

- Superstition is such a patent stupidity. Nevertheless, we humans are so prone to it. When we find that the true God as revealed in His Word does not meet with our expectations or desires, we chase after ephemera. However, we should not be unaware that ephemera are exactly that and when confronted with reality, they will fail us and be exposed. Therefore, 1 John 5:20-21.

- The hand of the Lord is alone powerful. We should seek out where He has displayed His hand most clearly, that is, in the person and work of Jesus. Eventually, He will display His hand in judgment as He has done in the past.

Suggestions for Preaching

Preliminary Preparation

The first bit of advice on preaching publicly on this passage is that you meet with the Bible reader well beforehand and explain what the passage means and how it is to be interpreted. Help them understand the hints of humour and iconoclasm in the text. If you cannot find the right public reader for this text in particular, read it yourself! If read well, it may well have people seeing the humour beforehand.

Ways Into the Text

There are a number of ways into the text. However, given the abundance and richness of examples of superstition in our society, the media, literature and entertainment, this could provide a strong and relevant way forward. An example or two would raise the issue and also give an opportunity to explore the nature of superstition and how we use it to give shape and order to our thought worlds. This would allow us to explain that superstition is as old as humanity and that as we examine their attitudes and actions we will learn from God about what He thinks of such things, we will also get some advice from God as to how to approach thinking about Him, the world, and our superstitions.

Moving Through the Text

The bulk of the sermon should consist of working our way through the passage in a way that makes it live for our people. If you are a natural story teller, then perhaps you could retell the story, highlighting the things in the text that carry the original meaning of the author.

Since the text appears to have two major sections (chapters 4 and 5), it would make sense to break the explanation with an illustration or application at the end of chapter 4. For example, you might pause to reflect with your hearers about how Christians can often be superstitious, such as in the way they think mechanistically about prayer rather than about the nature of the person to whom they are praying. The teaching of Jesus in Luke's Gospel on the nature of prayer would be helpful here. The story of chapter 5 might then be picked up again in its two major parts (5:1-5 and 5:6-12).

In explaining the text, the following two points should be highlighted:

(a) the author's references to 'hands', and
(b) the way the passage progresses from the defeat of Israel and therefore the apparent defeat of Israel's God through to the defeat of Dagon by the Lord and His humbling of the Philistines without any of His worshippers being present.

If this is done, it will be easy to move through to the big idea that there is only one true God and that in the face of His power and sovereignty, all alternatives look ridiculous. Since He is the real God, He is able to care for His people and wage war against His enemies without the help of His people. Observing this will be a helpful prelude to chapter 8 where Israel will ask for a human king to do this.

Biblical Theology and Application

A theologically and practically helpful way forward from this point might be to take up the notion of idolatry and briefly explore it in Scripture, perhaps using the mockery of idolatry seen in Isaiah or Daniel (although Isaiah might be more help, given its consistent use of the language of hands and carrying). The point could be made that no matter how sophisticated our idols are, they are the creation of our hands (or minds) and will fare no better than Dagon.

In terms of giving the sermon a strong Christocentric focus, the point could be made that in the face of human inability, God sent His Son to die in humiliation on the cross but thereby publicly disarmed the spiritual powers and authorities and triumphed over them (Col. 2:15). Such displays the great worth of our God and should cause us to hear and obey the words of 1 John 5:21, 'Dear children, keep yourselves from idols.'

Leading a Bible Study

For this Bible study, it will be helpful for the leader to supply some significant pieces of 'background information' that will help the participants understand the passage.

The three major elements are (1) the ark of the Covenant; (2) the Philistines; and (3) the journey of the ark. Information on each can be found in the earlier content of this chapter. Images of the ark are readily available in Bible dictionaries or online.

Read 1 Samuel 4:1-22 out loud in the group.

Verses 1 to 11

Observation

- Who does Israel think is responsible for their defeat in the first encounter?
- How do both the Philistines and the Israelites think that the second encounter will end?
- What do you think God is communicating to Israel through their defeat?

Verses 12 to 22

Interpretation
- What do you think verses 21–22 mean? What do they tell us about the ark and about God?

Read 1 Samuel 5:1-12

Interpretation
- What do you think the Philistines are saying by putting the ark in the temple of Dagon?
- What do you think God is saying by what happens between the ark and Dagon?
- How do you think the Israelites who listened to this account read out loud would have reacted to it?
- Who 'wins' the battle of the gods in chapter 4? Who wins in chapter 5?
- See if you can identify the times when 'hands' or the actions of hands are referred to in the account.
- Now read Isaiah 44:9-17, noticing the references to hands or the actions of hands. What is the difference between a real God and an idol?

Thinking it through
- Read Romans 5:6-8 and Colossians 2:15. What are the similarities between what God does in Jesus and what we see Him doing here in 1 Samuel 4 and 5?

Application

Break the remaining part of your time into two sections.

Part 1: Compare and contrast

Discuss the ways in which Christians can be like the ancient Israelites (e.g. superstitious). How can we encourage each other to be firm in faith and to keep ourselves from idolatry?

Part Two: The Rise of Samuel and Kingship

Part 2: Pray!

Share prayer points with each other. If possible, share prayer points related to the things that you've learnt from the passage and areas in which you need help.

Pray together.

9.
The Story of the Ark
(Part 2: 1 Samuel 6:1–7:17)

For the purposes of preaching and teaching the story of the ark from 1 Samuel 4–7, we have separated the four chapters into two sections of two chapters. However, given the tight integration of the whole four chapters, it will here be assumed that you have read them and understand the background and flow of the author's argument up until this point.

Listening to the Text

Context and Structure
As was noted previously, the larger structure is bound together with what comes before it by 1 Samuel 4:1a and then the chapter on kingship in 1 Samuel 8.

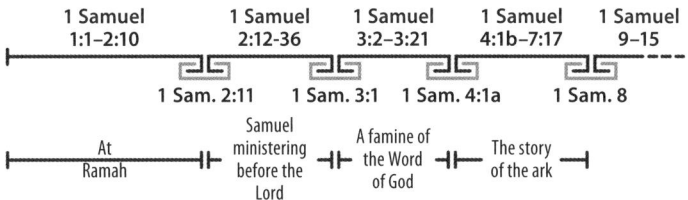

Within 1 Samuel 4:1b and 7:17 the first and the last chapter frame the rest, treat similar concepts and together prepare us for the introduction to kingship which will occur in chapter 8.

Content

The ark comes back from exile (6:1–7:1)

The previous chapter told us that the Philistines' experience of the presence of the ark was harsh. The first verse of chapter 7 lets us know the length of time – seven months. It also tells us of their desire to rid themselves of it.

The chapter can be divided into three sections:

    6:1-12   Ridding Philistia of a troublesome ark
         1-2   Crisis introduced
         3-9   Proposed solution (speeches)
         10-12 Resolution!

    6:13-21 Receiving the ark in Beth Shemesh
         13-16 Return
         17-18 Excursus: Tumours, rats, and a rock
         19-21 Trouble with the ark in Israel

    6:21–7:1 Temporary rest for the ark

As this structure indicates, the ark remains in focus in these verses. However, it remains troublesome until it is finally brought to temporary but long rest in Kiriath Jearim, a city lying at the juncture of the boundaries of Judah and Benjamin. It has been speculated that it might have had some sort of cultic background or connection.

Some of the more important things to note about the content of these verses are as follows.

- The speech by the Philistines is the longest by any Philistine in the whole of the Old Testament. It demonstrates what we have seen previously, that is, some knowledge of the Exodus and also of the care that must be taken in relation to the Ark and whom it represents (e.g. paying honour, guilt offerings, etc.).

- The Lord's interactions with both the Philistines and Israel in relation to the ark, indicate what we knew from Israel's time in the wilderness, that is, the ark—because of its association with the Lord's presence—is the desire of His people. However, His very presence can cause severe problems not only to His enemies but also to His people. For this reason, the plaintive cry of 'Who is able to stand before the Lord, this holy God?' (6:20 ESV) is one that perhaps captures the heart of this section, if not the whole ark narrative (after all, at the beginning we discover that Dagon cannot). It may also explain Israel's perceived need for repentance in the verse that immediately follows our section here (i.e. 1 Sam. 7:2).

- There is some textual variation about the numbers of people who die in verse 19. Some Hebrew manuscripts say seventy (reflected in the NIV translation here) whereas other Hebrew manuscripts and the Greek Septuagint say 50,070.

- The mention of Kiriath Jearim and the follow-on question in 1 Sam. 6:20—'To whom shall he go up from us'?—need further explanation. First, 'he' could equally mean 'it' as other translations indicate. Second, the next mention of this location is when David seeks to bring the ark up from there in 2 Samuel 6. He rapidly learns that even he needs to take care in relation to the ark and the Lord whom it represents (2 Sam. 6:5-8).[1] Third, the 'he'/'it' reference is picked up in the verse immediately after the one in 1 Samuel just

---

1. Intriguingly, Abinadab, who becomes custodian of the ark, is the father of Uzzah who dies as he reaches out to steady the ark as it is carried toward Jerusalem on a cart (2 Sam. 6:3-8).

mentioned, when David, wearing an ephod says, 'How can the ark of the Lord come to *me?*' The implication appears to be that while priests are normally the only ones who might stand before the ark, David can. In this sense, 1 Samuel 4-6 tantalisingly points us toward David. It may also explain the priestly reference in Psalm 110 where the Lord says to David in the context of war, 'You are a priest forever after the order of Melchizedek' (Ps. 110:4).

Israel learning dependence (1 Samuel 7:2-17)

The gap between verse 1 and verses 2-3 is marked in a number of ways. First, twenty years pass from the events of the ark narrative. Second, a change has happened in Israel during that period of time. Their apparent lack of interest in the Lord and His Word has been replaced by a heartfelt desire for Him that has brought 'all the house of Israel' to lamentation. Third, and perhaps linked with the previous two points, Samuel has reappeared and is active in leadership. In verse 3, he speaks to them the Word of the Lord which they apparently had little interest in earlier. Fourth, the section that follows has strong covenantal echoes.

Nevertheless, there are also echoes of the past in the narrative. For example, just as Israel in chapter 4 faced a problem that needed resolution (i.e. a military threat demonstrated by an initial victory of the Philistines in 4:1-2), so they also have a problem here. As observed earlier, the sense of distance from the Lord has resulted in lamentation.

There are also further links to be noted between the first and this last section of the ark narrative. For example, in both 1 Samuel 4 and 7 there is a consultation (initiated by the people with the elders in 4:3 but initiated by Samuel in 7:3). In both cases there is a proposal to involve the LORD and an expression of confidence or hope as a result. Nevertheless, there is a significant leap forward in this chapter in that chapter 3 had no real spiritual component whereas chapter 7 involves repentance and putting aside idols. Both incidents associate the ark of the LORD with saving from the hand of the Philistine enemies (4:3; 7:8 and, with slightly different language, 7:3).

The events involving Israel and the Philistines are also somewhat parallel. In chapter 3, the ark is brought with the Philistines already present. The sons of Eli are present with it and, without any hint of supplication, all Israel shouts so that the earth resounds but the LORD seems strikingly absent. He is not mentioned in relation to Israel except by the Philistines and Israel is soundly defeated. The contrast in chapter 7 is stark. Israel puts aside its idols, the LORD is openly served, prayer is given by Samuel and the Philistines come out against Israel. Israel fears, prays, offers sacrifice and cries out to the LORD for help for Israel and the LORD manifests Himself with loud thunder and the Philistines are thrown into confusion and flee before Israel's army (vv. 5-11).

The results are also very different. In the first, the Philistines are victorious, Israel is severely 'defeated' (4:10) and humiliated (4:10-11) and their leadership dies (4:11-18). This time, Israel is victorious, the Philistines are severely defeated (7:10) and subdued, such that cities previously taken are restored and they do not again 'enter the territory of Israel' (ESV) (at least in Samuel's time). Moreover, Samuel's godly leadership is endorsed (7:13-17).

Finally, both conflicts conclude with named memorials. In chapter 4, the named memorial is a child who is born and named 'Ichabod' or 'Where is glory?' and an explanation is given that 'The glory has departed from Israel' (4:21-22). Things are very different in chapter 7. There a memorial is made in naming a stone 'Ebenezer' (literally 'the rock of the helper') with an explanation that its meaning is 'Thus far has the LORD helped us' (7:12). Moreover, the language of the 'hand of the Lord' (7:13) returns for the first time since 1 Samuel 5:6 and 9.

Theologically, the impact is profound. The picture painted is one where Israel is faced with two different scenarios. They can forge their own way, independent of God (even if it is really a pretence) or they can cast themselves dependently upon Him. The former is as age-old as Adam and Eve, while the latter has its counterparts in Noah or Abraham or ... Hannah. Her approach modelled the right way and her prayer described how God would react. He would bring down the haughty and lift up the dependent, which is exactly how He has acted in the ark narrative, no matter who the haughty are. Hence, the beginning and end of the ark narrative contain two alternative ways in which God might be approached by the people of God.

Moreover, it also has some implied advice from the writer who penned these passages under the guidance and oversight of God, and who appears to be warning that there will be definite impact from lack of dependence and from pride. It may be that God will use the nations to rebuke His people just as He had done in the period of the judges. However, if and when they put Him at the centre by listening to His Word through His authorised prophet, then He will be exalted and glorified among His people and in the world. He will be united with His people and

He will be for them. As God's people listen to and read the beginning and the end of the ark narrative, they should take note and work out which way they will go. Will they trust in horses and military might (Ps. 20), or even in the kings that will follow soon? Or will they trust in the Lord who alone can solve their problems, even those of a military and/or political sort? Given the request for a king that is coming in the next chapter there may also be a pre-emptive rebuke here concerning that request.

Looking Back

The question put to Israel in this ark narrative is an ancient question. It goes back to the garden and to Israel at Sinai, in the wilderness, at the plains of Moab about to enter the promised land, and even as the people of Israel will later face nations mightier than them who threaten to wipe them out. The question concerns whether they will love the Lord their God with all their heart, with all their soul, and with all their strength (Deut. 6:2-4; cf. 1 Kings 11:2-4) and rely on Him rather than on others and their horses, war chariots, armies and the like.

Looking Forward

In the Hebrew canon, the book immediately before 1 Samuel is Judges, which ends with kings in view (Judg. 21:25). We then found ourselves in Shiloh with a barren woman who gives birth and prophesies about a messiah, that is, a king. She is the mother of the prophet whose word comes to all Israel but which Israel does not seem interested in. The ark is then taken from Shiloh and ends up in a backwater town waiting for a more permanent home. However, in the same context, we are pointed forward toward the king who is to come who will lead Israel against the Philistines and deliver them and establish the centre of his kingship in Jerusalem.

Of course, in the larger biblical theology of the Bible we know that we will need to look beyond David. This One greater than David will be from David's stock but unlike David *can* 'stand before the Lord, this holy God' (1 Sam. 6:20 esv) not only as prophet, priest, and king but also as His Son. We will also need to look beyond the ark and the city of Jerusalem to the city where there will be no ark nor temple but a heavenly Jerusalem, the holy city of God, where the Lord God Almighty dwells among His people and where their lamp is the Lion/Lamb of Judah (Rev. 5:6; 21:22-27).

The challenge is one still before us and which is picked up by the writer to the Hebrews who tells us that we must not shrink back (Heb. 10:37-39) but rather be those who believe that He is the rewarder of those who have faith in Him (Heb. 11:6). We not only enter relationship with God by faith, we go on in the same way, like those of old. We must be totally dependent upon God even if it pushes us to the edge. Isaiah called it a life of repentance and rest, of quietness and trust (Isa. 30:15). But it brings glory to our God and to His Son, the author and perfecter of our faith (Heb. 12:2).

From Text to Message

When we looked at 1 Samuel 4–5, it was assumed that the preacher might take chapters 4 and 5 on their own and then chapters 6–7 on their own and this is probably the most helpful way to preach these chapters. However, in my own preaching, I have approached preaching the ark narrative in a variety of ways, including:

1. One sermon on the whole narrative (i.e. chapters 4–7)
2. One sermon on each of the four chapters
3. One sermon on chapters 4 and 5, followed by another two sermons (6:1–7:1 and 7:2-17)

The same options are open to small group leaders as well as preachers. However, the advice that follows arises from the fact that I consider the best way to preach the chapters is to group them as I have done, that is, according to the third option above.

Suggestions for Preaching
Ways Into the Text
1 Samuel 6:1–7:1
Before telling you how I 'got into the text', it would be wise to explain that I am a natural storyteller. I love telling stories and people tell me that I do it well. If you are not like me, then the option that I'm suggesting here might not work for you. However, you could find an illustration that would have the same affect.

I began by telling the congregation that I was going to retell two stories from the Bible that I find confronting. The first comes from Joshua 7 which occurs just after God has won a great victory for His people at Jericho. However, when they go on to the next city, there is failure and God tells them that the failure is because one man kept some of the loot from the battle and that for his disobedience he and his whole family were to be stoned. The congregation were then asked, 'Who can stand before a God like this?' The second story was that of Ananias and Sapphira from

Acts 5 and concluded with the same question. Both OT and NT examples were deliberately used to make sure that those hearing noticed that God is holy in both Testaments. The congregation are then told that the same note is sounded by the men of Beth Shemesh at the close of chapter 6 and that we are going to look at what this passage says, and then reflect on how the Bible answers their question and ours.

1 Samuel 7:2-17

The way into the second passage was to tell a story from experience or from Scripture that raised the issue of alternative responses to God. After all, God is a God who is always putting alternatives to His people. He allows things to happen to them that draw out responses, knowing that He wants them to choose the godly response. God often does that to us in the circumstances of life and we must make choices. Moreover, those choices have ramifications as to whether God is honoured or dishonoured.

Moving Through the Text

1 Samuel 6:1–7:1

The major goal here is to (a) explore what actually happens in the passage, (b) work through what it is all about and then (c) pose the question raised in the introduction – 'Who can stand?' The implied answer of the text is, of course, 'No one can!'

From this point, it can be explained that this is the uniform position through the Old Testament. This is founded in Genesis 3, where we hear that because of sin it is impossible, without help, for Adam and Eve and their descendants to stand before a holy God. This appears to be at least part of what is meant by the cherubim guarding the

East entrance lest Adam and Eve attempt return. It may be that the cherubim woven into the sanctuary linen (cf. Exod. 26:1, 31; 36:8, 35) are meant to echo this.

1 Samuel 7:2-17

In this section of our second passage, I used a data-projector presentation to compare and contrast 1 Samuel 4 and 1 Samuel 7 in the way outlined earlier, concluding that there are two options for the people of God:

a) To look to their own ability while pretending to be dependent upon God. This will only result in dishonouring God.

b) To put God at the centre of their existence by putting His Word at the core of their lives and obeying it. This is expressed by hearing the bearers of God's Word and rejoicing in the exaltation and glory of God.

Biblical Theology and Application

1 Samuel 6:1–7:1

After explaining the text in its original context and touching, on the way, into the theology of the rest of the Bible, an appropriate connection can be made with the book of Hebrews. It is possible that at least part of the purpose of this book is to speak to people who find attractive the very tangible elements of Jewish faith and are tempted to drift away to it. In Hebrews 12:18-21, the writer reminds the readers that as Christians and not Jews, through Jesus they have come to a place where the promises of God have been fulfilled and they are spiritually in the very presence of God through the blood of Jesus. In verses 25-28, the writer reminds his readers that the day is coming when God will destroy the earth and the heavens, and that on that day believers in Jesus will not be swept away. However, he then reminds his readers that God is still a consuming fire.

This is a good point from which the preacher might remind people that without Jesus there is no hope of standing before this holy God and then apply the passage in the context of the whole Bible, by (1) reminding them that before the holiness of God we have nowhere to go without Jesus and that therefore, (2) they should heed the advice of the Philistine priests and diviners and not harden their hearts as the writer to Hebrews had similarly warned his hearers, (3) that they should renew their faith and trust in Jesus who alone can make us stand in the presence of the holy God; and (4) that we should encourage each other to keep believing in Jesus (cf. Heb. 3:13).

1 Samuel 7:2-17

Having outlined the alternatives for God's people, there could be some more theological reflection on what has been found in the passage. In a world of greater powers than their own seemingly fragile nation, they are fearful. However, Hannah has shown them the way forward and that is to trust in God who sometimes seems absent, knowing that it is not by strength that His people prevail but by trusting their God.

The point of course is that such trust is not easy because it demands a shift from our independence to making God the centre of our affections and faith (cf. Deut 6:2-4; 1 Kings 11:2-4). In relation to salvation, it means believing in His Son as being the only way of salvation. In relation to life as a whole, it is confidence that God exists, and that He alone is the rewarder of those who seek Him (Heb. 11:6).

Part Two: The Rise of Samuel and Kingship

Leading a Bible Study
1 Samuel 6:1–7:1
Welcome and introductions (5-8 minutes)
Two alternative starts to group time

A/1. Praying for each other (30 minutes)

It's normal in most small groups to pray in response to what is learnt. However, given the lighter nature of this passage, it may be helpful to spend time finding out how each other is doing, how God has been answering our prayers, what we can pray for each other.

B/2. *A quick quiz on 1 Samuel*
   1. Fill in the blank: 'And ... continued to grow in stature and favour with the Lord and with people'
   2. The name of the God of the Philistines who is mentioned in 1 Samuel 4 and 5 is...
   3. Name one of the sons of Eli (a bonus point if you can name both).
   4. What happens when Eli hears about the ark?
   5. What is the name given to Eli's grandson at birth? (bonus point if you can remember what the name means)
   6. What disaster happens to the Philistines when they take the ark of the covenant into their own territory?
   7. What were the names of Elkanah's two wives?
   8. Complete this sentence: 'In those days the .... was rare'.
   9. When the god of the Philistines falls before the ark of the covenant, what parts of him fall off?

10. What sin finally caused Eli to challenge his sons?

Read 1 Samuel 6:1–7:1 out loud in the group.

Observation

What three pieces of advice are given by the Philistine religious leaders as to what to do with the ark?

What do you think God is conveying through the incidents at Beth Shemesh? What do you think the Israelites should have learnt from the incident? What do they appear to have learnt/concluded?

Interpretation

- What is the question of the Israelites in the face of God's judgment upon sin and superstition (see 1 Sam. 6:20)? What is the implied answer?
- How does the New Testament answer this question? How can we stand before a holy God? Answer from Hebrews 10:19-22.
- What is one of the risks the Philistines faced that is similar to a risk that the Israelites and Christians face (read 1 Samuel 6:6 and Hebrew 3:1–4:11; look for a similar word that occurs in both passages)?
- How does the writer of Hebrews suggest that we avoid this risk?

Wrapping up together: Feedback from group work

Back to small groups

Break the remaining part of your time into two sections.

Part 1:

Discuss together what you can practically do to help each other stand firm in the faith and not drift into hard heartedness and superstition.

Part Two: The Rise of Samuel and Kingship

Part 2: Pray!
Pray together about the things you've learnt.

1 Samuel 7:2-17

Welcome and introductions (5-8 minutes)
Read out loud in the group 1 Samuel 4:1-22 and 1 Samuel 7:2-17. As you do, you might like to see if you can fill in the table below.

Observation
Chapter 4 and chapter 7 are the opening and closing chapters of what is called 'The ark narrative'. They have some similarities that convey some spiritual truths.

1 Samuel 4	1 Samuel 7
The Problem	
What type of problem is Israel facing here?	What type of problem is Israel facing here (7:2)?
Reflection and Consultation	
Who takes the initiative in sorting out the problem?	Who takes the lead in sorting out the problem?
Decision	
How do they decide to involve God and what do they hope the result will be?	How do they decide to involve God and what do they hope the result will be?
Event	

What action takes place (4:4)? Who is looking on (4:6)?	What action takes place (7:5-6)? Who appears in response (7:7)?
Battle	
How does Israel respond to the presence of the ark? How do the Philistines respond? Does God appear to be present or absent?	How does Israel respond to the presence of the Philistines? How does God respond? Is He present or absent?
Aftermath	
Who wins the battle and how well? What happens to the corrupt religious leadership of Israel (4:11-18)?	Who wins the battle and how well? What happens to the godly religious leadership of Samuel (7:13-17)?
Memorial and Summary	
What memorial naming occurs and what does it mean? What is the impact on Philistine activity?	What memorial naming occurs and what does it mean? What is the impact on Philistine activity?

Interpretation

- What do we learn here about the two options for God's people and the two results?

- How do these options show themselves in our lives as Christians?

Part Two: The Rise of Samuel and Kingship

Wrapping up together: Feedback from group work

Back to small groups

Break the remaining part of your time into two sections.

Part 1: Talk

Talk about the areas where you and your Christian friends are placed in situations where there is the risk that you move God out of the centre of your life and try to 'do it yourself' or move God out of the centre.

How can we encourage one another and support one another?

Part 2: Pray!

Do you need prayer for these things?

Is there someone that you should be praying for in relation to these things (don't necessarily mention them by name).

Pray together for the things that you have learnt and shared together.

10.
Moves Toward Monarchy
(1 Samuel 8:1-22)

Massive Changes

Each of the countries in which I have lived for a significant part of my life have had strong links with Britain: Vanuatu, Papua New Guinea, Australia and Singapore. Each, for one reason or another, have experienced change in that relationship. In the case of Singapore, there was the Second World War itself, the tussle afterwards, the new Constitutional Agreement in 1958, a brief incorporation into the new federation of Malaysia in 1963, final separation from that federation on 9 August 1965 and the declaration of the Republic of Singapore on 22 December in the same year. Such events changed Singapore forever and the nation as it stands today is the result of those events.

This passage of Scripture reflects a similar level of change. However, this nation caught up in this change is a nation chosen and called by God, His holy nation and special possession, a nation called into existence by Him (Exod. 19:1-6). It is therefore a change that needs serious thought and consideration, not just for the nation itself but also for the rest of the world for whom God wishes this nation to be a blessing (Gen. 12:1-3). For this reason we will slow down a bit in comparison with the previous chapters and give due focus and attention to this important event and its implications.

Listening to the Text

Context and Structure

Previously we noted that the story of the ark was demarcated by the transitional passages of 1 Samuel 4:1a and chapter 8. After 1 Samuel 8 has been settled and kingship formally integrated into the Lord's relationship with His people, we will focus in on the appointment of Saul through to God's rejection of his kingship over Israel and the choice of one better than Saul (1 Sam. 15). Both the introductory and concluding narratives of this next section are characterised by 'rejection'. In chapter 4, it is Israel's rejection of the Lord (v. 4) whereas in chapter 15, the Lord's response to the rejection of His Word is the rejection of Saul (vv. 23 and 26). This is picked up and reiterated in the beginning of the following section where David is chosen to replace Saul (16:1, 7).

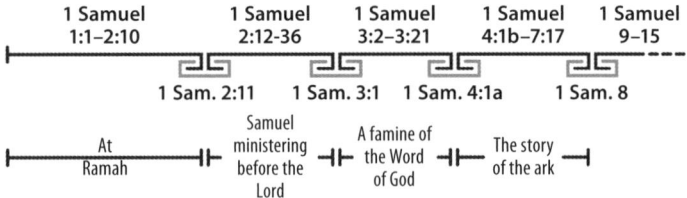

Content

Further background: The need for a king?

The chapter we are looking at raises the issue of Israel and kingship. As we have seen, the prospect of a king is raised as early as Hannah's prayer in 1 Samuel 2 where she connects her experience with an 'anointed one', that is, a messiah or king. Succeeding chapters have made a few other things clear to us.

- Hannah's son and the future anointed one are entwined with each other.
- There are *internal* problems within Israel (e.g. a corrupt priesthood) that demand leadership of some sort.
- Some *external* factors seem to reinforce the need for leadership, such as the aggressive Philistines.

However, the last few chapters have taught us that the LORD can counter the Philistines and humiliate them on their own turf without Israel's armies. Moreover, if the attitude of His people is right, the LORD can work in and through war as well, causing His people to be victorious.

In other words, much of what we have read since chapter 2 has told us that kingship is not necessary for either external or internal reasons. Moreover, Israel itself acknowledges that the LORD Himself can accomplish all of this when Samuel takes a stone in 1 Sam. 7:12, sets it up and says:

'Till now the LORD has helped us' (ESV).

The point is that the LORD is their King, Saviour, and help. They need nothing else.

Judges, judging, Samuel and the LORD (1 Samuel 8:1-3)

To understand these verses, it is helpful to understand the language related to 'judging'. Up until this point in the Old Testament, the language of judging has been used in several ways in relation to humans. Key among them is the appointment of judges to help Moses judge disputes among the people of God (Exod. 18:13-27). Such language is taken up in Deuteronomy where the Lord instructs Moses to appoint judges (16:18). Their main task appears to be maintaining harmonious relationships between Israelites by solving disputes and ensuring justice. Those involved in the task of judging must be godly themselves (Exod. 18:21; Lev. 19:15; Deut. 1:16-17; 16:18-20; 25:1) and they are often considered to be part of the core of leadership within Israel (Josh. 8:33; 23:2; 24:1).

While being a 'judge' in the book of Judges uses the same language, the role of the judges in Judges is different. They are raised up by the Lord Himself rather than appointed by Israelite leaders (2:16-19), often empowered by the Spirit (e.g. 3:10; 14:6, 19; 15:14) and act as deliverers of the people (e.g. 2:16, 18; 3:9, 15, 31). It has been argued that Samuel is pictured as this sort of judge in 1 Samuel and there are certainly elements of his service in chapters 4–7 that have echoes of the judges in the book of Judges.[1]

This background raises the question about what Samuel is doing in 'making his sons judges over Israel' (8:1 ESV). Even though he sometimes appears in a military context (1 Sam. 7) and there may be echoes elsewhere of his doing book of Judges style things, even in this chapter his actions look more like that of Moses in Exodus 18 (e.g. 1 Sam. 7:6, 15-16; 8:1). It is therefore likely that he is appointing his sons for the same Moses-like task.[2] However, like so many fathers in the books of Samuel,

---

1. David Jobling, *1 Samuel*, ed. David W. Cotter, Jerome T. Walsh, and Chris Franke, Berit Olam Studies in Hebrew Narrative and Poetry (Collegeville, MN: The Liturgical Press, 1998), p. 51.

2. Possible references back to role in the book of Judges can be found in 2 Sam. 7:11 and 18:19.

this father has unruly sons who therefore do not meet the demands of Deuteronomy. Moreover, he appears to be making the role hereditary.

The request for a king (1 Samuel 8:4-9)
Given the background just outlined, the request of verses 4-5 can make sense. His actions cause 'all the elders of Israel' to gather together to make an alternate proposal for leadership: 'Now appoint for us a king to judge us like all the nations' (v. 5 ESV). In other words, instead of making judges hereditary their alternative solution is kingship, which is what other nations have. Such a proposal would mean a move from a loose tribal confederacy to a State ruled by (possibly hereditary) kings.[3]

In verse 6, Samuel is displeased with their proposal. One possibility for the displeasure is that it is a rejection of his own proposal. This possibility is reflected in the comment by God later that 'they have not rejected you, but they have rejected me' (v. 7 ESV), although it is unlikely as the following analysis shows.[4]

There are three elements highlighted in the text: 'a king', 'to judge us' and 'like all the nations.' Although many commentators consider that the problematic clause is 'like all the nations', that is unlikely because verse 6 explicitly tells us what displeased Samuel and it is that they said, 'Give us a king to judge us' (ESV). This would fit with Deut. 17:14-15 which does not find 'like all the nations' objectionable in a request for kings over Israel.

---

3. Of course, the narrative of the books of Samuel will go on to indicate that hereditary kings will not be any better and may themselves need discipline (2 Sam. 7:14).

4. Contrary to a previously held view; Reid, 1 & 2 Samuel, p. 47.

After Samuel turns to God in prayer (v. 6), the LORD responds to Samuel and our list of plausible causes of objection reduces further, the LORD speaks only of the request for a king, noting that this amounts to a rejection of Him as King (cf. 1 Sam. 10:19). In other words, His people's allegiance to Him is being overturned by an act of idolatry, which makes it very surprising that He then accedes to their request in verse 9, albeit urging Samuel to 'solemnly warn them and show them the ways of the king who shall reign over them' (v. 9 ESV). The focus thus falls on the nature of the kings, not the office itself or even the request. God accepts kingship but knows what humans are like and therefore what kingship by humans will look like. As we will see, this will be confirmed in the echoes of the language used here by the LORD when He rejects Saul in chapter 15. One further note is that the LORD has changed the language of the people. The people wanted a king to *judge* us but He speaks of a king who will 'reign (as king) over them.'

The ways of the king (1 Samuel 8:10-18)

Not 'giving' but 'taking'

The speech of verses 10-18 is striking in a number of ways. First, the narrator has already told us that the sons of Samuel stretched out their hands for dishonest gain, took bribes and wrested justice from people. In other words, their object was self, and they did this by wresting things from others. Now he tells us the 'ways' or 'policies' (lit. 'judgment') of their kingly ruler.

They may have wanted a king for benefits to themselves but the LORD's response is to tell them that the flow will run in the opposite direction. In the Hebrew of the passage the word for 'take' is used four times. Their king will take 'your sons' (v. 11), take 'your daughters' (v. 13), take 'the best of your fields and vineyards and olive orchards' (v. 14 ESV), and take 'your male servants and female servants and your donkeys' (v. 16 ESV). He will 'give' but it will be to his servants (v. 14) and administrators/eunuchs (v. 15).

Strikingly, the fourfold repetition of the Hebrew word used for 'taking' here is used four times of a king and his actions toward one of his subjects in 2 Samuel 12. The rich man in Nathan's parable (i.e. David) 'takes' the poor man's ewe-lamb (v. 4) because he did not want to 'take' (v. 4) one of his own. In verse 9, Nathan then gives David the Word of the LORD and says to him that he has 'taken' Uriah's wife as his own and despised the LORD by 'taking the wife of Uriah the Hittite' as his own.

The Word of judgment from the LORD to David is that: 'Right before your eyes I will ***take*** your wives and ***give*** them to your friend.'

Return to slavery

Second, it is important that we do not miss the reference to slavery in verse 17. The force of the passage is not that the king will be their servant but that they will be his servants/slaves. In other words, kings could easily mean a return to the bondage of Egypt.

The loss of immediate access

The third implication flows into Israel's immediacy of access to God. The escape from Egypt began with Israel's groaning. The people groaned out under the burden of slavery and God heard their *groaning*, remembered His covenant, saw their plight and knew (Exod. 2:23-25). The same was true under the judges (e.g. Judg. 3:9, 15; 6:6-7; 10:10) and Samuel (7:8-9).

However, verse 18 says that this immediacy will be gone; the LORD will not listen. Under the burden of Israelite kings who take and enslave (v. 17), they will cry out. However, when they do, 'because of your king, whom you have chosen for yourself ... the LORD will not answer you in that day' (v. 18 ESV). The tragic irony is that Israel is about to forfeit something precious for a king and doesn't even seem to notice.

The response of the people (1 Samuel 8:19-22)

The speech of Samuel is clear and unrelenting. However, the reaction of the people is also as clear as it is unequivocal. They 'refused to obey the voice of Samuel' (v. 19 ESV) and effectively chose the path that will be full of kings who are as human as they are and therefore as prone to asserting their own rights. As Samuel has indicated, it will be a rough path. Samuel listens, repeats their rejection to the LORD, does not name a date or time, and sends them home. The implication appears to be that he will do what is necessary to find them a king.

Theological Themes

The theological themes within this passage are strong and robust. First, God is a good King. He has the good of His world and His people in mind. He even warns His people of the costs of human kingship but, as we shall see, still ties it into His covenant relationship with them.

Second, the strongest theme here is human sinfulness. On the one hand, we see it in their desire to do what they think will work best for them, despite what God might think. Their request is full of such self-assertion and God makes this clear in verses 7 and 8. However, the grimmest portrait in this chapter is that of their kings who will be unlike God the good King and who will instead be bent on taking rather than giving. In other words, the kings will also do what they think is good for them at the cost of their people. Self-rule is going to be like hell for them, full of people like themselves – self-interested, bent on 'taking' and using others for their own interests.

Listening to the Whole of Scripture

Looking Back

The independent mindset shown here in Israel is as old as Adam and Eve in the garden. Even if all the evidence is of God being good and great and able, it is hard to not think that He might withhold from us something that really is better for us (such as the fruit of a tree or a king). Demonstrated in countless places and by countless people in Scripture, it seems it is a human disposition to be unsure that God can be trusted to do what is best for us.

Looking Forward

The best antidote for this streak of independence and lack of trust is to go to the place where God displays His kingship most clearly, in His Son. Jesus is God in human form, thinking as God thinks and acting as God acts. Jesus knows as His Father does, that we are people with a passion for self-rule and that a world filled with such people is hell on earth.

In Jesus we see God the Son as true human and true king. He submits to the Father and comes into the world as a true human. He lives the perfect human life. He acts as a true king should in that He does not *take* but instead *gives* His life on behalf of His people, taking upon Himself the punishment due to them because of their commitment to self-rule. He dies in their place and shows us a picture of the rule of God in action. He may be physically descended from David, but unlike David and his successors, He does not 'take' but gives. In this, He is like His Father.

From Text to Message

The 'big idea' of this passage is plain: humans have a passion for self-rule and despite God indicating clearly that He has the best interests of His people in mind and the ability to save and secure them, they feel insecure. Moreover, having humans rule will only expose them as subjects to the vagaries of the all too human dispositions of their rulers, that is, self-interest and selfish gain. In preaching, we will need to demonstrate that this is the main thrust of the text.

However, on the other side, we will need to demonstrate that God the King is different. In order to do this, we need to take the congregation to a descendant of both David and Adam and Eve, the sinless Jesus who, on the cross, gives rather than takes and in doing so enables salvation for those who believe in Him and His work. A Christian is, therefore, one who sees their nature, who abandons self-rule, and who accepts the kingship of Jesus and the gift won on the cross by Him. They then turn *away* from self-centred 'taking' and turn *to* live a life like His of self-sacrifice for the well-being of others.

A sermon based on this text, therefore, provides great opportunity to do three things: (1) to explain the nature of God's kingship and benevolence; (2) to explain the heart of human sin; and (3) to show how the kingship of Jesus is the clearest demonstration of the kingship of God. The application can be directed equally well to both Christians and those who are not yet Christian.

Suggestions for Preaching

The importance of 1 Samuel 8 for biblical history and biblical theology is evident. It interacts decisively with the story of Israel begun in the garden, continued in history, taken up in Judges, and that then flows on into kingship. It, therefore, inevitably points toward the kingship of Jesus. For this reason, as well as systematically working through the books of Samuel, you may use it in other contexts as well (e.g. a Bible overview series). However, because of its importance, it is probably best preached as one unit on its own.

Ways Into the Text

The way into the text of this passage rather depends upon the purpose for which you want to use the passage. For example, if you were going to use it evangelistically, your way in might raise a question that is suited for that application, such as how the hearers might think about themselves or even God. As a preacher, I have used it for a variety of purposes and therefore developed a more generic introduction that speaks of pivotal moments in a nation's history (such as at the beginning of this chapter).

When preaching it in an Australian local church context in the early years of this millennium people still had memories of a constitutional debate and referendum on whether Australia would become a republic. I recalled that event and noted that if the change had been made then many fundamental aspects of who Australians thought they were, how they governed themselves, and Australian national identity would have changed. I reflected that this was the sort of level of change that Israel was contemplating in the chapter we were going to look at in chapter 8.

Moving Through the Text

Moving through the text of 1 Samuel 8 in preaching is relatively straightforward. The major sections are clear in demarcation, and although not without problems, their intention seems obvious and can be easily explained as has been indicated.

For the purposes of exposition, the text easily divides into clear sections. Verses 1-3 allow the preacher to set the larger Biblical context and to remind the hearers as to the important background of the passage, that it is set in the days of the judges. A decision will also need to be made and explained as to what Samuel is doing when he makes his sons 'judges'. Is he doing something God should do (as in the book of Judges) or is he doing something similar to Moses' actions under the advice of his father-in-law back in Exodus 18? Astute hearers will want to know whether Samuel's actions are legitimate or not and this will need to be addressed and explained.

The second section of text is verses 4-9 and again there are problems as to what the critical issues are in the debate. Most importantly, what is it that displeases Samuel? The preachers will have to make a decision and communicate the basis on which that decision has been made because it significantly affects meaning and therefore application. For example, should the preacher think (as many commentators do) that the displeasure is caused by the phrase 'like the nations' then that could significantly affect how these verses or even the whole sermon is applied.

Part Two: The Rise of Samuel and Kingship 175

As indicated above, the view here is that the issue is the request for a king and the implicit rejection of God as King (v. 7). The preacher who concludes this may then have to explain why God allows Israel to move ahead with this incredibly significant change.

As indicated under 'Listening to the text', the key points that need to be pushed home in verses 10-18 are (1) that kings will be characterised by 'taking', (2) that it will effectively mean a return to slavery such as their last experience under an earthly king in Egypt; and (3) that their immediate access to God and rescue will be affected as He will not answer their cries. The point is that human kingship will be human and therefore bound together with all the sinfulness of humans.

The third section of the text is verses 19-22 where the people fail to listen to Samuel and press on with their request to which the Lord accedes.

Biblical Theology and Application

The core of good preaching that is rich in biblical theology is not simply placing the story in the larger storyline of Scripture that finds its centre and focus in Jesus. Rather, it is about pondering what is happening theologically. Once we have done this, we can then see how this theology fits into the larger biblical theology of the whole Bible that has its centre and focus in Jesus. In this case, the focus is clearly on human sinfulness. Samuel is presented as a failed father, Israel as a group wanting to reject the kingship of God and future kings as being self-interested and self-serving people who 'take' rather than give. Even David, as 2 Samuel 11 indicates, is like this and so we must look for another, that is, Jesus, who gives rather than takes and whose rule is dominated by giving. As indicated above, this leaves things quite open for applying the text broadly to a variety of people within a church congregation and affords a wonderful opportunity to help them place their hope in Jesus alone.

Leading a Bible Study

Introduction to 1 Samuel 8:1-22

Welcome and introductions (5-8 minutes)

Ask people to summarise what has happened so far in 1 Samuel 1–7. Explain the difference between those chapters and chapter 8. Use this to introduce the fundamental nature of what is happening in chapter 8.

Read 1 Samuel 8:1-22 aloud in the group

Observation (perhaps in smaller groups)

Verses 1-5

In the group, brainstorm all that you know about the appointment of judges in the book of Judges (if you need a good brief overview passage, try focussing on Judges 2:6-23 and the summary diagram below).

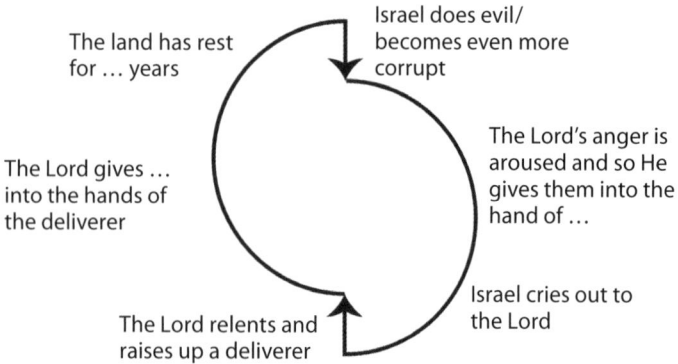

Part Two: The Rise of Samuel and Kingship

In the light of this background, what is unusual about what Samuel is doing in these first five verses?

What is the big request put to Samuel by the people? What reasons or underlying motivations lie behind the request?

Verses 6-7
Verse 6 says that Samuel is displeased. What are some of the options as to what might cause this displeasure?

What does God think is the reason for Samuel's displeasure (v. 7)?

Verses 8-9
How is Israel's treatment of Samuel similar to their treatment of God?

What is God then saying that Israel's request for a king amounts to?

What is striking about what God does in response (v. 9)?

Verses 10-18
Why did Israel want a king?

Read verses 1-18 again. This time, see if you can notice which word is repeated over and over again in relation to the king (hint: 'He will …').

When Israel was under a king (i.e. Pharaoh) in Egypt, what was their experience like? What does God say it will be like with an Israelite king ruling over them?

Think about the book of Exodus and the Judges again. When Israel cried out to God for rescue from harsh rule, what would happen? What does this passage say is going to happen under an Israelite king when they cry out to God?

How is Israel going to lose out with human kingship?

Getting back together in the larger group to discuss verses 19-22

A Passion for self-rule

As a group leader, you might then open up the conversation as to what the central point of these verses is and how the Lord responds. What is surprising? Why? What does it tell us about God?

Application (back to small groups)

When you return into small groups, break the remaining part of your time into three sections.

Part 1: Compare and contrast

How does the kingship of Jesus differ from the kingship of the kings outlined in 1 Samuel 8:10-18?

Part 2: Praise and thanks

Pray together thanking God for the kingship of Jesus. Praise God for the things that you mentioned in Part 1.

Part 3: Pray for each other

Spend time hearing from each other about personal items for prayer and then praying together.

Part Three:

THE BEGINNING AND END OF SAUL'S KINGSHIP

(1 Samuel 9:1–31:13)

11.
Israel's First Human King
(1 Samuel 9:1–11:13)

We have now reached the second major section of Samuel. Having laid the groundwork with Hannah's story and then her prophecy/prayer, we saw God send His Word to His people who had little time or inclination to listen to it. He humiliated the Philistines in the absence of His people and led them through Samuel. However, in the face of his growing age and the absence of any prospective successor, they appealed for a king. Samuel resisted it, but God accepted it.

Listening to the Text

Context and Structure
The concept and practice of kingship had been coming for a long time. In some sense it could be argued that it has been in prospect since Genesis 1, when the presentation of humans as vice-regents over God's world, under God's rule was made (Gen. 1:26-27). Moreover, it was promised that kings would come from Abram and Sarai (Gen. 17:6, 16). As we have seen, Deuteronomy anticipated the appointment of kings (Deut. 17:14-20). The previous chapter of Samuel

concluded with the LORD outlining what kingship would look like in reality for Israel, but the leaders still said they wanted a king for what they perceived as the benefits (1 Sam. 8:19-20). The LORD then urged Samuel to get on with the process and Samuel told the leaders of Israel to go home, presumably while he went about preparations.

It is therefore with anticipation that we reach chapter 9. Surely, we will hear of Samuel indeed 'making them a king' at some gathering. Instead, Samuel is strangely absent as we are led by our author into a corner of Israel, to a tribe that had almost disappeared at the hand of fellow Israelites during the period of the Judges (Judg. 20). We are transported to the ordinary family life of a Benjaminite man of wealth. The narrative that follows is delightful, albeit a bit strange to foreign ears at times. It is also striking because of the variety of places and the number of separate encounters there are with different people. The preacher or teacher more at home with New Testament epistles may struggle to know how to deal with this narrative passage in a way that will do it justice. It is vital that we do not simply reduce it to three flattened points or a series of propositions.

The passages under examination here fall into two clear sections: 9:1–10:16 and 10:17–11:14 (although the terminating point of the second section varies among commentators).

1 Samuel 9:1–10:16

The structure of the first passage can be approached from a variety of perspectives. For example, if there are geographical or journey markers between the starting point of his family in Benjamin (9:1-4) and the return to

Part Three: The Beginnings and End of Saul's Kingship 183

the family (10:13-16), then this finds its centre in the meal in 1 Sam. 9:22-24.

Alternatively (and preferably for preaching), the structure can be considered from the perspective of a series of quests.[1]

Quest 1: Saul's search for the lost donkeys of Kish, his father
Begins at 9:1

Quest 2: Saul's search for a nameless 'man of God'
Begins at 9:6

Quest 3: Samuel's search for 'a man from the land of Benjamin' to be anointed 'prince'
Begins at 9:15-16

Quest 3: Resolved at 9:17 when Samuel finds Saul

Quest 2: Resolved at 9:18-19 when Saul finds Samuel

Samuel promises a resolution to Saul's Quest 1 but only after some important things happen. These important things concern Israel's quest for a king, the 'desire of Israel'.

Various discussions happen with various groups of people but most significant are the four persons or groups of persons that Saul will meet on the way home:

(i) Two men who will tell him that Quest 1 has been resolved (10:2).

(ii) Three men who will offer him food, therefore resolving the food problem raised in 9:7 (10:3-4).

---

1. The analysis here draws significantly from J. P. Fokkelman, *Narrative Art and Poetry in the Books of Samuel: Volume IV: Vow and Desire (1 Sam. 1–12)*, Studia Semitica Neerlandica, 31 (Assen, The Netherlands: Van Gorcum, 1993), pp. 356-435.

(iii) Saul will come to a location where there is an outpost of the Philistines. There he will meet a group of prophets with whom he will also prophesy (10:5).

(iv) The Spirit of God will come on Saul in power, and he will be changed (10:6), at which point he should 'do what your hand finds to do' (10:7 ESV).

(v) Saul is then to go to Samuel in Gilgal and wait for him there (10:8).

Saul then returns home and has a discussion with his uncle, and for the first time in the whole narrative, the notion of kingship/kingdom is mentioned by the narrator (10:16).

1 Samuel 10:17–11:13

The larger context for this chapter is set by chapter 8, where Israel asked for a king and the LORD promised them one. Moreover, He told Samuel to make them a king. In the previous section we were given something of a private glimpse of the LORD bringing His appointee to Samuel and in the first half of this section we've seen Saul receive some signs of God's choice. At this point the process that appeared to have stalled at the end of chapter 8, has resumed with the introduction of God's king to God's people.

There are two major sections within the narrative here: 10:17-27 and 11:1-13. It is hard to be certain whether 11:14-15 fits with what precedes or succeeds it, although the weight would seem to fall on verses 14-15 introducing the occasion (the renewing of the kingdom) at which Samuel then delivers the speech contained in chapter 12.[2]

---

2. Matitiahu Tsevat, *The Meaning of the Book of Job and Other Biblical Studies: Essays on the Literature and Religion of the Hebrew Bible* (New York: Ktav Publishing House, 1980), pp. 77-99.; Dennis J. McCarthy,

The structure of this section falls into two clear parts:

10:17-27	**Saul becomes king at Mizpah**
11:1-13	**Threat to Israel and Saul's demonstrated leadership**
1-3	The Nahash threat
4-5	Messengers arrive and speak; result: weeping
6-8	Spirit-initiated response by Saul
9	Messengers arrive and speak; result: gladness
10-11	Deliverance
12-13	Honour to whom honour is due

Content

1 Samuel 9:1–10:16

Although this passage is long, it should be kept together. It is important that we help people grasp the drama of the various quests and the flow of the story. From another perspective, however, it is also important that they do not get lost in the dramas so that they miss the main point of it. The main point is that through these various interactions with a broad variety of people, God is doing something very important. God has heard the request of His people for a king and He is answering that request. In the third and central quest observed previously this is picked up (1 Sam. 9:16) when the Lord tells Samuel that he is to

---

'The Inauguration of Monarchy in Israel: A Form-Critical Study of 1 Samuel 8–12', *Interpretation* 4 (1973), pp. 401-412; J. R. Vannoy, *Covenant Renewal at Gilgal: A Study of 1 Samuel 11:14–12:25*, Dissertation (Amsterdam: Free University, 1977); Fokkelman, *Vow and Desire*, pp. 481-92.

anoint a leader. The Hebrew verb 'anoint' is the word that lies behind the Hebrew word for Messiah (and the Greek word 'Christ'). In other words, God is in the process of finding an anointed one, a Messiah, a Christ. Saul is the first of these.

If this is the main point, there is also a subsidiary point, and it is critically important in reading Samuel to understand this (and to help our congregations absorb it). That point is that God's primary agent under God here is Samuel. However, something very important happens within the narrative that Saul and readers need to recognise. At the beginning of the narrative, Saul is a son under the direction of a father. However, at the end Saul is under the direction of God through His prophet (and not even Saul's family can control or deflect that – 1 Sam. 10:16). The point is that God's new leader is a man under authority who must live under the direction of God through His Word. That is emphasised by the use of 'prince' (9:16 or 'leader') rather than 'king'.

There is also a tantalising possibility that leaves us wondering. First, Saul's appointment as king is meant to be connected with delivery from the Philistines (9:16). Second, in the list of events that Samuel said will happen, there is one that does not. When all the signs happen, Saul is meant to 'do what your hand finds to do'. However, he meets the prophets, the Spirit of the LORD comes upon him, but the writer does not tell us of anything that he does. The only real possibility in Samuel's instructions appears to be the outpost of the Philistines. Given that Saul was appointed to 'save my people from the hand of the Philistines', perhaps Saul is meant to be like a judge at this point and engage in battle with them (as his son will later). Third, we do not hear of Saul going to Gilgal as indicated. Why not? Is this linked to his failure concerning the Philistines?

Finally, there is something that readers should observe about the story. It has an unusual level of human involvement, including a father, the servant, some girls, a cook, two men with news, three men with food, the prophets, and the uncle. Few of them are aware that God is using them in this incredibly important event in the history of His people.

1 Samuel 10:17–11:13

1 Samuel 10:17-27: The people summoned to Mizpah; Saul becomes king

It appears that if the chain of events had happened as Samuel expected, then Saul would have gone down before him to Gilgal (10:8). Instead, Samuel calls the people together to the Lord at Mizpah. He recalls with the same hint of negativity, the sentiments espoused about kingship in chapter 8. Speaking for the Lord, he reminds them that the rescue from Egypt had been from the Egyptians and 'all the *kingdoms* that were oppressing you' (ESV). Samuel adds in his own words that now they are wanting a king. The implication? To ask for a king is to foolishly reject God.

Nevertheless, lots are drawn, and Saul is eventually isolated only to be found to be hiding. Saul is found by the people and then stands tall above them. Strikingly, the first explicit use of the term 'king' concerning Saul in these chapters is not on the lips of Samuel but on the lips of the people (v. 24). Given the echoes of the Torah in the early verses of this passage, it would seem reasonable to assume that the 'rights and duties of kingship' conveyed by Samuel to the people could be those reflected in Deuteronomy 17:14-20. They are written down and deposited before the Lord after which the people are sent or return home. In an unusual insertion of his own opinion, our author tells us of 'some ***worthless*** fellows' (ESV) who despise Saul. However, the insertion not only reflects the author's opinion but lets us know that not all will be smooth sailing for Saul.

1 Samuel 11:1–13: Threats to Israel and Saul's demonstrated leadership

When Israel's request for kingship was first issued, Samuel was asked to 'appoint for us a king to *judge* us like all the nations' (1 Sam. 8:5 ESV). It was a strange request in some ways. Nevertheless, given that the Philistines were in view and that it was previously Samson of whom it was prophesied that 'He will *begin* to deliver Israel from the hand of these mighty Philistines' (Judg. 13:5), it is possible that judge-like figures were the way in which they conceived of kingship and expected it to function. This may explain what the people are looking for in this chapter and the way Saul is portrayed. It may also explain something of the refrain captured in the final verse of Judges 21:25: 'In those days there was no king in Israel. Everyone did what was right in his own eyes.'

The text itself needs little explanation of its content. Nahash has in mind not simply the eyes of the men of Jabesh Gilead but the humiliation of all Israel (v. 2). The right eye may have been chosen because ancient soldiers held their shields over the left eyes which means that gouging out the eye might not only humiliate but weaken the army in battle.

Notice that it is not just one messenger who comes to Gibeah of Saul but *the* messengers (v. 4), whom Saul then sends out 'to all the territory of Israel' (v. 7 ESV). This appears to be what Israel was after in the appointment of a king and the corporate weeping before he arrived would seem to emphasise this. As in Judges, the Spirit of God rushes on Saul (v. 6).

Given what has happened, the difference in the people captured in verse 9 is striking. They themselves give the message to the people of Jabesh Gilead. Saul organises the people and the victory is complete. Saul's kingship is endorsed by the people. Questions are put to Samuel by the people but the answer comes from Saul, the man who had to be dug out of the baggage a chapter earlier. Saul acts wisely and also ascribes victory to the proper person – the LORD who worked salvation.

Theological Themes

The dominant theme of these passages is kingship. As we will see, this must be closely linked in with prophecy and the relationship between the two will be a matter of significant exploration in the chapters that follow. As far back as 1 Samuel 2 we have seen bonds between notions of kingship and the Messiah (1 Sam. 2:10) as well as a faithful priest (2:35). Such links will need to be explored and highlighted as we continue to work our way through Samuel and then explored as part of a larger biblical theology.

However, for our purposes in these chapters, it is significant to notice a pattern within the narrative of the appointment of the first king. First, we are told that God chooses the king (1 Sam. 9:16; 10:24). Second, He involves the prophet by having him anoint the king (1 Sam. 9:16; 10:1). Third, His king is endowed and empowered by God's Spirit (1 Sam. 10:6, 10; 11:6). Finally, His king is publicly affirmed in public mighty acts of deliverance (1 Sam. 11:1-11).

The pattern just observed is repeated with David. He is chosen by God in 1 Sam. 16:1; anointed by the prophet Samuel in 1 Sam. 16:13; endowed with the Spirit in 1 Sam. 16:13 (and the Spirit taken off Saul in 1 Sam. 16:14) and finally performs public mighty acts of deliverance in 1 Sam. 17.

As we will see as the books of Samuel and kings unfold, Saul's kingship is tainted almost from the start and David's is not without flaw. Neither fully fulfil the requirements of kingship that were outlined in Deuteronomy 17, and the books of Kings show us that their descendants follow in their footsteps as the summary in 2 Kings 17 demonstrates. The end result is the punishment of the exile.

Listening to the Whole of Scripture

Looking Back

As we look back in Scripture, we see the notion of kingship is strong right from the opening passages. Although the language of kingship is not used in Genesis 13, the notion is present in such places as Genesis 1:26-30, which is then picked up in Psalm 8. It appears that such delegated human rule is designed to flow through God's king (e.g. Psalm 2) and yet they too fail as we have already observed.

Looking Forward

The question posed by the troublemakers of 1 Samuel 10:27 is a good one: 'Can this man save us?' It could perhaps be addressed to all the kings of Israel with both the narrative books, the prophetic books, and the book of Psalms giving the same answer. Such kings may be able to save from occasional armies, but they are in the end tarred with the same brush as the people over whom they rule, who are descendants of Adam and Eve.

The New Testament takes both these streams— humans as a whole and the kings of Israel as God's appointed rulers—and indicates that the Lord Jesus fulfils them both. This is picked up concerning humans in Hebrews 2:5-18 (which reflects on Psalm 8). However, the gospel narratives also indicate that while we may never have seen other Israelite kings following the pattern we observed in Samuel, we do see it in the ministry of Jesus. He is a descendant of David who is God's choice (Matt. 12:15-21). He comes to the prophet for recognition of His appointment (Matt. 3:13-17), is anointed by and filled with the Spirit and equipped for ministry (Matt. 3:13-17; Luke 4:17-21), performs mighty acts of deliverance for the people of God (Matt. 4:23-25; 12:22-29) and acts as the true king of Israel, obeying God and being a servant for the good of the people of God.

Vannoy raises the tantalising possibility of an allusion here to Genesis 3:15, given that the Hebrew word for 'serpent' in Genesis 3 is the same as 'Nahash' and that his actions here are to strike out aggressively against Israel's first anointed king (i.e. Messiah).[3] In this case, we see that in this first skirmish between Israel's first messiah, the Lord has indeed fought for His people and 'given

---

3. J. R. Vannoy, *1–2 Samuel*, CBC (Carol Stream, Ill: Tyndale House, 2009), p. 104.

strength to his king and exalted the horn of his anointed' (1 Sam. 2:10; cf. Rev. 12:7-17; 20:1-3).

From Text to Message: The Big Picture

It might be possible to preach the whole of 9:1–11:13 in one sermon. However, I think that this might be too large a task and runs the risk of stripping the passage of some of its drama and key points. The alternatives might be:

Option 1		Option 2	
Sermon 1	1 Samuel 9:1–10:16	Sermon 1	1 Samuel 9:1–10:16
Sermon 2	1 Samuel 10:17–11:13	Sermon 2	1 Samuel 10:17-27
		Sermon 3	1 Samuel 11:1-13

No matter what the choice (we will be focusing on Option 1), it will be important to keep our people in tune with where we are. The narrative detail and textual complexity mean that each sermon in the whole series on Saul will constantly need to remind people where each segment falls within the whole. The story grows as it goes, as do the relationships and people, and our hearers (whose lives are often busy and filled with complexity themselves).

Suggestions for Preaching

1 Samuel 9:1–10:16

The most important advice that can be given about this passage is to urge as strongly as possible that the preacher not take the punch and drama out of the narrative or reduce it to a series of points. It is a story. If you are a born storyteller, this passage is made for you! If not, then avoid the temptation to reduce it to a series of points. Treat this passage more like reflections on the weekend at morning tea on Monday rather than an agenda at the board meeting on Friday afternoon.

Ways Into the Text

A possible way into the text is to talk about the whole process that we inevitably go through in life when making decisions. If life has been particularly full of decisions of various sorts, you might even reflect personally on them and the impact that they have had. The purpose would be to illustrate that we often divide life into 'big' and 'small' decisions.

There may be another way in, that has a similar purpose, and that is to raise the question as to which are the really important decisions in life and which are the ones to which we give little time. Suggest that the passage being looked at might throw some fresh light on the way we think about these matters.

Moving Through the Text

No matter how the passage is introduced, it is important to remember to orient/reorient people as to what has happened so far. Start with Hannah and quickly retell the story up to this point. Remind them that at the end of chapter 8 the people have been sent home after being promised a king. They are therefore in waiting, as we the hearers are. The sort of questions we have are … How will God appoint? Whom will He appoint? etc.

Introduce the passage as a story of quests and quickly move through the text summarising the key elements of each. Having done this, get people to note what the main point is and what the subsidiary point/s are.

After this, you might note the vast variety of people involved and how most of them did not know the big picture as we do. Unbeknownst to them, they are caught up in God's big plan for His people and His world.

Biblical Theology and Application

After this has been done a possibility would be to move on to speaking about God's sovereignty, even noting the observation in Acts 2:22-24 that God can even work out His purposes in and through His Son, through the evil deeds of people.

A good way to apply the text would be to return to the ideas raised at the beginning, that it is often the ordinary and mundane decisions of life that matter most. It might possibly be that this is why the Bible does not focus on the ones we often think are important such as career, who we marry, how many children we have, etc. Instead, the focus is on issues of godliness.

1 Samuel 10:17–11:13

Ways Into the Text

While it may not be the most encouraging way to start a sermon, one way into the passage is to talk about the main emotion that is raised by part of the text – that of despondency. Many people will resonate with this, and it will be helpful for them to hear that in the passage you are about to explore, God's people experience it and that God heard, saw, and rescued. That said, it would be good to tell them that this will be returned to, that there will be an explanation of how this helps us as God's people.

Moving Through the Text

There are two major sections in the text. The verses and my headings were: (1) A Candidate (10:17-27) and (2)

Part Three: The Beginnings and End of Saul's Kingship 195

The First Test (11:1-15). In the first section, you might simply move through the text explaining it quickly and emphasising the question raised by the worthless men in verse 27. In the second section, it will help to do what was done with the narrative in the choice of Saul, that is, retell it in a way to catch the drama and pathos. Both sections could be done relatively quickly.

Biblical Theology and Application
The next section might contain a summary of what has been observed in the whole narrative about Saul that has been under scrutiny, that there is a pattern of divine choice, anointing, empowering by the Spirit, and public mighty acts of deliverance.

This would open up opportunities for biblical theology in that the same pattern is observed in David but then not observed again in the Old Testament. In fact, what is observed is that Saul and David fail as do their successors (see above for argument and references). However, the pattern is picked up in Jesus who spectacularly succeeds.

The application would be that 'this fellow *can* save us' and that we can look to Him for salvation and kingship that is lasting, and we can also look to Him in the difficulties and despondency of life and not give up.

Leading a Bible Study
Study 1: 1 Samuel 9:1–10:16
Welcome and introductions (5-8 minutes)
Orientate people again to kingship in Israel and warn them that there is much reading to be done. Then read 1 Samuel 9:1–10:16 aloud in the group, answering the questions as you go.

Observation
What are the outstanding features of Saul?

Three quests
Observe that there are three quests in the passage that we are looking at and that you have identified them below. Explain to group members that you want them to read the passage together and answer the questions related to each one.

Quest 1 (v. 3)
Whose quest is it? What is its goal?
List its progress…

Quest 2 (v. 6)
Whose quest is it? What is its goal?
List its progress…

Quest 3 (vv. 15-16)
Whose quest is it? What is its goal?
List its progress…

Saul's homeward journey (1 Samuel 10:1-16)
What four signs will Saul have on the return journey?

1. (v. 2)   ☐
2. (vv. 3 and 4)   ☐
3. (v. 5)   ☐
4. (v. 6)   ☐

What is Saul meant to do when they are fulfilled?
Are all the signs fulfilled (tick the ones that are)?
What, if anything, does Saul do when they are fulfilled?

Part Three: The Beginnings and End of Saul's Kingship   197

Interpretation
(perhaps these could be divided among smaller groups)

Some things to think about (1)

Think back to where we have been.

- Why did Israel want a king?
- Brainstorm about the pattern set in the book of Judges. What is the pouring out of God's Spirit associated with in the book of Judges?
- What happens when God's Spirit is poured out on Saul? In what way is he different from the judges who preceded him?
- What do you think Saul should have done when the signs were fulfilled?

Some things to think about (2)

- Is Saul God's choice (cf. 1 Samuel 10:24)?
- Who is the boss in this new incorporation of kings into God's relationship with His people?

Some things to think about (3)

- How many people did you meet in the narrative?
- Did God use them to fulfil the quests?
- What were they doing at the time God used them?
- What does this teach us about the ways of God in the world?

Report back briefly into the large group

Application (back in smaller groups)

Talk with each other about your needs in terms of prayer. Spend time praying for each other.

Particularly pray for each other in the 'ordinariness' of life.

Share any ways in which you see God active in the 'ordinariness' of your lives.

Pray for your honouring of God in all parts of life.

Thank God for the ideal King, Jesus, who did what Saul and David did not do.

Study 2: 1 Samuel 10:17–11:13

Observation
Read 1 Samuel 10:17-27 aloud

Looking for a king

Verses 17-19 give a prophetic denunciation of Israel. If you were writing up a charge sheet of the sins of Israel on the basis of this passage, what sins would they be guilty of?

If a prophet gave such a denunciation and then gathered the people together, what would you suspect might come next (particularly when tribes are then chosen by lot; cf. Joshua 7:16-18)?

What happens instead?

We are not told why Saul is hiding in the baggage Any guesses as to why? Any evidence?

Apart from his hiding in the baggage, there are three things we are told about Saul. What are they?

1.

2.

3.

When they are combined, what is the overall picture of Saul we are given?

Part Three: The Beginnings and End of Saul's Kingship

Note: In verse 25 we are told that Samuel explained to the people 'the rights and duties of kingship' (ESV). Although we are not told explicitly here what they are, it is reasonable to assume that they would be the same or similar to Deuteronomy 17:14-20.

Read Deuteronomy 17:14-20 and summarise in one sentence the 'rights and duties of kingship' as outlined there.

Read 1 Samuel 11:1-13

Here are some hints that might help with understanding this story.

- Traditionally ancient soldiers held their shields in their left hand over their left eye. Gouging out their right eye would not only have brought humiliation but also weakened them in battle.
- The setting of the story is the question of the scoundrels in 1 Samuel 10:27: 'Can this fellow *save* us?' The same Hebrew word for 'save' is used in verse 3 (NIV 'rescue'), verse 9 ('delivered') and verse 13 ('rescued').

List how Saul is like a judge in this passage.

Interpretation

Thinking about Israel's first king

Finish these sentences ...

Saul is God's .... (1 Samuel 9:16; 10:24)

Saul is anointed by .... (chapter 9)

Saul is endowed with and empowered by .... (chapters 9 and 10)

Saul is affirmed as he does .... (chapter 11)

The same pattern is repeated with David (1 Samuel 16:1, 3; 13; chapter 17) but with no other Old Testament kings that follow them.

However, neither Saul nor David fully fulfills the duties of kingship.

Think about the early ministry of Jesus. How and where is the pattern seen in Saul and David fulfilled in Jesus? Can you find Bible references for these?

Prayer

Thank God for God's perfect King, Jesus.

Share prayer points and pray for each other.

12.
King and Covenant
(1 Samuel 11:14–12:25)

As students of the Bible and disciples of the Lord Jesus, the language of kingship is something with which we are very familiar. The language we use with each other, the songs that we sing, the names by which we know the Lord Jesus, are often linked with the language of kingship. Although kingship has sat below the surface in the Bible until the last few chapters of Samuel, all that is about to change. Kings are about to be sewn into the way in which God's people envisage and speak about God and a key moment in that development is this section of Scripture that we are about to examine. Kingship from this point will be incorporated into the Lord's covenant with Israel.

Listening to the Text

Context and Structure

Because these chapters and their stories can sometimes seem somewhat disjointed, it is helpful to orientate ourselves again. As we have seen, the book was probably divided into two for pragmatic reasons of space, with the first book finishing at the death of Saul and the second one beginning with the matter of succession to the throne. We have already noted that within that larger picture there are chapters that form overlapping links between the sections.

```
|------------1 Samuel------------|-------------2 Samuel-------------|
1    7  9    14 16              31 2  4 5:6 8 9              20 21 24
      ⌐⌐         ⌐⌐                 ⌐⌐   ⌐⌐
       8          15             2 Sam.1  5:1-5
```

The section we are examining lies between these two series of events:

(a) The inauguration of kingship by God in chapter 8 followed by the appointment of Saul as the first king, and

(b) God's formal rejection of him as king in chapter 15 (although he remains king until chapter 31), along with the announcement of a successor: 'a neighbour of yours, who is better than you' (1 Sam. 15:28 ESV).

Subsequently, this neighbour is introduced as David in chapter 16 and he is anointed in the same chapter, although he does not formally become king until sometime after the death of Saul in chapter 31.

Between chapters 9 and 14 there are various other critical moments. One such moment is captured in verses 14-15 of chapter 11. These verses provide a transition point between the actions and reactions of the previous chapter and the formal speech of chapter 12 wherein the actions of the previous chapters are made concrete in a covenant renewal. Diagrammatically, we could represent it as follows.

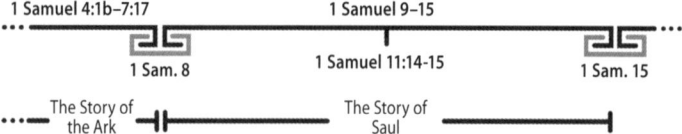

Part Three: The Beginnings and End of Saul's Kingship   203

After the request for a king in chapter 8, we have seen Samuel tell the people 'all the words of the Lord' about kingship and its costs (8:10-18) and heard of Israel's willing acceptance of those costs (8:19-22). Since then we have seen:

- The Lord's selection of Saul and his apparent failure to engage the Philistines as expected (9:1–10:16)
- the public introduction of Saul by Samuel (10:17-24)
- the people's acclamation of him as king (10:24)
- Samuel's outlining of the rights and duties of kingship (10:25-27)
- the threat of Nahash and Saul's triumph over him, along with the acknowledgement by Saul of the victory having its source in the Lord
- Saul's kingship welcomed and endorsed by the people (11:1-13)

Content

1 Samuel 11:14-15

These critical verses mark a transition toward chapter 12. After the success over Nahash, Samuel calls for the people to gather at Gilgal and 'renew the kingship' (11:14). This term raises significant problems – whose kingship is being talked about?

One choice is that it is Saul's kingship. However, we haven't heard anything so far that has indicated that Saul has actually begun to reign, and the term 'renew' generally means to repair something broken or in need of repair (e.g. Ps. 51:12; Isa. 61:4; 2 Chron. 15:8; 24:12; Lam. 5:21). Moreover, if Saul had a kingdom over which he ruled, one might think that a message might come direct to him rather than to 'all the territory of Israel' (v. 3). Moreover, the messengers do not appear to come directly to Saul but to 'Gibeah of Saul' and his hearing of it seems circumstantial, that is, he notices weeping when 'coming from the field behind the oxen' (v. 5 ESV). Therefore, it is unlikely that 'renewing' the kingdom in verse 14 refers to Saul's kingship, in which case it might refer to the kingship of the LORD.[1] This would make sense given the threats that human kingship posed to the kingship of God, as intimated by the LORD Himself (8:7), Samuel (10:19) and the people of Israel (as reported by Samuel in verse 12).

The solution is to formally make Saul king 'before the LORD' with sacrifices and celebration (v. 15). Such an action would not only affirm the LORD's kingship but also renew the covenant and acknowledge Saul as a human king envisaged in such places as Deuteronomy 17:14-20. Therefore, what is spoken about briefly here is what will be formally carried out in the next chapter and explains the content of that chapter. Gilgal is noteworthy given that it was the place where the sins of the wilderness were put aside and the men born in the wilderness were circumcised in accord with the covenant (Josh. 5:2-9).

It is hard to know how significant it is, but Samuel who has never seemed very happy with the move toward kingship is not included among those who 'rejoiced greatly' in the final verse of chapter 11 (ESV). We will need to look at what Samuel says in the ensuing chapter to see if we can ascertain why that might be.

1 Samuel 12
Verses 1-5

The first five verses of chapter 12 have the shape of a legal declaration with some key elements.

---

1. A change of mind from a previously held position; Reid, *1 & 2 Samuel*, p. 68.

The 'take' which Samuel used four times concerning the coming kings is now used here four times as well. Three times, Samuel uses it concerning his ministry, asking Israel to testify against him if he has 'taken'. The response of the elders in verse 4 is to assert that he has not defrauded, oppressed or 'taken' anything from any man's hand.

Samuel has exercised leadership within Israel, and that will continue. However, as shall be explored later, that leadership will now take a different shape from what it has until now.

Verses 6-19
In verses 6-19 the focus shifts in Samuel's speech away from himself and toward the LORD and Israel. It takes the form of a monologue that stretches to verse 17 and consists of a survey of Israel's history from the time that Jacob went into Egypt until settlement in the land, the period of the judges and finally the incident with Nahash the Ammonite. The words 'And now behold…' form a break in the middle at the beginning of verse 13 (ESV) (with ten references to YHWH/LORD in verses 1-12 and another ten in vv. 13-17).

Samuel's central contention in verses 6-12 is that the LORD was their King during that period but that they had found that insufficient and therefore asked for a king. Strikingly, in verse 13, he introduces Saul as 'the king whom you have chosen, for whom you have asked' (ESV) before going on to say 'behold, the LORD has set a king over you' (ESV) and then outlining to them the two options for proceeding from where they are ('If you will … But if you will not …'; vv. 14-15 ESV). These binary options outline the conditions of the covenant in this new era: kings are included. However, the emphasis on the involvement of both king and people in sin or obedience, indicates that in the end not much has changed by adding a king. The people must still be obedient themselves as well as their king.

Having set out the binary options of 'fear/service/serve/obey/follow' and 'not obey/rebel', Samuel stands before them and tells them to 'stand still and see this great thing that the Lord will do before your eyes' (v. 16 esv). The language of standing still and looking is used in Exodus 14:13 of God saving His people as He fights for them. Here it is ominously used of His action toward His own rebellious people. To ensure that we know the severity of what happens, we are told that Samuel highlights with the people that it is the time of wheat harvest (i.e. a time when thunder and rain would cause significant damage and have longterm impact). Moreover, Samuel explains the reason for the judgment – their great wickedness, done in the sight of the Lord and involving their request for a king (v. 17). There is something of an irony here in that their request appears to involve a lack of trust in God the King and His ability to protect and care for then. He judges them by casting the elements at them and acting toward them as a divine warrior (cf. Exod. 14:1–15:21; Deut. 28:15-68; Ps. 18). It appears that the long rebuke, full of the Lord, has its desired effect. Israel acknowledges the evil of their request for a king (v. 19).

Verses 20-25

The final verses of the chapter summarise many key matters raised in this chapter and the ones preceding it. First, at the heart of the matter is the sin of not trusting the Lord or serving Him. They therefore need to be exhorted to cast aside such an attitude, which underlay their request. Second, specifically they are to turn aside from 'empty things' (ESV), such as a kingship isolated from trust in God's care and provision. Third, they are to find comfort in their election as a people chosen to be 'a people for himself' (v. 22 ESV). Fourth, he promises them his continued intercession for them and finally, he urges them to remember that they are the LORD's covenant people who are called upon to be faithful to Him. While His hand is filled with good things, He will punish wickedness, even in His good gift of kings.

Summing up
The passages that we have looked at in this chapter are critical. When we view 1 Sam. 11:14–12:25 as a whole, we can see an extraordinary shift. That shift involves a move away from the time of the judges and to something which has been looked forward to since at least Genesis 17 as well as being strongly hinted at in the formulaic refrain toward the end of the book of Judges (e.g. Judg. 17:6; 18:1; 19:1; 21:25) – the time when Israel will have kings.

Significantly, what happens here is done by the LORD and by Samuel within the context of covenant renewal. In other words, despite the sinfulness of God's people in the manner and means in which they have gone about gaining kings, we see here, in the context of covenant renewal and under the guidance of His prophet, how the Lord sews kingship into His relationship with His people. At the same time, the story emphasises that only where God is acknowledged as true King over Israel can there be any room for human kingship.

Theological Themes
The major theological themes of this chapter are clear. First, we have humans acting as they have since Genesis 3,

that is, seeking to act independently of God. This passage declares that such action is reprehensible and deserves judgment, particularly when the humans involved are those who know God and His ways and have experienced His love and mercy in abundance.

Second, we see God who is sovereign. He is able to accomplish His purpose even without human hands or involvement. This is of great comfort, for we know that a sovereign God can forge His purposes even through human sinfulness.

Listening to the Whole of Scripture

Looking Back

As we look back in Scripture, we can see that the things we see in our passage are not new. In Genesis 1 we see God creating a wonderfully rich world and placing humans in it to rule it under His rule (Gen. 1:1-31, particularly vv. 26-27). This rule is a remarkable gift celebrated in places such as Psalm 8. However, we see humans stepping out from under God's benevolent rule and exercising independence, that is, doubting His good rule and seeking to be free from it. We also see God judging sin but, as we see here, tempering His judgment with mercy and promise (such as the promise of 'offspring' (lit. 'seed') in Genesis 3:16 amongst the promises of judgment).

This pattern of sinful people used by God in His sovereignty to accomplish His purposes for His world and His people is evident constantly in the stories that follow. For example, the promises given to Abram of land, children and blessing (Gen. 12:1-3) are almost immediately threatened by Abram's actions in leaving the land of promise, fleeing to Egypt where he puts his wife (and the promise of children by her) under threat, and his actions also cause Pharaoh to be afflicted rather than blessed (Gen. 12:10-20). Nevertheless, five chapters later the Lord promises Abram and his descendants/'seed' an everlasting covenant (Gen. 17:7). Through Sarah will come a son, nations and even 'kings of peoples' (Gen. 17:16).

This promise of 'offspring' and 'kings' continues on through the Pentateuch and is picked up in various sections therein, including the blessing of Judah by Jacob (Gen. 49:9-10) and even a tantalising reference in the prophecy of Balaam (Num. 24:17-19). Kings are also clearly in prospect and allowed in the sermons given by Moses on the plain of Moab before entry into the land (Deut. 17:14-20). The location of these sayings (i.e. set within the covenantal context of Deuteronomy) and their general thrust is clear. When kingship eventually came to Israel as anticipated, it was to be different from that seen in other nations. Like human kingship, it was to be exercised under the overarching kingship of God and therefore subservient to His Word. Moreover, it was a mechanism for exercising the Lord's kingship over the Lord's people. Like His rule, it was to be just, righteous and benevolent.

Looking Forward

As we look forward in Scripture, we will see that this first king—Saul—was not all that was desired or anticipated. We will, therefore, look for another. He will come from the line of Judah and his rule will look like the rule of God. Without pre-empting the story too much we will find that Saul is noted for not letting God's Word rule and David is a move in the right direction. While Saul was God's choice (1 Sam 10:24), David was a distinct move in the right direction – a man loved by God, who loved God and was willing to live under His Word and to be corrected when he did not. Nevertheless, he was also tainted with the same brush as Saul and the same flaws prophesied by Samuel in chapter 8. He was still inclined to 'take' with all the self-interest that those words reflect. We must, therefore, look for another, who will be from his line but who will not 'take' but give.

The prophets of Israel, many of whom lived and ministered in the wake of the spectacular failure of Israel's kings and the results of the exile, began to look for another who would fully live subject to God's kingship and with the manner and style of His kingship (e.g. Isa. 9:6-7; Jer. 23:5-6; 30:9; 33:15-17). The New Testament announces His coming by specifically observing His descent from David (e.g. Matt. 1:1-16), the endorsement of God and His prophet (Matt. 3:13-17), His determination to live under the rule of God and His Word (Matt. 4:1-11) and His humble, dependent, sacrificial, 'giving' rule exercised in life and in death (Matt. 12:18-21; 20:24-28; cf. Phil. 2:5-11).

From Text to Message

One of the significant dangers of moving from text to message is that of rushing to fulfilment in Christ. The central message, as we have explored above is (a) the sinfulness of humans and (b) that the Lord is a just and benevolent God who will forge a future for His people and His world despite human sinfulness. God will eventually do it in such a way that will deal with their sinfulness and give them the reign of a King who will be like God Himself. On the cross He will be both just and merciful as He is here and will accomplish it finally by *giving* rather than *taking*.

Suggestions for Preaching

Ways Into the Text

There are lots of ways in, which might engage your congregation concerning this passage. Being a lover of great rhetoric, I began by getting people to think about some of the great speeches in human history. I gave examples of people and places, making sure that I touched on one or two recent ones that had shaped either the world or a particular country. Given that this volume was written in days of the presidency of Donald Trump, you might even give some examples of an inferior but still potent modern equivalent – the 'tweet'!

The idea behind this is to get people into the frame of thinking about how speeches capture or define pivotal moments in history. From this perspective, you can talk about 1 Samuel 8 as a critical moment in Israel's history—the inauguration of human kingship—and how this is defined by the speech of God's prophet.

Moving Through the Text

In this passage, there are four major areas to be addressed if you are to preach an expository sermon on the passage.

Context (1 Samuel 11:14-15)

First, you should set the context and remind people of where they are in Samuel. Fortunately, because of the way I consider that the passage is broken up, verses 14-15 give this in a nutshell and enable the hearers to be refreshed in terms of context. One of the main things to point out is the question about whose kingship is spoken about in verse 14. You might even say that it is somewhat ambiguous and, on that note, move into the passage to see if a conclusion can be reached.

Examining the participants (1 Samuel 12:1-11)

The second area to be addressed is the participants in the passage (my heading was 'Examining the Participants'). Here, I put three subheadings: Samuel (vv. 1-5), God (vv. 6-8), and Israel (vv. 9-13). In preaching, I briefly summarised the key points of the text, illustrating from the text and showing them that what I was saying was really there. I gave a summary point for each of the participants:

- Samuel, the judge, has been true, honest, and faithful
- God, the LORD, has been faithful to the covenant He made with His people
- The people of Israel have been characterised by unfaithfulness and sin

The Nahash episode (1 Samuel 12:12-13)

The third area addressed in the exposition was the Nahash episode (vv. 12-13). I had two headings:

- Expectations

I went through the passage and explained that it is couched in the pattern set in the book of Judges and that the normal expectation in such stories is that Israel would repent and call on God for deliverance. However, Israel's response is to ask for a king.

- Reality

The reality is no repentance, not calling out to God but instead, spurning God and asking for a king. Israel is very sinful. They have spurned God. However, He gives them a king (theologically, although they were faithless, He remains faithful).

Covenant and kingship (1 Samuel 12:14-18)

The fourth area addressed in the exposition was 'Covenant and Kingship' (vv. 14-18). Here a number of things were pointed out, such as…

- The covenant language; and
- The thunderstorm and its untimely/ unseasonal appearance and possible impact

The main point of the passage was then explained, that is, that kingship comes from a sinful disposition, but that God is going to incorporate it into the covenant. He had already pre-empted that in Deuteronomy and said that prophets are to be covenant guardians for kings.

Aftermath (1 Samuel 12:19-25)

Here I made sure that the message was heard that Israel was sinful but that the Lord remained committed to the relationship. The key thing was that the people and their king recognise that the covenant has obligations, blessings, and curses.

What hope is there?

In this final section, I emphasised that the kings that followed were sinful, even David. Why? Because they are human, just like Abraham and Sarah, Adam and Eve, and us. I then pointed out that the book of Samuel begins with a barren woman in a helpless situation and that God acts to deliver her. This is what God has done for us in Jesus, even if we sometimes don't realise our plight. In Jesus and the cross, we see God's true King in action, being like God, *giving* rather than *taking*.

Leading a Bible Study
1 Samuel 11:12–12:25
Introduction to this section

What's going on in 1 Samuel 11:12-15? (5 minutes)

- Great speeches
- What happens
- Three participants

Observation (in smaller groups)

Participant 1 (Samuel: 1 Samuel 12:1-5)

How does Samuel's leadership differ from that of the coming kings? (look for the word that is repeated here by Samuel and which he also repeated concerning the coming rule of kings in 1 Samuel 8:10-18)

Who affirms and/or witnesses (or called upon to affirm/witness) to the truthfulness of Samuel's claims?

What word might you use to summarise Samuel's actions with God and Israel?

Participants 2 and 3 (1 Samuel 12:6-11)

The other two major participants in this story are God and Israel.

What word(s) might you use to summarise God's actions with Israel?

What word(s) might you use to summarise Israel's actions with God?

The Nahash Incident (1 Samuel 12:12-13)

The normal cycle from the book of Judges looks something like the diagram on the next page.

Read 1 Samuel 12:12-13. From the diagram, what would the presence of an external oppressor normally indicate?

What would be the expected response of Israel to this oppressor?

What does Israel do instead and what does their action amount to?

How does God respond to Israel's actions?

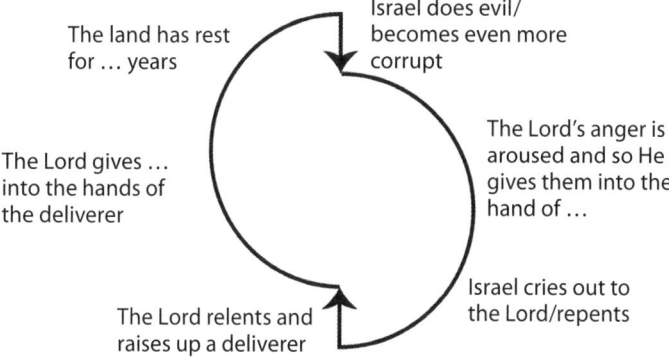

Footnote: What is strange about what verse 13 says about Saul?

Covenant and kingship (1 Samuel 12:14-18)

In these verses, God sews kingship into His covenant relationship with Israel. What are the rules for kingship within that relationship? Do you think that this is any different to the rules of the covenant prior to this (e.g. Deuteronomy 28)? How?

What do you think the thunderstorm is about?

Back in the large group

Together look at and summarise the aftermath of … in 1 Samuel 12:19-25.

Application

As Christians, what things do we use to avoid calling on God alone for help (i.e. where else are we tempted to put our hope and confidence)?

How can we help each other in this?

> What can we pray for each other to help? Pray together about these things.
>
> Don't forget to thank God for the help He gives to us the helpless ones.

13.
The Reign of Saul as King
(1 Samuel 13:1–14:52)

A Lengthy Passage

The question as to how much to cover in a sermon is a significant one for the preacher. As indicated earlier, Mark Dever has done us a favour in not retreating from trying to preach each book of the Bible in one sermon. Sometimes preaching large slabs is necessary and helpful in order to help our people understand what is going on or to see the cohesion of the whole or to grasp the main point when it comes not from the individual parts but a larger whole. An example of when you might do this is the instructions about the building of the ark (Exod. 25–31) and then the narrative about its actual building (Exod. 35–39), perhaps with a separate sermon on the golden calf incident together with God's self-revelation in chapters 32–34. Another less lengthy candidate is the passage before us, which stretches across these two chapters of reasonable length. Although I have preached it in three, two or one sermons, I am convinced that the last alternative is the best and will proceed on that basis here (while suggesting an alternate breakup as well).

Another possibility that presents itself, given the length and content of the passage, is to make room in preaching through Samuel to have one sermon devoted to Jonathan which might be preached between any series on the two halves of Samuel, or after the song of 2 Samuel 1. The reason for saying this is that the narrative of Jonathan begins here, is intriguing, and occurs in a book where there are relatively few characters who escape the criticism—either explicit or implicit—of our author. One is Hannah. Others might possibly be Samuel or Abigail (although she doesn't get much space). But the one who gets significant space but doesn't seem to get *any* bad press explicitly or implicitly is Jonathan, and so he needs some focus at some point and perhaps even a sermon just on him. Such a sermon would be beneficial for our people and would also pick up some of the items we will need to skim over in this sermon on chapters 13–14.

Listening to the Text

Context and Structure

Context

Concerning context, there are some important things that we need to keep in our minds as we approach this passage.

First, we must not lose sight of 1 Samuel 2 and the song of Hannah! The important things she taught us in prayer are: (a) the Lord is a God who exalts the humble and humbles the proud (2:2-9); (b) that principle applies particularly to kings and therefore it will not be by might that kings will prevail, rather they will recognise the Lord's judgment and depend upon Him to judge (2:9-10).

Second, remember at Saul's first contact with God's prophet Samuel he was explicitly told that he would come to a particular location where there was a Philistine outpost and when the expected signs were met Saul was to 'do what your hand finds to do, for God is with you' (10:7 ESV). However, we heard of nothing happening.

Third, Saul is specifically told by Samuel that he shall go down to Gilgal ahead of Samuel and that when Samuel arrives, he will offer sacrifices. Saul is to wait for him and then Samuel will tell him what to do (10:8). Again, this has not happened yet that we know of.

Fourth, in the immediately preceding chapter, kingship had been formally included into Israel's covenant relationship with God as anticipated in Deuteronomy 17 and two particular things appear clear there: (a) kingship is subject to prophecy and not the reverse and (b) kings are to be subject to the same covenant boundaries as the people (hence the 'you and your king' of 1 Sam. 12:25). If they do not observe the Word of the LORD, they will be 'swept away' (12:25 ESV).

The structure of this section can be summarised as follows:

13:1-23	Saul and the Philistines
13:23–14:52	Jonathan and Saul against the Philistines
13:23–14:15	Jonathan's partnership with the LORD
14:16-23	Consequences
14:24-35	Saul's oath
14:36-46	Aftermath
14:47-52	Summarising Saul's reign

Content
1 Samuel 13:1-22
Some textual difficulties

There are two textual difficulties with the Hebrew text of 1 Sam. 13:1, as noted by most English translations.

They involve Saul's age at the beginning of his reign and the duration of his reign. It appears that all textual traditions we now have are corrupt. The Septuagint simply removed the whole verse. English translations propose various alternatives based on other sources or proposed amendments. Acts 13:21 shows that the apostle Paul was aware of a tradition that Saul reigned for forty years.

There is a further textual problem in verse 15 as a comparison with English translations will indicate. Hence, the translation given in the NIV84 reflects the Hebrew text but has a footnote that follows the Septuagint's version while the ESV has things the other way around.

When preaching, unless it is something that stands out for our people (as verse 1 does in the ESV translation) or that raises interpretative issues, such things probably don't need to be raised in a sermon but may sometimes need to be dealt with in a small group Bible study. The point of the original, whatever the years were, is probably that Saul's reign had not begun until the covenant renewal ceremony of chapter 12.

The Philistines

We have already been introduced to the Philistines in the earlier chapters of 1 Samuel and their growing prominence through the time of the judges. Moreover, the Lord's action in appointing Saul is explicitly linked with Saul and salvation from the Philistines (1 Sam. 9:16). In chapter 13 we learn why Israel was fearful of them: (a) they had already established a strong presence within Israelite territory (at Geba, a Benjaminite city; Josh. 18:24); (b) they possibly had outposts in a number of locations (cf. 1 Sam. 10:5; 1 Chron. 11:16); (c) they were dominant militarily in armed

Part Three: The Beginnings and End of Saul's Kingship   221

forces (compare Israel's 3,000 in v. 2 with the Philistines' chariots, charioteers and unable to be numbered soldiers in v. 5) and technology (v. 19-22).

What happens

The story itself is straightforward and can be run through quite quickly in a preaching or teaching context. However, apart from the elements already mentioned above, a few more will involve a particular focus or explanation.

First, Saul (apparently still at Gilgal; v. 7b) chooses three thousand men and splits them between himself and Jonathan, who is based at Gibeah. In verse 3, Jonathan does what Saul was meant to do back in chapter 10. The credit is given to Saul (v. 4), and the Philistines assemble with an enormous number of chariots and soldiers that terrify the Israelites (vv. 5-6a). Saul waits out the seven days as instructed by Samuel. However, his men begin to scatter and so he takes things into his own hands and offers the sacrifices (v. 9). Finally, Samuel arrives and Saul goes out to greet him, is rebuked, and offers a defence (v. 10-12).

Verses 13-14 are critical and have elements that need careful explanation. First, if Saul had obeyed the prophet's Word, which is critically called 'the command the Lord your God gave you', then the same Lord would have established his kingdom 'for all time' (v. 13). The point appears to be that as Israel was to live by every Word that came from the mouth of God (Deut. 8:3), so was Israel's king. Perhaps it is critical that this be emphasised with the first king. In any case, instead of establishing his kingdom, the Lord will replace Saul with 'a man who is after his own heart' (v. 14). These two terms, 'for all time' and 'after his own heart' need careful explanation when teaching or preaching since they have default meanings in English that are probably significantly different from their meanings in Hebrew.

Elsewhere in Samuel, the Hebrew behind our phrase 'for all time' does not mean what the English means (e.g. 1:22; 3:13-14; or 27:8, where it is refers to the past and is translated 'from of old' or 'for a long time') and the sense here is probably 'permanently'.

In English, the default meaning for a person who was 'after someone's own heart' would be that the person concerned shared the same tastes, interests, opinions and the like. However, when the Hebrew concept is used elsewhere in Scripture (e.g. 1 Sam. 14:7; Ps. 20:4; Jer. 3:15) and when its equivalent is used in other Ancient Near Eastern literature, it often has connotations of choice.[1] Hence, the focus in verse 14 is not on David and his disposition or inclinations but on the LORD who is searching for someone who fits His desire or disposition for a king, that is, His will. It is the language of elective choice. This is quite different from the mixed language that we hear used of Saul and kings in general, who can be said to be chosen by God or by the people (e.g. 1 Sam. 8:18; 10:24; 12:13). With David, the man after the LORD's own heart, we do not have mixed language. Instead, we have this statement in verse 14, a story of election (1 Sam. 16:1-13) which climaxes in a statement by the LORD ('Arise, anoint him, for this is he'; 1 Sam. 16:12 ESV) as well as human declarations of the LORD's choice of him (e.g. 2 Sam. 6:21; 16:18).

---

1. For a full exploration of the Ancient Near Eastern background to this language and its implications for this passage, see Athas, '"A Man After God's Own Heart": David and the Rhetoric of Election to Kingship', *JESOT* (*Journal for the Evangelical Study of the Old Testament*) 2/2 (2013), pp. 191-98.

The remaining verses of the chapter continue to show Israel's diminished state, troop movements and Israelite weakness. Of particular note, particularly given the story of chapter 14, is the Israelite inability to forge or even sharpen their own metal and the fact that only Saul and Jonathan had sword or spear.

1 Samuel 13:23–14:52
Jonathan's partnership with the LORD (13:23–14:15)
The same two armed men are the focus of this passage. There is a Philistine detachment at Michmash but Saul, who was raised up to defeat the Philistines (1 Sam. 9:16), is staying (literally '*sitting*') under a pomegranate tree at Michmash without God's prophet, and in company that is not exactly prestigious (1 Sam. 14:2-3). Ahijah is unusually and inexplicably linked with Ichabod and it is possible that the author does so deliberately to suggest some similarities between the situation here and the loss of glory there (1 Sam. 4:21-22).[2]

In contrast, Jonathan is not sitting but is set on fearlessly engaging the Philistines. The contrast begun here between the two men will continue as a focus throughout the chapter. In verse 6, Jonathan's attitude and approach to the LORD is like that of Hannah and that lauded by her prayer. The sense of dependency and God giving the victory is heightened throughout, particularly in that Jonathan does not even have to raise a sword. He had explicitly requested God's presence and the Hebrew of verse 15 captures God's

---

2. The reference to 'pomegranate' may possibly be to 'the rock of Rimmon' (lit. 'Pomegranate Rock') of Judg. 20:45-47, which may be close to Gibeah; Patrick M. Arnold, 'Migron (Place)', in *Anchor Bible Dictionary*, ed. David N. Freedman (New York: Doubleday, 1992), pp. 822-23.

involvement by using the word for 'trembling' or 'shaking' three times, with the third time attaching the Word 'God' to it (lit. 'Then *trembling* came upon .... They *trembled* ... It was a *trembling* of God').

Consequences (14:16-23)

These verses shift the focus back to Saul with marked contrast. The boldness, confidence and action by Jonathan compared to the attention to roll-calling and talking by Saul is profound. However, eventually Saul instructs the priest to 'withdraw his hand' and he too joins in. Three marks of God's activity and the response to Jonathan's dependence and leadership are evident. First, the lack of swords is made up for by the Philistines raising swords against each other (v. 20). Second, the apparent Israelite defectors turn against their allies the Philistines, joining Saul and Jonathan (v. 21). Third, Israelites who had deserted Saul and hidden in the hill country of Ephraim joined in (v. 22). The confidence of Jonathan expressed in verse 6 is vindicated.

Saul's oath (14:24-35)

The bright light that has shone in Jonathan and that is credited to the LORD in verse 23 is quickly snuffed out by the author as he turns to Saul's actions and their impact on the men of Israel in verse 24. Apparently, before this Saul had bound his people to an oath of abstinence from food. However, Jonathan is oblivious, finds honey, tastes it, and when informed of the oath criticises his father as one who has 'made trouble' (cf. Josh. 6:18; 7:25; Judg. 11:35; 1 Kings 18:17-18). Additionally, as Jonathan makes clear (v. 29) his oath lessened the possible victory. Moreover, it led to the ensuing sin of verse 32, which in turn leads to the construction of an improvised altar for slaughtering the animals (vv. 31-35).

Aftermath (14:36-46)

In the flush of a longed-for victory after the despondency apparent in the previous chapter, Saul and his troops are keen to press on and pursue the fleeing Philistines. When the priest suggests consulting God and it is done, there is no answer (vv. 36-37). The following comments by Saul show that he assumes that the non-answer is due to the presence of sin and therefore lot-taking is engaged in to isolate the sinner. Ominously, Jonathan's name is explicitly included (v. 39) and the lot-taking exposes him (vv. 38-43).

The question 'What have you done?' occurs in two locations in the larger passage: First, where it is put to Saul near the beginning, it is met by obfuscation and excuses (1 Sam. 13:11-13). Second, where it is put to Jonathan here near the end, it is met by direct acknowledgement. Moreover, Saul, who was willing to excuse himself, is quick to indicate punishment will be carried out concerning Jonathan and does so by taking another oath. The contrast between these two responses further heightens the differences between Saul and Jonathan evident throughout our section and leaves Saul isolated, the battle incomplete, and the advantage over the enemy petered out.

Summarising Saul's reign (14:47-52)

The darkness of the contrasts in this whole section is a little redeemed in the final section. Israel wanted a king for a purpose and Saul achieves that purpose. However, the long narrative from chapter 8 to this one have indicated that kings come with a cost and that cost will often have to be paid by others.

Theological Themes

The dominant theme of these passages (if not the whole of 1 and 2 Samuel) is that of kingship both divine and human and how the two are related. Such continues here with the focus falling on a comparison and contrast between the first formally appointed king, Saul and his son Jonathan. Because we have explored the larger biblical picture of kingship previously, our focus here will fall on the theological development that is happening within the book itself. Although in one sense it is still 'looking back', we will call this 'Looking within'.

Looking Within

Chapters 13–14 of 1 Samuel are key theologically. Although we know and have already examined how God has planned kingship for some time, we have now seen the formal inauguration of the first king and his inclusion within the LORD's covenant community. As a result, we might expect that there would be a rigorous exploration of kingship in Israel in general and this king in particular. That is indeed what we have and it comes in two forms. First, our writer examines Saul's own actions and then second, he explores them through a contrast provided by his son, Jonathan.

Assessing Saul's actions theologically

When examining Saul, we have clear guidelines in three places. First, we have the guidelines from Deuteronomy 17:14-17. In addition to them, we have Hannah's prayer and the just-enacted covenant arrangements of chapter 12.

In Deuteronomy 17, we learn that Israelite kings are to be distinct from kingship in the surrounding nations (i.e. not 'like the nations around us'). They are to be 'from among your own brothers' and not 'a foreigner', 'must not acquire great numbers of horses' for themselves or 'make the people to return to Egypt to get more of them', and 'must not take many wives' lest his heart be led astray or 'accumulate large amounts of silver and gold' (vv. 14-17). Kings in Israel must be familiar with God's will as revealed in the Scriptures so that they might 'revere the Lord', 'follow carefully all the words of this law and these decrees' (v. 17:19) and not 'turn from the law to the right or to the left' (v. 20). Moreover, a king in Israel must not 'consider himself better than his brothers' (v. 20).

It is to be observed that the most repeated element within these instructions are those related to God's Word. Fundamentally, kings are to be governed and directed by God's will as expressed in His Word. Obedience to God's will expressed in His Word will result in 'he and his descendants' reigning a long time over God's kingdom in Israel (v. 20).

Hannah's prayer in 1 Samuel 2 made clear that pride must be eschewed and that humility and dependence were the right approach to life before God the Creator, the God who weighs all deeds and is able to both humble and exalt, guard the feet of His saints and silence the wicked (vv. 3-9). The bottom line is that opposition to the Lord will result in His judgment (v. 10a) and the implication is that all of this applies to His 'king' and 'anointed' should they not take the theological advice given in the prayer (v. 10b). Jonathan, who is without a 'throne of honour' (1 Sam. 2:8) because of the actions of his father in the previous chapter (1 Sam. 13:13-14), is explicitly dependent on the Lord for saving (1 Sam. 14:6, 10) and acknowledges His activity, humbly giving credit to Him and wanting glory for Israel

(1 Sam. 14:12). In other words, he is an ideal candidate for a future king although he has been deprived of it.[3]

Already Samuel has explained to both the king and the people about how kingship would work, written this down, and 'deposited it before the LORD' (1 Sam. 10:25). Samuel outlined that the key things for both people and king was fear of the LORD, serving and obeying Him, not rebelling against His commands. Disobedience would be met with their being 'swept away' (1 Sam. 12:25).

A final manner in which the writer wants us to assess Saul is to do so in contrast to Jonathan. Although masked by most of our translations, chapter 11 uses the Hebrew words related to the root for 'save'/'rescue' (1 Sam. 11:3, 9, 13) three times in relation to Saul's victory and three times of Jonathan's (1 Sam. 14:6, 23, 39). In chapter 11 one reference has the source as being the LORD whereas in chapter 13 all references are explicitly related to the LORD.

Looking Forward

As we look forward theologically, this passage has given us a model of what kings should not be like and what they should be like. In this Jonathan comes out unflawed according to the criteria outlined so far in the book. Without a throne of honour, he puts his faith and trust in God who does what He promised in chapter 2. He exalts Him, fights before Him and fights for Him. Beside Saul, he provides a clear contrast as well as a clear model for future kings. Moreover, he will die beside his flawed father, loyal to him to the end.

---

3. In further support of the link between 1 Sam. 2:1-10 and 1 Sam. 14, the word 'foundations' in verse 8 is found in only one other place in the Old Testament, 1 Sam. 14:5.

If anyone is a precursor to, or type of Christ here, it is Jonathan. He is humble, has no apparent self-interest, courageous in his dependence upon the LORD, an agent of salvation that is ascribed to the LORD, willing to suffer for others, zealous for God and not zealous for fame, fortune, honour or kingship. He is a model for the man with whom he will make a covenant, the future king David. However, more than that, he is a precursor of Jesus who refused to grasp at things for Himself but humbled Himself and became obedient to the point of death, even death on a cross (Phil. 2:5-11) and who did not come to be served but to serve and give His life as a ransom for many (Mark 10:45).

From Text to Message

As indicated earlier, it seems preferable to preach the whole passage as one sermon. However, should you wish to preach it as two or three, the suggested breakup would be as follows:

Two sermons:
    Sermon 1: 1 Samuel 13:1-23
    Sermon 2: 1 Samuel 14:1-52

Three sermons
    Sermon 1: 1 Samuel 13:1-23
    Sermon 2: 1 Samuel 14:1-23
    Sermon 3: 1 Samuel 14:24-52

Some Hints About Preaching Narrative

Since we have not as yet spoken about preaching Old Testament narrative texts, it will be helpful to do so now as many preachers are more at home in the pericope-restrained Gospel sections or the epistles of the New Testament.

Most importantly, do not denude narrative by reducing it to propositions. Help it to live for your listeners. If you are a natural storyteller, then retell the story summarising its interpretation as you do. Furthermore, if you work from full notes, make the notes easy to read in a way that will not cause you to lose eye contact with your congregation. My own practice as a preacher is to have the text large, to have one sentence paragraphs and, unless it is impossible, to try and restrict sentences to 10-12 words. I also set my paragraphs to have 8pt spacing before and after and to set the line spacing at 1.15.

Here is part of the text of my own sermon on this particular passage.

In verse 16 the focus shifts back to Saul.

And the contrast is marked.

Saul sees the tumult in the Philistine camp.

But he doesn't join in with God and Jonathan.

No.

Instead, he engages in a roll call and brings up the ark.

Finally, he sees sense.

He makes a quick decision that he will take advantage of the situation and go into battle.

And when they do, they find that the havoc caused by God is overwhelming.

It is so overwhelming that the Philistines are 'striking each other with their swords' (v. 20).

And that is just as well.

After all, chapter 13 told us that 'on the day of the battle, not a soldier with Saul and Jonathan had a sword or

> *spear in his hand; only Saul and Jonathan had them'*
> *(13:22).*
>
> *Friends, this is the God Hannah celebrated.*
>
> *He is the God of reversals.*
>
> *In chapter 13, verse 5, Beth-Aven was a place of distress and desertion.*
>
> *But not now.*
>
> *Now it is a place of the Lord's rescue and where troop numbers have swelled (14:22-23).*

Suggestions for Preaching

Ways Into the Text

One way to preach on this passage is to have it framed around the hero of the passage, that is, Jonathan. The key thing about Jonathan is that he knows and loves God, wants to depend upon Him and takes risks in doing so. He is, therefore, not unlike some great missionaries or Christian leaders in history. So, you could find one such person and retell their story of costly risk-taking for the sake of the gospel. The telling of such stories can then lead into saying that such stories are of the same shape and order as what is seen in 1 Samuel 13 and 14. Express that your hope is that we might be inspired to line up with such people in our service of God. However, you might like to warn your hearers that you are going to cover a lot of ground.

Moving Through the Text

Concerning the major sections of the sermon, the best way to break it up is into 1 Sam. 13:1-23a and 1 Sam. 13:23b–14:52.

In the first section, it might be wise to tell people that in order to really understand the passage there are three clues to be understood: (a) Remember Hannah! (b) Remember 1 Sam. 10:5 (Samuel's instruction to Saul); and (c) Remember chapter 12 and that kings are subject to prophets and not the reverse. This will set you up for the rest of the story. You may also need to introduce the Philistines if you haven't already done so.

Once you have done all of this, the text can be traversed quickly, perhaps highlighting verses 13-14 and then summarising what the chapter is all about, that is, Saul's disobedience and that he is therefore an ungodly king.

The second section might be broken up into the following sections:

- Jonathan's partnership with the Lord (13:23b–14:15)
- Consequences (14:16-23)
- Saul's oath (14:24-35)
- Aftermath (14:36-46)
- Summarising Saul's reign (14:47-52)

The summary might be that although Saul is a man in decline, he's not a total disaster and God did use him to accomplish something of what they wanted. However, there were costs and key among them were that kings are self-interested humans.

Contemplating Jonathan
This section is used to explain to people the function that Jonathan plays in the narrative, that is, offering a contrast to Saul who has so much but who lacks faith, trust and obedience to God. Jonathan ends up 'saving' Israel.

Biblical Theology and Application

This section should make explicit links through to the New Testament. My personal approach was to see Jonathan as a precursor of David as we see him in 1 Sam. 17 and also a precursor, a type of Christ as indicated above. Concerning application, you might return to the example Christian(s) mentioned earlier and stress that what God wants in His people is the humility and courage demonstrated by Hannah, Jonathan and other godly saints in history. This *may* result in success or even honour. But equally it *may not*. Nevertheless, it is such humility and dependant trust and obedience that God loves and that will be of eternal value.

Leading a Bible Study

1 Samuel 13:1–14:52

Introduction

In the introduction to the study, leaders might note the length of the passage and the exhortation in Scripture to give attention to its public reading. The purpose of this study is therefore to read the passage and to come to some broad conclusions about its meaning and significance.

It would be helpful to remind the group that there are two helpful scriptural perspectives from which we can read 1 Samuel.

The *first perspective* is the story of Hannah and her song. In many ways, Hannah is the hero/heroine of 1 Samuel. Her acts and her prayer give us a picture of what it means to live positively before God (that is, in dependence and trust). The *second perspective* is the passage about kingship in Deuteronomy 17:14-20, which tells us how kings should live (and not live) before God.

However, it will be helpful to give people the one other clue that might help them in reading 1 Samuel 13–14, the reminder of what Saul should have done when he was filled with the Spirit and saw the Philistine outpost back in 1 Samuel 10:5-13. Bible study group participants could be urged to keep an eye open for a Philistine outpost and who does something concerning it.

Observation

The main object in this study is to read the whole story and to work out who is/are the hero/heroes and who are not.

Using the grids below and the clue from 1 Samuel 10:5-13, read through the whole section and for each of the following characters, list the positive and the negative things in favour of their character/godliness.

At the end, list any questions that people have about the whole story and perhaps discuss them at the end of the study (or a leader might go away and do some further work between this session and the next to find answers).

The main sections of the text are: 1 Samuel 13:1-23; 13:23–14:15; 14:16-23; 14:24-35; 14:36-46.

Saul	Positive	Negative
Jonathan	Positive	Negative
Samuel	Positive	Negative

Questions for Group Leader (and responses from the Group Leader)

Praying together

Make sure that you finish reading through the passage leaving a good amount of time to spend gathering prayer points and praying for each other.

14.
The Rejection of Saul as King
(1 Samuel 15:1-35)

If you had to assess the hardest chapter in the books of Samuel to understand and then preach or teach to a Christian congregation, this chapter would be up near the top if not at the top. It is quite complicated, very nuanced in its interactions, and raises theologically significant and complex issues. Nevertheless, it has great pastoral opportunities in teaching God's people central things about themselves and Him.

Listening to the Text

Context and Structure
This chapter must be seen as part of a larger story that began in chapter 8. In 1 Sam. 8, Samuel is old, and Israel's elders make the request for a king to Samuel, who turns to the Lord in prayer. The opening comment by the Lord to Samuel is that he should listen to the people, followed by a note that their rejection is not of him but 'they have rejected me as their king' (lit. 'from being king over them'). In 1 Sam. 16:1 we have a matching statement by the Lord to Samuel concerning Saul, their first

king, where the LORD says, 'I have rejected him as king over Israel' (lit. 'from being king over Israel'). The same Hebrew word for 'reject' occurs in both places. Moreover, the same or similar words are used in the centre of chapter 15 where Samuel tells Saul that the LORD 'has rejected you as king' (v. 23) and again that the LORD 'has rejected you as king over Israel' (v. 26).[1] Samuel listening to God's Word in chapter 8, resulting in Saul's appointment, is mirrored in Saul's failure to listen in this chapter (something which we will see is highlighted throughout the chapter). This is made explicit in our chapter in verses 23 and 26 where the same Hebrew word for God's 'rejection' of Saul is used of Saul's 'rejection' of the Word of the LORD.

The larger context also prepares us for this chapter and the focus on listening. Saul has been notably reticent in listening to God and His prophet. He failed to listen and obey concerning action against the Philistine garrison (1 Sam. 10:7; 13:3) and did not wait for Samuel as he was told to (13:8-10, 13).

The structure of the passage is straightforward:

15:1-9   Saul under command
    15:1-3   Now listen
    15:4-9   God's Word and Saul's actions

15:10-35 Samuel under command
    15:10-12   The Word of the LORD comes to Samuel
    15:13-19   Initial interaction
    15:20-23   Second interaction
    15:24-29   Third interaction

---

1. Fokkelman, *Vow and Desire*, p. 337.

15:30-33   Fourth interaction
15:34-35   Separation of king and prophet

Content

Saul under command

The first verse sets the scene for the whole and it is loaded with words that clearly set up the story, its characters, and their relationships. A more literal translation highlights this: 'Me ... the Lord sent ... to anoint you ... as king ... over his people ... over Israel.'

'Me' emphasises Samuel's importance; 'the Lord sent' indicates that his importance is derived from the Lord; 'to anoint you king' emphasises that it is this same Lord who is responsible for Saul's position as king; and the separation of 'people' and 'Israel' emphasises that Israel is not Saul's people but God's people.

The first command after this introduction is strong and because of the stress on sounds throughout the chapter it is helpful to know that it literally says that Saul is to 'hear the voice/sound of the words of the Lord.' The command is straightforward and invokes the word that was used in the book of Joshua for what Israel was to do to in battle with the inhabitants of the land (e.g. Josh. 2:10). It has the sense of irrevocably giving something or some person over to the Lord, sometimes by totally destroying them, which is explicitly indicated here. In this case, it is commanded because of the way the Amalekites acted toward Israel when they were coming out of Egypt (Exod. 17:8-15), something which resulted in a particular, written down memorial in 'the book' (Exod. 17:14). It is what Moses commanded Israel to do concerning the Amalekites in Deut. 25:17-19 and it was prophesied by Balaam (who also mentions the Kenites) that when a ruler comes out of Jacob 'Amalek ... will come to ruin at last' (Num. 24:15-21). Saul is being called to be an agent of the LORD in engaging in His war against Amalek.

If the key elements explicitly devoted to destruction in verses 2-3 are compared with Saul's actions in verses 4-9, it is clear that he has not done what was commanded. However, his actions toward the Kenites (a Midianite tribe) who had been friendly toward Israel are laudable. Some notable Kenites include the wife of Moses, her father, and Jael (Exod. 2:16, 21-22; Judg. 1:16; 5:24-27). Saul has again failed to listen to or obey the prophetic Word and instead of living under God's Word has stood over it.

Samuel under command
Verses 10-33 turn our focus to how Samuel and the LORD respond to Saul's actions and how Saul responds back. However, before looking at the details, attention needs to be given to a key Hebrew word ($nḥm$) used four times within the remaining verses of the chapter (vv. 11, 35 and twice in v. 29) and is critical for interpreting the chapter. In English Bibles this word is variously translated according to context. Hence, in this chapter it is translated in the NIV84 as 'grieved' (vv. 11 and 35) and 'change his mind' in both occurrences in verse 29. The only other occurrences of the word in the books of Samuel are translated in the NIV84 as 'sympathy' (2 Sam. 10:2, 3), 'comfort' (2 Sam. 12:24), 'consoled' (2 Sam. 13:39) and 'grieved' (2 Sam. 24:16). As a starting point, we will use 'regret' for all occurrences of the word in the chapter.

In verse 10, the Word of the LORD comes to the prophet of the LORD again. It results in Samuel becoming angry (with whom, we are not told). Then it drives him to entreating the Lord all night, clearly without success as he then goes out to meet up with Saul in verse 12, only to find that he had gone to Carmel to erect 'a monument for himself', a clear indicator that he thought the battle was his battle rather than the Lord's.[2]

Initial interaction

In the initial interaction with Samuel, Saul acts like the archetypal sinners, Adam and Eve, and blames others for his actions. Samuel stops the self-justifications (v. 16) and describes where Saul's kingship began and has ended up. It began humbly, resulted in the Lord anointing him as king but ended in his casting aside or disobeying the Lord's Word and doing evil in His eyes (vv. 17-19). The wording of verse 15—'the Lord *your* God' (see also vv. 21 and 30)—is strange but may be indicative of that which has appeared evident from the beginning, that is, that Saul's relationship with the Lord is distant at best. Alternatively, it could be more shifting of blame, with which the verse is replete.

Second interaction

In the second interaction, Saul responds by highlighting the thing that he did do (destroyed the Amalekites) and again blaming the men for taking sheep and cattle (the best of which he says would have been devoted to God and sacrificed at Gilgal). However, Samuel has already been told that Saul did not head off to Gilgal to sacrifice but to Carmel to build himself a monument. His priorities were elsewhere, and Samuel will have nothing of his excuses – kingship is about obedience and the arrogance seen in Saul is like the evil

---

2. Vannoy, *Samuel*, p. 143.

of idolatry (v. 23). Significantly, when Saul does attempt to defend himself, he again uses the language of 'the LORD *your* God (v. 21). Samuel concludes his indictment by announcing punishment. One rejection (Saul's rejection of God's Word) will be met by another (the LORD's rejection of Saul as king).

Third interaction

Until now the major voice of Saul has been one of defence. A confession of sin marks the third interaction. Earlier Saul had claimed that he had obeyed the LORD but here he admits sin and acknowledges its content: violating the LORD's command and His prophet's instructions. Nevertheless, unlike David who readily admits his sin when confronted by God's prophet and independently and directly goes to the LORD (2 Sam. 12:13, 15-17; Ps. 51), Saul is somewhat tentative in taking responsibility and also dependent upon Samuel. Such dependence is demonstrated by his request for forgiveness and for company in worshipping the LORD (vv. 24-25). Samuel refuses and announces sentence. Rejection of God's Word has led to the LORD rejecting him as King.

In verse 27 there is an interruption to the long dialogue: Saul seizes the hem of Samuel's robe and tears it. His robe was a mark of his consecration (1 Sam. 2:19) and elsewhere in Samuel it signifies a person and perhaps their rank or position (1 Sam. 18:4; 28:14; 2 Sam. 13:18) and cutting it merits repentance (1 Sam. 24:5, 11). Perhaps Saul's grasping at what symbolised Samuel's dedication to God is, therefore, a fitting mirror of what the LORD has announced and its permanency.

Fourth interaction

Here, still grasping at any possibilities, Saul confesses again but also begs for some fragment of his kingship and honour before the people, which Samuel grants (vv. 30-31). Finally, he does what Saul had not done with Agag before the LORD (vv. 32-33) and then the final two verses of the chapter announce the end of the relationship between prophet and he who once was the LORD's king. The LORD will now send Samuel to find and anoint another better than Saul (1 Sam. 15:28; 16:1).

Separation of king and prophet
The last two verses are full of grief and pathos. The two human participants of this chapter leave for their relevant places and for a permanent separation. Samuel returns to his family base at Ramah while Saul returns to his at Gibeah. The depth of the separation from Samuel will apparently grieve Saul so much that later he will seek to break God's law again in order to seek Samuel's advice (1 Sam. 28). However, even from beyond the grave Samuel reinforces the resolute decision of the LORD along with Saul's death.

The announcement of the LORD's grief/regret frames the whole of the encounter between His prophet and His nation's king (cf. vv. 11 and 35). It is a dark and tragic moment that captures the seriousness of sin, particularly among those given responsibility by God to lead God's people under His leadership (James 3:1; cf. Matt. 18:6).

Theological Themes

Voices, listening, and kingship
There are many key theological themes in the chapter. A critical one is that which hangs around the 'sounds' or 'voices' that are referred to within the chapter and they need to be heard in a larger context. The Hebrew noun for 'sound' or 'voice' occurs thirty-seven times in 1 Samuel. The greatest number of those references are in chapters 12 (five times), 15 (six times), and 28 (five times). Chapter 12 is where kingship

is included into the covenant and if we follow through a more literal translation of these verses we hear that Samuel is told to 'listen to the *voice* of the people' and give them a king (v. 1 ESV).[3] In verse 14, the LORD indicates that the people must 'fear the LORD, serve him, and obey his *voice*'. The concluding part of the verse speaks of 'both you and the king who rules over you' and that double point of address apparently carries over to verse 15 where the warning is given that 'if you do not listen to the *voice* of the LORD and if you rebel against what the LORD says, the hand of the LORD will be against you…' (ESV) In verse 19 the narrator appears to recall 1 Samuel 8:19 where 'the people refused to listen to the *voice* of Samuel' (ESV) and declared 'No! But there shall be a king over us.' However, in the very last verse of the chapter the LORD says to Samuel, 'Obey their *voice* and make for them a king' (ESV).

There are no more uses of the Hebrew word used in chapter 12 for 'voice' until the first verse of chapter 15 where Samuel reiterates chapter 12 by coming to Saul and telling him to 'Listen to the *voice of the words of* the LORD.' In verse 14, he asks Saul, 'What is this *voice*/sound of sheep in my ears and the *voice/sound* of cattle that I hear?' and then, in verse 19, 'Why have you not listened to the *voice* of the LORD?' to which Saul responds in verse 20, 'But I have listened to the *voice* of the LORD.' Samuel is firm in verse 22 as he poses the question to Saul, 'Does the Lord delight in burnt offerings and sacrifices as much as in obeying the *voice* of the LORD…' Finally, Saul confesses, 'I have sinned. I violated the LORD's command and your *words* because I feared the people and listened to their *voice*' (v. 24).

---

3. In order to demonstrate the connections that the original hearers might have made, I have supplied my own more literal translation in various places or used italics to show the connections.

This summary shows that a key element of this chapter, when combined with chapter 12, is what voices the kings of Israel will listen to. As far as the LORD is concerned, it is His voice as heard in and through His prophet, and as expressed in His covenant, that must be most important, and this first king has not listened rightly. Kingship among God's people is built on obedience to God's Word.

'Regretting'

As indicated earlier, there is a Hebrew word (nhm) that is used four times in this passage and it might be a helpful start to use the word 'regret' in all four occurrences (the RSV version uses 'repent' in all four). Verse 29 uses the word twice, with both indicating that God does not do this activity. However, in verses 11 and 35 we are told by God (v. 35) and then by the narrator (v. 35) that God *does* do it. More exploration is needed.

Although we know that most words can have a broad range of meanings, the original hearers of the passage would have heard the word said three times and heard what has been highlighted above. This alone should warn us to take care how we use verse 29 (e.g. such as using it to make a systematic theology assertion). Some possibilities of resolution might be that it is a word that is particular to Saul at this time (e.g. pastorally necessary for him). For example, it might be that Samuel is saying to Saul, 'God is not going to regret over this in your case. He has found a replacement who is better than you and he's not going to be vacillating like some humans are. He's sticking with this.' In other words, this is about the choice of David.

Alternatively, there is the option that what Samuel says does not have the endorsement of God. This does not really appear likely given the context and tenor of what is being said.

A final possibility is that our author is deliberately wanting us to understand this word in the light of the other two occurrences in verses 11 and 35. Whatever it is, we know that we need to treat it carefully.

Listening to the Whole of Scripture

Looking Back and Looking Forward

Kingship, voices, and listening

In this chapter, we have seen the announcement of the end of Israel's first king and a promise that God will not turn back from this action. The underlying reason is human sinfulness. Saul has been particularly human, listening to other voices as Adam had done (Gen. 3:17), and standing above rather than under God's Word. The voices that he gave attention to have been the wrong voices when only one matters, the very one he had treated with disdain. He exalted himself above God's Word and therefore above God and thereby became a rejecter of the one true God and an idolater (vv. 10 and 22-23). This is also demonstrated in his setting up a monument in his own name and his language of '*your* God' (v. 15).

Of course, he was not alone. The Lord had already observed that Israel's wish for a human king amounted to a rejection of Him as king by His people and that this had been obvious in their idolatry from the day they came up out of Egypt (1 Sam. 8:7-8). But that can be traced back even further in that they were simply being human and following in the steps of Adam and Eve (Gen. 3). In such actions, it is therefore not difficult for us to find ourselves in Saul, even if we have not sinned as blatantly or with as high a hand.

So, while chapter 15 forces us to 'look back' from the passage to see Adam and therefore ourselves mirrored here, so too it also points us forward in hope as it speaks of one coming 'who is better than' Saul (1 Sam. 15:28) and as we will meet that coming one—David—we do indeed find something 'better'. Nevertheless, we will also find him guilty of 'taking' as God indicated kings would do (1 Sam. 8:11-17; 2 Sam. 12:1-10) and 'despising the word of the LORD by doing what was evil in his eyes' (2 Sam. 12:9). His descendants will continue in the same vein with the result that Israel will be expelled from the promised land even as Adam and Eve were expelled from the garden. The final indictment given in 2 Kings 18:1-12 indicates that the exile came 'because they had not *obeyed* (lit. '*listened* to the voice') of the LORD their God, but had violated his covenant – all that Moses the servant of the LORD commanded. They neither *listened* to the commands nor carried them out.'

The great news is that as we take the notes of kingship, voices, and listening and pursue them through Scripture, we eventually arrive at the one truly and comprehensively 'better than' Saul, Jesus the Messiah, the descendant of David. As the psalmist had prophesied, He came into the world to do what others had not done, the will of God (Heb. 10:5-9; citing Ps. 40:6-8) and through that to make believers in Him holy through 'the sacrifice of the body of Jesus Christ once for all' (Heb. 10:10).[4] His

---

4. As we have observed the notes of 'listening', it is intriguing to note that although Hebrews quotes the Septuagint of Psalm 40:6-8, which talks of a 'body', the Hebrew uses the language of 'ears' that have been 'hollowed' out or 'cleared', perhaps therefore meaning 'open' or 'listening'.

human obedience to God's will is picked up throughout the Gospels and epistles as the mark of His human life (e.g. Mark 14:32-39; John 6:38-40; Rom. 15:12-19; Phil. 2:1-11).

'Regretting'

The gloom of the passage that we have looked at here is overwhelming. However, there are some flickers of light related to God's regret. The first such flicker is found in God's treatment of the Amalekites. Many years have passed since the sin was committed and God had held off judgment, although it did indeed come, as this chapter makes clear. Moreover, the punishment promised to Saul here was also a long time in coming. God allowed him to continue as king for quite some time yet and also allowed his dignity to be preserved.

However, the history of Israel holds out even more hope. The word used for 'regret' in verses 11, 29 and 35 has a long history and is also used in the Old Testament to express God's grief and turmoil over sin. For example, as we look back in Scripture it is used in Gen. 6:7 to express God's grief or 'regret' over the creation of humans but then chapters 6–9 tell us how God's mercy triumphs over judgment through Noah whose name is a play on the very same root word used for 'regret' (Gen. 5:29). Moreover, after the sin of the golden calf we are told that the Lord observes His stiff-necked people and asks Moses to 'leave me alone' so that His anger can burn against them (Exod. 32:10). Moses intercedes in verses 11-13 and requests that the Lord 'relent' (v. 12; same word as used in 1 Sam. 15). Then, in verse 14, the narrator tells us that He does indeed 'relent.'

Soon after, Moses asks for a revelation of God's glory and is given it not physically but in words in Exod. 34:6-7. The words of that revelation are thereafter echoed on various occasions but also occasionally cited. When Jonah does this, he combines the *story* of God 'relenting' with the *statements* of grace and mercy in chapter 34 (see the combination in Jonah 4:2) and says that he knows that God's steadfast love will incline Him toward mercy, even toward repentant Ninevites! He may 'relent', as He does in Jonah 3:10.

From Text to Message

The complexity, depth and difficulties of this text make the choices quite broad in terms of preaching. Whichever way we go regarding application, it is critical that the text is explained well and compassionately. The drama, pathos, harshness, and strength must be preserved.

One possibility is to follow the thread that is prevalent in the text, that is, of sounds or voices and the question as to whom people will obey. Saul failed as humans before and after him failed. However, there was a perfect human who gave full attention to listening to the voice of His Father and was obedient to the point of death, even death on a cross (Phil. 2:1-11). The difficulty will be then tying this into the work of Christ and application in a way that reflects the text of 1 Sam. 15.

Another possibility would be to pursue a more Christological approach in which you might highlight Saul's failure but God's continued pursuit of a godly king. This is one option that arises out of one interpretation of verses 27-29. The risk here is making sure that the rest of the text is fully explained in context of this verse. The preacher/Bible study group leader would also need to deal carefully with what the reference to 'one better than you' means, which probably means dealing, at least in part, with the next chapter.

Yet another possibility might be to go ahead in such a way as to demonstrate that even in proceeding with David as the future king, there is still room for His mercy, which is displayed in allowing Saul to survive for some time after this incident. Of course, we see the same tension in the cross of our Lord Jesus Christ. We know that God is inclined toward mercy and, at the same time, we know that He desires to forgive. On the cross, God does not 'relent' from dealing with human sin as it deserves. However, at the same time He does relent and allow mercy to triumph over judgment (Rom. 3:26). It is this option that we will pursue in 'Suggestions for Preaching' below.

Suggestions for Preaching

Ways Into the Text

There are a variety of ways into the text. One could be to talk about the seriousness of sin among the leaders of God's people, perhaps even by giving an example of what it has led to. However, another way is to take on board the tragedy and seriousness of this passage and to let people know its significance and impact. Occasionally, it helps to explain to our people how affected we are by the texts we spend a week working on and why. This sets the background for then explaining the difficulties.

Moving Through the Text

If this approach is taken, then in the next section you might explain what you think the main problems of the text are. This way, you are helping people into the passage and highlighting both its inherent problems and also acknowledging the issues that they raise (e.g. the harshness of God; Samuel's apparent anger or trouble with what God tells him to do as expressed in the ESV and NRSV translations; the comments about God changing His mind; etc.).

Having raised these issues, the preacher or teacher would take his hearers through the major sections of the passage and explain them. My own approach was to do this under the heading of 'What I know about this passage', making sure that I not only interpreted the passage but was honest about the difficulties (e.g. the judgment of the Amalekites, the interaction with Saul which highlights his sinfulness and the universality and seriousness of sin, the 'regret' of God; etc.).

Biblical Theology and Application

Having raised the issues of the text, the preacher/teacher could then reflect more widely from the rest of the Bible about the difficulties raised, perhaps in the light of not only biblical theology but also systematic theology. Here you might address the issue that although the judgment of the Amalekites might seem harsh, God has held off judgment for a long time. Also, although the judgment of Saul seems tough, God allows him to continue as king for quite some time, just as He allows his dignity to remain intact (it's a private encounter between God's king and God's prophet, not a public one). Finally, you might explain that God's regret is often in Scripture linked to His regret over judgment (e.g. Exod. 32–34) and His relenting from judgment (e.g. Jonah 3–4).

The approach just outlined enables the preacher or teacher to talk about how these tensions are met and resolved in the cross of Christ, which then leads into the application. Since my approach to the sermon was quite personal, I said three things concerning application:

(1) That while my sins may not be the same as those of Saul, they are real and I make excuses for them as he does.

(2) That I know my sin and what I deserve.

(3) However, I am also aware that in the cross Jesus takes my sin upon Himself and enables God to be just and the justifier of those who have faith in Jesus (Rom. 3:26).

Finally, this could be pushed home by saying that true repentance should not be shallow or filled with excuses and passing of blame like that of Saul, but instead followed by rigorous dealing with sin and determination to grow in godliness.

Leading a Bible Study

Study 2: 1 Samuel 15

A foretaste of this week

In leading a Bible study, it would be helpful to set the context for this passage, explaining that it centres around three central characters and that a literal translation of the first verse highlights the important people and relationships.

> 'Me ... Yahweh sent ... to anoint you ... king ... over his people ... over Israel.'

The Bible study leader might then give people the following questions to ponder or talk about with each other: What is the order of authority implied by this sentence? Who is first in authority ... second ... third ... etc?

Part Three: The Beginnings and End of Saul's Kingship   251

Some important background information

For this passage to be understood, a second important element is some background about the Amalekites. It would therefore be helpful to read Exodus 17:8-16 and then ask the following questions: What does God tell Moses to write down? What does Moses remind the people of in Deuteronomy 25:17-19? It may also be helpful to explain that the Kenites are non-Israelites, the descendants of Cain. Through Moses, who was married to a Midianite/Kenite, a bond was formed between Israel and the Kenites.

Observation

A big picture

Read the whole of the chapter aloud from beginning to end, without stopping. Now read it again but this time look for all the references to voices, sounds, or similar. What are the various sources of noises/voices/sounds/etc. within the chapter? What do we learn about Saul from the way these occur and are used in the story?

God's Word and Saul's practice (vv. 1-9)

Here are some sentences about what God said. Put the matching words beside them which describe what Saul did.

'Do not spare …' (v. 3)	
'Put to death …' (v. 3)	
'Totally destroy everything …' (v. 3)	

God's Word and Samuel's response (vv. 10-12)
How does Samuel respond to God's Word about Saul? To whom do you think this response is directed? What does he *do* as a result?

Encounters (vv. 13-33)
Give your own summary of each of the encounters between Samuel and Saul. What are the main areas of change between encounters?

    Encounter 1 (vv. 13-19)
    Encounter 2 (vv. 20-23)
    Encounter 3 (vv. 24-29)
    Encounter 4 (vv. 30-33)

Three principal characters (34-35)
We began with three principal characters: God, Samuel, Saul. We finish with three principal characters. Summarise how this chapter finishes for each of the three characters.

Back in the large group
Hear back from groups. Give some input about the topic of 'regretting' and how people should hear it/respond to it.

In smaller groups
Praying together (1) about 'hearing' and 'doing' God's will and (2) for each other.

15.
The Anointing of David
(1 Samuel 16:1-23)

Perhaps you have met that rare breed of person that everyone seems to love. For some unknown reason when they walk into a room, attention focuses on them. People like something about the way that they look and the words that they speak. They follow them, love to be with them and seek to be led by them. This chapter introduces us to such a man for the first time: David. As we see in the chapters that follow, people from all sorts of backgrounds fall at his feet: soldiers, women, enemies. Some open up their houses or townships. Others put up with his supposed madness and give him shelter and a home. Some make covenants with him against the wishes of their loved ones while others are willing to die for him because he expresses a wish that he would like a drink of water from a memorable place for which he has affection. But not only is he lovable. More significantly, he is the ancestor of our Lord and Saviour, Jesus Christ.

The story of David is entrancing, and its beginning in this chapter is fundamentally important for the books of 1 and 2 Samuel and the history of God's plans for His people and the salvation of His world. It is a story that is straightforward and well known but not always understood. Moreover, it is one that cannot be divorced from the demise of Saul, whose kingship will overlap with David's story for 16 chapters.

Listening to the Text

Context and Structure

Chapter 16 of 1 Samuel is divided into two major sections: 16:1-13 and 16:14-23. The first section links backwards, tying David into the anticipations expressed in chapter 15. The second section looks forward as it ties David into the court of Saul and the inevitable comparison that such proximity and intersection will invite. We have already seen how Saul had failed virtually from the first day, and so the question in the minds of readers is whether David is indeed 'better' and if so, in what way?

The context is further set by the opening verse which lets us into the mind of God and the feelings of Samuel that we had already glimpsed in the previous chapter (1 Sam. 15:11b, 35); Samuel is mourning for Saul. However, the LORD tells Samuel to stop looking back and that He has 'rejected him [Saul] as king over Israel' and chosen one of the sons of Jesse of Bethlehem 'to be king.' Samuel is, therefore, to take up his horn with oil and be on his way. In the first half (vv. 1-13) of the chapter, David is chosen by God. In the second half (vv. 14-24), David is chosen by Saul. For the rest of 1 Samuel, the conflict between David and Saul will dominate, and the readers will wait to see how the will of God voiced here in His choice finally bears fruit. Having accomplished his task, Samuel will now drift into the background (except for a brief appearance posthumously to rebuke his first appointee).

Part Three: The Beginnings and End of Saul's Kingship   255

Content

Verses 1-13 David is chosen by God

The content of verse 1 holds something that most English translations do not make clear. When Israel first asked for a king, the Lord had, more literally, told Samuel to 'appoint/install *for them* a king' (8:22). The Hebrew more literally says, 'for I have *seen* among his sons *for me* a king.' However, even if we could not pick that up, the source of the new appointee looks promising given that it does not seem to be Benjamin but Judah, from which we know rulers will come (Gen. 49:10; also note the explicit links with Bethlehem and Jesse in Ruth 4:11-22).

To assuage the fear felt about wandering around presumably with his anointing horn looking for a replacement for Saul (v. 2), the Lord suggests the camouflage of offering a sacrifice (i.e. coming as priest rather than a prophet). Verse 3 again reminds us of the contrast with Saul as the Lord speaks of an anointing 'for me.' Samuel then arrives in Bethlehem, assuring them of his coming in peace for the sake of sacrifice, an ironic but beautiful preface to what will come much later through David's descendant, the Prince of Peace.[1]

Samuel has his horn of oil and is in Bethlehem with the family of Jesse and his sons. All that remains of the task outlined in verse 1 is finding the appointee. Samuel does not even wait when confronted by the sons. In the last chapter, we had a play on voices/sounds and hearing. In this chapter, we have a play on the Hebrew root word for

---

1. M. R. van den Berg, *Het eerste boek Samuël. Van koeienjongen tot voortvluchtige messias. Deel 2: hoofdstuk 16–31* (Amsterdam: Buijten & Schipperheijn, 1996b), pp. 18-19, in Vannoy, *Samuel*, p. 156.

'seeing', something particularly apt since the leading figure is Samuel, the 'seer' (1 Sam. 9:9). This began in verse 1, as we noted earlier. It continues in verse 6 when 'Samuel *saw* Eliab', followed by three references in verse 7 and then two more (vv. 17 and 18).

As we look at verse 6, it is not clear from the verse itself what it was that Samuel saw and was impressed with. However, verse 7 seems to indicate that it is height and/or appearance related things. With this in mind, it is helpful to look at a more literal translation of the extant text of verse 7.

> But the Lord said to Samuel, 'Do not consider his appearance or the height of his stature, for I have rejected him. For it is not what man *sees*. Man *sees* [what is before] the eyes but the Lord *sees* [what is in] the heart.'[2]

The default reading of the text is that what the Lord sees is not a person's outwardly impressive features (e.g. Saul) but something else related to their heart. Another possibility is that the heart is referred to at the end of the verse is the Lord's heart.[3] Our view here is that within the larger narrative both perspectives need to be held together. So, while the reference to 'a man after his own heart' (1 Sam. 13:14) *is* the language of choice and election, there is something 'better' in David (1 Sam. 15:28) as well and this is what is being referred to in verse 7. God is flagging here what the narrative that follows will make clear.

---

2. The sentence is further loaded with words related to visual perceptions. The word translated 'consider' is more literally 'look' and the word translated here as 'appearance' is related to the word translated as 'see' in the verse.

3. Woodhouse, *1 Samuel*, pp. 286-87.

The broader context of Samuel may supply us with other hints as to what it is that God might have seen. For example, the prayer of Hannah specifically praises humility and dependence and decries arrogance and wickedness and applies this to kingship. The impression is that this is what will result in a king being strengthened and his horn being exalted (1 Sam. 2:10). We know that Saul has not looked like this and perhaps the LORD knows David to be like this. David certainly appears to be like this in the psalms to which his name is attached. Moreover, as we shall see, when confronted with the prophet of God speaking the Word of God, his attitude and response are worlds away from what we saw with Saul in the previous chapter. Finally, even physically he is different, and this is captured by the contrast between him, his brothers and Saul. Saul is described with superlatives in the Hebrew and English of 1 Sam. 9:2 and his height is stressed. The word used there for height only appears in two other places in the books of Samuel. The first is in Hannah's prayer where its repetition is used to form a superlative, urging people not to speak 'very highly' (i.e. haughtily) and the second is in verse 7 of this chapter where Samuel is urged not to look at 'the height of his stature' (ESV), or 'his tall stature'. The associations are, therefore, profound and are emphasised when David is described, using another superlative that is the opposite of this one. He is the 'littlest', which may do double duty for him being the 'youngest' of the sons but possibly even a contrast with his oldest brother physically, that is, in height. He is not a prime candidate as far as human choice would be oriented. He is the 'littlest' who has the lowlier task of shepherding.

In any case, when David finally arrives, it is not that his looks are not fine. He is said to be 'ruddy' or 'reddish' (which could refer to a number of things such as skin tone [e.g. red-cheeked] or hair colour, such as is used of Esau in Gen. 25:30-34). He is also said to have 'a fine appearance and handsome features' (lit. 'beautiful [of] eyes' and 'good of appearance'). However, what matters is not what appears to humans but what is known to the Lord and it is He who tells Samuel to, 'Rise and anoint him; he is the one' (v. 12b). Samuel does so in the presence of David's brothers and the Lord then gives him the sign of kingship, His Spirit who comes in power upon David (v. 13; cf. 18:12, 14, 28).

Verses 14-23 David is chosen by Saul

A note on a troublesome theme

The corollary of the Spirit coming in power on David is the departure of the Spirit from Saul noted in verse 14. Linked with that is the matching statement in the same verse that the Spirit was replaced by 'an evil spirit from the Lord' that 'tormented him.' This is an unusual statement and will probably need explanation to contemporary hearers and a warning about being hasty about reading New Testament language into the term 'evil spirit.' Rather, the way ahead is to try and understand it in its immediate context first, then within the Old Testament as a whole, and then the New Testament if it has something to add.

Instruction here might proceed in the following manner. First, the 'Spirit of the Lord' is simply said to have 'departed from Saul' (v. 15), presumably because 'the Spirit of the Lord came upon David in power' (v. 14). Second the text makes clear that the 'evil spirit' has its source in the same Lord who caused the Spirit's departure from Saul. Third, the Hebrew word translated here as 'evil' can have a broad range of meaning such as ethical or moral evil (e.g. 2 Sam. 12:9) but also circumstantial or uncomfortable badness, misfortune or trouble, such as can be found even in the use of the same Hebrew word in the rest of Samuel. For example, the same word used of the spirit here and in succeeding chapters is also used of the 'meanness' of Nabal (1 Sam. 25:3), the deeds David might do that would 'displease' the Philistines (1 Sam. 29:7), the good or 'bad' words that Absalom never said to Amnon (2 Sam. 13:22), and the inability of a person in old age to be able to tell 'good or bad' in taste and hearing (2 Sam. 19:35).

The preacher or teacher might then make the point that the term 'evil' here does not necessarily mean what we might read it to mean, which raises the question: Is this spirit inherently 'evil' or simply disturbing, hurtful or 'bad' in some way? Certainly, it is overwhelming and at least internally injurious as is indicated by the word 'tormented' in verses 14-15 (perhaps better translated as 'terrorised/ terrorising' or 'overwhelmed/overwhelming'). However, it may be too much to say that it is an 'evil spirit' in the sense used in the New Testament where the source is not God but the devil or his demons (e.g. Mark 1:23, 26-27; 5:1-13; Acts 5:16). It might then be observed that this understanding appears to be supported by the fact that it is dealt with and alleviated through music (vv. 17-23).

Interpreting the rest of verses 14-23
The next verses need to be read from the perspective of verses 1-13 which were a private affair in the household of his father, Jesse. However, while we the readers know of the private affair, Saul does not. We, therefore, note the irony (and the difficulty created) as God's chosen king is introduced without knowledge into the court of

the one whom he will replace in order to give him relief from another action from the Lord. Ironically, he will also introduce pain and grief that will spread throughout the court of that same king.

We began exploring this chapter by noting David's winsomeness and how people loved him. Now, we find the first one of whom this is said: Saul (v. 21). Later, it will be used of his children, Jonathan (1 Sam. 18:1) and Michal (1 Sam. 18:20, 28) and of all Israel and Judah (1 Sam. 18:16). Such love will give rise to fear and result in David becoming an enemy (1 Sam. 18:29). In other words, David's winsomeness and giftedness which gave relief will eventually cause Saul grief, such that David becomes an enemy. In this way, the two halves of this chapter prepare the reader for the chapters that will follow.

Theological Themes

When we put the dominant threads in the text together, the central point or big theological idea is clear: God sees things as humans do not. Humans invariably look for 'bigness' or impressiveness but He looks for other, better things. We have seen this throughout the chapter as we noted the words for seeing, the words that contrasted big with little, external with internal, appearance with being.

Having said that, as we worked through the text above, we saw that although there was no certainty about what the 'better' thing was about David, we *do* know from the narrative and the poetry of the book of Samuel that kings pleasing to God would be humble and dependent (perhaps we could say they would be 'little in their own eyes'). We could add to this the outline of the law on kingship in Deuteronomy 17 and the information given in 1 Samuel 12 when kingship became incorporated into Israel. Israelite kings would also be those who heard God's Word and expressed their dependence upon Him by being dependent on His Word. Not listening to the right sounds was where Saul failed. Not looking for the right things in humans is where Samuel stumbles here.

Listening to the Whole of Scripture

Looking Back

One way ahead as we think of this passage and the rest of Scripture is to notice that chapter 16 is a pair with chapter 15. Both have to do with human senses. Chapter 15 is all about sounds and right listening. Saul listened wrongly and did not obey what came from God. He, therefore, could not be king over God's people.

Chapter 16 is all about sight and right seeing. Samuel is infected with the spirit of every age in the sense that he is impressed by size and stature, things that are external. However, God is not interested in those things. Instead, He is interested in things internal.

When we look at the whole of Scripture we see humans getting sight and sound-related things wrong all the time. They wrongly listen and wrongly see and God constantly urges them to get this right. If we think of Genesis 1–3, we can understand this. Chapter 1 paints a beautiful picture of God creating a good world with everything in right order. He puts humans in this world and allows them to rule that world under His rule.

In chapter 2, humans fail to hear and see rightly and this is the essence of their sin. Their failure to see and hear rightly leads them to sin. In verse 16 God gives them freedom to eat of all except the tree of the knowledge of good and evil and a warning as to what will happen should they do so. In chapter 3, the woman *hears* a voice other than that of the LORD God. She *hears* a disputing word and *sees* that the fruit on offer was 'good for food and pleasing to the eye and also desirable for gaining wisdom' and takes and eats (Gen. 3:1-6). Her husband willingly joins her in her sin.

The failure of Israel throughout the Old Testament is not properly listening to God's Word and obeying it, not seeing things as He sees them and acting accordingly. Hannah's brilliance in Samuel was that in her desperation she saw that dependence upon God was the right way to go rather than defiance or doubt. Saul's big problem was that he failed in seeing things as God saw them (emphasised through the contrast with Jonathan, who saw things as God saw them) and in hearing God's Word through God's prophet.

Looking Forward

As we look forward from here into the coming chapters in Samuel, we will see the contrast between David and Saul. It will be particularly obvious in chapter 17 where David *sees* things rightly where Saul does not. Subsequently, he will refuse to take the kingship off Saul by force even though he has the opportunity to. Later, when God's prophet rebukes him for his sin, he will *hear* God's Word and rightly respond to it. However, he will not do so perfectly and nor will those who follow him. The Old Testament will, therefore, end with the sorrowful tale of Israel's failure to see and hear properly.

As you can see, hearing and seeing rightly or wrongly is a fundamental way of thinking about what God desires of those He has created. To see yourself rightly is to see yourself in relation to God and not so much in relation to humans. To hear rightly is to be guided and governed by God through His Word. Underneath both of those things is an attitude of humility. Moreover, underneath human failure in both areas of sight and sound is our infatuation with ourselves. Again, the only antidote for this is humility. Humility willingly sees things as God sees them and delights in it. Humility knows God's Word is from God. It hears it willingly and obeys it. Humility sees things from His perspective.

When we get to the New Testament, we see Jesus as the perfect example of what it means to be human. The Gospels portray Him as living under God's Word Himself, hearing God and obeying God, seeing things as God sees things and obeying God to the point of death, even death on a cross. Philippians 2:5-11 explores Jesus being human and talks about it in terms of humility, obedience, and suffering. We are told that although He was in the form of God, He did not regard equality with God as something to be grasped. Rather, He emptied Himself and became obedient to death, even death on a cross. Here is a human king whose interests are God's interests, one like the king prophesied of by Hannah.

From Text to Message

In the scenario above, I have given one possible approach for appropriating this passage as Christians. The flow-through is to combine the two threads from chapters 15 and 16. One arises from the 'voices' of chapter 15, to which Saul fails to listen. In other words, he is a false king. The other comes from the 'seeing' of chapter 16, which Samuel gets wrong. He is overly impressed by stature and status and does not see things as God sees things. He needs reorientation.

How does Jesus fit into this? Well, on the surface that is easy. He is the descendant of the David we meet in chapter 16. However, that may be where Jesus fits in the *storyline* or *plotline* of the Bible as a whole, but it is not where the passage has been heading. It *does* want us to identify David as the coming king and as the ancestor of our Lord and Saviour. However, it is doing much more. It is engaging us in the story of two individuals who get things wrong and calling us to interact with them as well. On the one hand, there is Saul who hears wrongly. On the other, there is Samuel who sees things wrongly. These two failures betray all too common human traits that are not found in our Lord, Jesus Christ.

For example, consider Samuel's failure as a prophet. Prophets were meant to be 'seers', that is to see as God sees and proclaim it. Samuel saw wrongly and needed correction. Jesus, on the other hand, sees humans with God's eyes. He sees them rightly.

Jesus as the true human sees the human condition well. Jesus, as true human and true king, hears the Word of God, obeys to the point of death, even death on a cross. However, as true God He knows the human heart. As true human, God will finally exalt Him as true King and bestow on Him the name above every other name.

However, following through to Jesus as true, exalted King is not the end of this exercise in biblical theology. After all, the apostle Paul used an ancient hymn for a purpose and that was to illustrate true humility and to urge the Philippians to have the same attitude of humility themselves and to let it flow through to having the interests of others in mind as Jesus did (Phil. 2:1-5).

Part Three: The Beginnings and End of Saul's Kingship 265

Suggestions for Preaching

Ways Into the Text

There are many and varied ways into this text and sermon or Bible study. At the most basic level, if you are a good storyteller, you could simply imagine Samuel approaching the household of Jesse with all the personal grief of 1 Sam. 15:34-35, the fear of 1 Sam. 16:1-2a, the resolution of verses 2b-3 and the cautious or hesitant greeting of verse 4.

Once, when preaching this passage to ministry workers in training, I began with a story of the leadership advocated by Adolf Hitler and Benito Mussolini. I gave an outline of their program to produce the 'new man' and ended with a quotation as to what such men would look like. It was a picture of hard, tough, resilient men. I then asked them to think about what a true leader looks like in any form of rule, including church leadership. This led into saying that Samuel is all about leadership and that the passage being studied would give a glimpse into God's mind about good leaders.

Moving Through the Text

As we move through the text, the things to emphasise are clear. First, God has a clear idea of what He is about; anointing a king *for myself* (v. 1). Second, Samuel is fearful. The anointing of David is a critical task carried out by a somewhat reluctant but obedient prophet.

The important things moving through the passage are those already pointed out, including particularly verses 6-7 and the notes throughout the chapter about 'seeing'. You will need to slow down here and explain some of the difficulties and intricacies and perhaps even bring in some other passages in Scripture to support the position you take as to the meaning and significance of these verses. You may even need to make sure that your people understand the big picture of the previous chapters in Samuel, explaining that Saul had been a failure in the sense that he had not lived under God's Word and not listened to God's Word. It may be necessary to explain that God is searching for someone 'better'.

Having done this, you will need to move through the rest of the chapter and explain how the first half fits with the second half.

Biblical Theology and Application

As indicated above, if you consider that David is indeed 'better than' Saul, you need to explain what that means and the consequent ironies inherent in the passage. You may even need to give a quick overview of David as king throughout the books of Samuel, explaining that he is not perfect but that at his best he is like the vision painted by Hannah. You may particularly note the difference between Saul and David when confronted with their sin. Saul is remote from God and asks the prophet to intervene where David goes running to God in repentance and prayer. He also submits to His will. Although not perfect, at his best, David is humble and dependent.

The preacher or teacher here may then choose to look at the wider context as we have above and notice that chapters 15 and 16 give us insights into how to listen and see rightly. Right seeing and listening is a critical attitude for God's people throughout Scripture and is exemplified by the submission of Jesus to His Father and His Father's will. This could then lead to Philippians 2.

The application when speaking to a group of people preparing for the ministry of the Word among the people of God was that they should cultivate their character and that their chief focus should be Christlikeness, particularly in relation to humility and dependence. I noted that such were often not the things denominations and churches were looking for, but it is what God thinks they need. To push it home to people, I observed the adjectives that were appended to the names of people speaking at Christian conferences (e.g. 'gifted', 'experienced', 'influential', etc.) and urged them rather to develop humility. I suggested that Christian leaders should prize and cultivate humble dependence upon God, that is what will most benefit God's purposes and people.

Leading a Bible Study

Introduction
In the group, name two people who are heroes to you in public life and even in Christian circles. What is it about them that makes them so outstanding? What do you admire? How would you be like them?

Pray
Have one or two people pray about this Bible study, that God would use it to form you more into the likeness of Jesus.

Read 1 Samuel 1-13 aloud in the group
- Without looking back, see if you can corporately remember what happened in (1) the immediately preceding chapter; (2) the last three or four chapters. Once you have exhausted your memory, look back at the chapters and refresh yourselves.

- What three things is Samuel told by God to do in chapter 16? What is his response? Why?
- How does God help Samuel in his fears?

A note for leaders

It may be helpful for you to note with your group that a more literal translation of verse 1 reads … 'I have seen (i.e. 'provided') *for myself* a king.'

Get people to look back at when Israel first asked God for a king. There God said to Samuel, 'Appoint *for them* a king' (1 Sam. 8:22). Make the point that something very special is going on here and talk about whether your group can see a similar sentiment in verse 3.

Questions for the groups

- Why do you think the elders ask Samuel if he comes in peace?
- What sorts of things does Samuel appear to be looking for in an able leader of God's people? What sorts of things does God appear to be looking for?
- Write down the characteristics of David that are highlighted in the verses 11-12.
- How does God endorse the anointing of David?

A note for leaders

Again, it would be worth helping your people understand how our writer is playing with us a bit. We and the original readers know that 'the youngest' is David. However, he is not named until his name can be tied up with God and His Spirit.

Interpretation questions

- Do we yet have any indication as to what is 'better' (1 Sam. 15:28) about David compared to Saul? Perhaps we

might find some help in thinking what was unsatisfactory about Saul? What can you remember about Saul that seemed unsatisfactory? List things. Only when you've done this, check out the summary of Saul in 1 Chronicles 10:13-14.
- Now think back through Samuel. Who have the heroes been? List their characteristics.
- Read Jeremiah 17:10. How does it support the general principle that appears within this passage?

A note for leaders

It is important not to read too much into this passage. It is not talking about salvation or the like, but a choice of a king over God's people. In such matters, God looks at the heart.

Back in the large group

Thinking biblically

Read Philippians 2:5-11. List the characteristics of Jesus, our Lord and King. How does He rule over His people? In what key characteristic are we to be like Jesus (**hint:** check out the immediately preceding verses in Philippians 2).

How do your heroes from the beginning of this study measure up? How does the world's concept of heroes measure up?

Praying together

Pray for two things: (1) that as individuals and a church, we might be characterised by growth in the characteristics God is looking for; (2) pray for our leaders, that they might be marked by likeness to Jesus in these areas.

Gather prayer points and pray for each other.

16.
Seeing as God Sees
(1 Samuel 17:1–18:5)

The passage that we look at in this chapter has a story that is still one of the great short stories of world literature. Its characters can still be used in book titles in order to draw people in and to comment on such things as fighting against obstacles and disadvantages, discrimination, disabilities and assorted other battles that beset us as humans. Paired together 'David and Goliath' are still recognisable and their story vaguely known. More than that, the narrative is still used to teach ethics and attitudes to children, to illustrate significant points in sermons or even to critique methods of interpreting Scripture.

For this reason, preaching on it is both immensely enjoyable and also fraught with danger. More importantly, it is full of profound theology reflecting timeless theological insights and highlighting how the lad of chapter 16 was a wonderful choice of God, despite Samuel's lack of sound 'seeing'.

Listening to the Text

A Preliminary Note
Although it is not necessary in teaching, the preacher or teacher approaching this passage should be aware of some

matters of significance that may be raised about this text and the possible need to consult commentaries on their resolution. The most significant of these are as follows.

There is a significant difference in length (and some details) between the Masoretic Hebrew text and the Greek text of the Septuagint. The view taken here is that the Hebrew text is more likely to be the original.

There are some apparent differences between texts in Scripture as to who killed Goliath. For example, in 2 Sam. 21:19 and its parallel in 1 Chron. 20:5, we are told of a certain 'Elhanan son of Jair-Oregim the Bethlehemite killed Goliath the Gittite, who had a spear with a shaft like a weaver's rod'. The difficulties can be resolved, but it may be helpful to be forearmed and to read through commentaries on this if you think that it might be a matter for discussion or questioning from those who read their Bibles carefully and well.

There is one place where the difference between the Hebrew Masoretic text (MT) and the Greek translation, the Septuagint (LXX), is of intriguing interest and may be of interest in the context of a Bible study – the height of Goliath. The calculations below are based on the following considerations:

- The cubit varied in length according to different times and places and was more a matter of order of magnitude than precision.
- The distance between the extended tip of the little finger to the tip of a thumb is a span, which is half a cubit, also considered to be the length from the tip of middle finger to the elbow.
- Cubits can range from 16 inches (40.6 cm) to 20 inches (50.8 cm) with the standard generally being 18 inches (45.7 cm).

Part Three: The Beginnings and End of Saul's Kingship   273

Text	Cubits	Spans	Imperial Height			Metric Height		
Where a cubit =			16 in	**18in**	20in	40.6cm	**45.7cm**	50.8cm
MT	6	1	8ft 8in	**9ft 9in**	10ft 10in	2.64m	**2.97m**	3.3m
LXX	4	1	6ft	**6ft 9in**	7ft 6in	1.83m	**2.06m**	2.29m

By way of comparison, at the time of writing the tallest living man in the Guinness Book of Records was 8ft 2.8in (2.51m) and the tallest ever recorded and chronicled by the same book was 2.72m.

Context and Structure

In the previous two chapters, we have witnessed some critical events. The first was the rejection of Saul as king in chapter 15. The second was the choice of David by God, his anointing, the coming in power of the Spirit upon him and the departure of the Spirit from Saul (1 Sam. 16:12-14). In the second half of chapter 16 we are told that David's gift of music will bring relief to Saul. However, the subsequent narrative will tell us that this same gift will mean that David's presence in Saul's court will also be a constant source of grief for Saul until his death in chapter 31.

The passage we now examine will add two more elements. We have previously noted that God chose Saul (1 Sam. 9:16; 10:24). He was anointed by God's prophet under God's instruction (1 Sam. 9:15-16; 10:1), endowed with His Spirit (1 Sam. 11:6) and publicly affirmed by victory in battle against Israel's enemies (1 Sam. 11). Three of these signs were repeated with David in chapter 16: chosen by God (v. 12), anointed and endowed with the Spirit (v. 13; accompanied by the departure of the Spirit from Saul in v. 14). However, there has as yet not been any sort of public affirmation in victory over

Israel's enemies. This missing element will be the focus of chapter 17.

One further and unforeseen element will be added in the first five verses of chapter 18 where we observe that the physical heir to the Sauline kingship will effectively abdicate his right to inherit the throne. In other words, by the end of the passage under focus here we will have everything in place for David to assume kingship, and yet the story will continue until Saul and Jonathan's death in chapter 31. We therefore know (as Saul will admit before too long) that David will eventually inherit the throne over all Israel at the Lord's hand. Nevertheless, David will not be king over Judah for fourteen tension-filled chapters and over all Israel for 3 chapters more.

In the light of these observations, we can again outline our developing structure of the book. Chapter 15 is, therefore, another transitional chapter and will introduce us to David's time in Saul's presence before David retreats to the wilderness until the death of Saul at the end of the book.

```
    1 Samuel 9–15              1 Samuel 16–31
···─────────────────┬─────────────╔═╗────────────────────────···─┤
      1 Samuel 11:14-15          1 Sam. 15

···──── The Story ─────────────┤├────────── The Struggle to Come ────┤
         of Saul                                to the Throne
```

Content

Given the familiarity that we might have with this chapter and its interpretation, it is incumbent upon the reader and preacher/teacher to take particular care with our observations of the text, making sure that we do not impose pre-existing conclusions upon the text. As always, we should observe the text well, fire questions at it, and ponder why the author might have included or excluded certain elements. How do such choices indicate how he wants us to understand the passage?

Context: Gathering for war (17:1-3)

Earlier we noted the words of the divine messenger to Samson's mother in Judges 13:5. He would be the one who would 'begin' to save Israel from the hand of the Philistines. In 1 Samuel 9:15 the Lord indicated that Saul would save his people from the hand of the Philistines, and while he and Jonathan have had some success (1 Sam. 14:1-23, 47) the task is still to be completed and will not be completed in the days of Saul (1 Sam 14:52). Since then we have heard that the Lord has rejected Saul and replaced him with a keeper of sheep (1 Sam. 16:11).

With this as background, the opening verses set the scene. The battle against the Philistines has turned to full and open confrontation. Apparently being threatened in the south of his domain, perhaps with the Philistines pursuing a strategic goal of separating the tribes of Judah, Benjamin, Ephraim and others from those further north, Saul mustered a significant force for a critical battle. The last time the two nations had drawn up in battle lines like this Israel was severely defeated (1 Sam. 4), and the ark of the covenant captured. We, therefore, wonder what will happen now that kings have arrived.

A Philistine champion (17:4-11)

Having set the scene for the conflict, there is a slowing down in the narrative as we are introduced to a lone figure, a single-fighter or champion. Goliath is impressive in every way. Like the leader of Israel—Saul—he is tall, although most probably at least another 'from his shoulders upward' taller than Saul (1 Sam. 9:2 ESV). Then there is his heavy armour, javelin, spear shaft like a weaver's rod, tipped with an iron tip weighing about seven kilograms. Moreover, his mouth spews heavy and threatening words which challenge Israel to a preliminary skirmish such as that which happened back in chapter 4. Victory or defeat at such an encounter may have been read as a forerunner or omen of the final result (cf. 1 Sam. 4:1-22; 8:10-11; cf. Josh. 7:7-9).[1] The result of his presentation is conclusive: dismay and terror (v. 11). However, these verses also introduce a word that will be used throughout the chapter to describe his fundamental attitude: defiance (vv. 10, 25-26, 36, 45).

The lad from Bethlehem (17:12-24)

In verse 12 we flip back to Israel's forces, and the contrast is marked. In the previous chapter, we were presented with David as the 'youngest/littlest', and that note of diminution and contrast is preserved with the same possible double-entendre used in the previous chapter (oldest brother versus youngest in verses 12; height of Goliath versus lack of height). Such contrasts are further picked up between the oldest brothers following Saul while David goes back and forth to tend sheep (vv. 14-15) and the references to Goliath as 'champion' and 'fighting man' (vv. 4, 23, 33) while David is but a 'boy' or 'lad' (33, 42, 55, 58).

Such contrasts between bigness, arrogance and bluster versus smallness, humility and dependence continue throughout the chapter. David is marked by dependence, personal humility but confidence in a great God who

---

[1] Suggested by Moshe Garsiel, *The Book of Samuel: Studies in History, Historiography, Theology and Poetics Combined*, Part 1: The Story and History of David and His Kingdom (Jerusalem: Rubin Mass, 2018), pp. 71-72.

should be known in all the world (17:46-47). He is in marked contrast to the Israelites who, when they see Goliath, 'all ran from him in great fear' (v. 24).

'Who is this uncircumcised Philistine?' (17:25-31)

Verses 25 to 31 pick up a new theme and emphasis. While the first 24 verses have been dominated by narrative, verses 25-57 are dominated by dialogue and centre around the speech of David rather than the bluster of Goliath. Where Goliath's speech is bold and defiant, David's is inquiring and curious as well as affronted with the impact of Goliath's words. His questioning about rewards and the removal of disgrace from Israel as well as his questioning of the defiance of the armies of the living God bring about a rebuke from his older brother but also arouse the attention of Saul who sends for him (v. 31).

David in Saul's presence (17:32-40)

The contrasts between David and Israel's leadership and people, remains stark. They are fearful (vv. 11 and 24) while he urges them to be like him and not lose heart; he 'will go and fight him' (v. 32). It is hard not to see the same contrast that we observed earlier when Saul does not engage the Philistines when the Spirit comes upon him, but Jonathan does so with boldness and the same confidence that David expresses here (1 Sam. 13:23–14:23). Fear is replaced by this confidence, and something of a climax is reached when, for the first time in the chapter, the Lord is mentioned (v. 37). Significantly, it is only after this that Saul himself invokes His name (v. 37).

Of particular importance in this section but often missed is the mention of sheep and shepherding in verses 34-40 ('keeping ... sheep', going after enemies of sheep and killing them, delivering sheep, taking up the staff, 'the pouch of his shepherd bag' and his sling). The presentation of his actions is that of a shepherd protecting sheep. It is as though David is acting as a shepherd to his people just as God is his Good Shepherd (Psalm 23).

The fall of the Philistine champion (17:41-53)
The language of animals (but not of shepherding) continues in the mouth of Goliath. He speaks of beasts of the field, birds of the air and dogs. Goliath mocks David's armour and curses David by his gods (vv. 41-44). As readers of Samuel we have already seen a type of this before and so we might anticipate what might happen. In chapter 5 the Philistines bring the representation of God's presence and power into the temple of their god (i.e. the ark). The image of Dagon, that is, his representation, ends up headless and handless before the representation of the real God. Similarly, here David comes without sword, spear or javelin before Goliath, bearing only the LORD's name. He stones the one who has blasphemed, as the law required (Lev. 24:15-16).

The other link between chapter 5 and this one is that both allude to the exodus. In 1 Sam. 4:7-8, the Philistines allude to the exodus. In the plague narratives, we are told that the LORD's actions in raising up Pharaoh and striking him and his people were that Pharaoh might 'know that there is no one like the LORD our God' (Exod. 9:14) and that his 'name might be proclaimed in all the earth' (Exod. 9:16). Similarly, David here declares that God's actions against Goliath and the Philistines might be so that 'the whole world will know that there is a God in Israel' (v. 46). As often in Scripture, God's working salvation for

His people has a focus on both Israel and others knowing Him.

With their hero and representative slain, the Philistines flee with the men of Israel and Judah pursuing them and then plundering their camp.

Identity and relationship (17:55–18:5)

In this final section of the story, a few key things occur. There is an enquiry by Saul as to the identity of David, the revelation by the commander of the army that he has no idea, and the search to find out. Finally, he is brought to Saul and announced as 'the son of your servant Jesse of Bethlehem' (v. 58). We are not told how it was that Saul who was placated by David's music (1 Sam. 16:21-23) did not know who his father was. However, it is important to note that the question is not David's identity but the identity of his father that is requested. Perhaps now that he has a promise to fulfil that might involve a marriage (1 Sam. 17:25), it may be entirely appropriate to find out some more![2]

In the first five verses of chapter 18, we meet Jonathan again. We know that if kingship is to be dynastic, then he would have been a good candidate for the throne. He is a good and godly man who thinks as God thinks and has God's glory in mind. However, we as readers know that the throne will be taken away from Saul and as a result Jonathan will not inherit it. We also know that Jonathan

---

2. David W. Gooding, in *The Story of David and Goliath: Textual and Literary Criticism: Papers of a Joint Research Venture*, ed. Dominique Barthélemy, Orbis biblicus et orientalis, p. 73 (Fribourg, Suisse, Göttingen: Éditions Universitaires; Vandenhoeck & Ruprecht, 1986), pp. 19-20.

does not like some things he sees in his father. However, we have no hint that Jonathan knows that the LORD has chosen David.

Perhaps it is that Jonathan looks at the heart as God does and that he loves what he sees in David. In any case, Jonathan enters covenant with David here. Moreover, he takes his robe, which is probably a symbol of his future rule and gives it to David, along with other parts of his kingly dress (18:4), possibly thereby formally giving to David his rights as crown prince. For his part, David, who has refused the armour of Saul, apparently accepts the armour of Jonathan. Saul, for his part, gives David authority over the army.

Theological Themes

As we have emphasised, one of the great risks in pursuing biblical theology in Scripture is that we impose an outside framework upon the text rather than considering how the theology of this particular passage fits into the larger theology of the Bible as it is revealed in the emerging plotline of Scripture. In passages like this one, the result is that biblical theology can look imposed upon the text rather than arising from the text. Our approach has been to exegete the text, try and work out what is happening theologically within this passage, and then to see how it fits into the larger theology of the Bible. We have then sought to see how this relates to what has preceded this passage and then how it goes on to find its centre, focus and end in Jesus Christ.

With this in mind, let's consider what is happening theologically within the passage. Our quick survey has highlighted a number of things.

First, there is a constant play on big and small. Even before we came to this chapter, our author had clearly wanted us to have David's small position and perhaps even small stature on our minds. This finds a strong contrast in chapter 17 where big is what matters. However, what matters to David is not 'bigness' but faith and confidence in a capable God who can overturn things. In other words, David thinks theologically as Hannah has thought and reflected in her prayer. This causes David to put trust in a great God rather than in great humans or in military might.

Second, we cannot fail to hear the mocking tone of the Philistine champion as he terrifies Israel through his arrogance. Here, as elsewhere in Scripture, such mocking of God's people incurs God's wrath and judgment (vv. 26, 36, 45; cf. Zeph. 2:8-11). Moreover, as observed, blasphemy of God is to be punished by God's people.

Third, there are the references to beasts and shepherding throughout the chapter. The point is that Goliath through his mocking and his terrifying is a threat to God's people, God's sheep. As David himself indicates, Goliath is simply like a threatening lion or a bear, and as a shepherd, he knows how to deal with threats to sheep (cf. 2 Sam. 24:17).

It appears that the text is, therefore, presenting David as a man who thinks as God thinks. He sees God's people harassed as sheep without a shepherd and wants to help. He sees them afflicted by a beast that needs to be dealt with and so he trusts in God and steps up to do the job. In this sense, he is a true shepherd of God's sheep. This is specified within Samuel in 2 Sam. 5:2 (ESV), which appears to reflect on this passage and interpret it as it speaks of David as one 'who led out and brought in Israel' and to whom the LORD said, 'You shall be shepherd of my people Israel'.

Listening to the Whole of Scripture

Looking Back

We have already observed above how our passage picks up themes from 1 Samuel 1:1–2:12. Saul does not look dependently to God as Hannah indicated people and kings should. He is worried by demonstrations of power and does not turn in faith towards God. He thinks that it *is* by strength that one prevails and he does not trust that those who oppose the Lord will be shattered and judged (1 Sam. 2:9-10). David, on the other hand, here looks like a king should in 1 Samuel 2. He believes that, 'it is not by strength that one prevails' and that, 'those who oppose the Lord will be shattered' and that, 'He will thunder against them from heaven', 'judge the ends of the earth' and, 'give strength to his king and exalt the horn of his anointed'.

As we have seen often in our explorations, such attitudes are constantly praised and lauded in Scripture and in this sense, David, at least here, is of the same mind as God. He sees things as God sees them.

Looking Forward

It is in this sense observed above that David foreshadows his greater Son, Jesus Christ. When He came into the world, He came to a situation where Jews were tired of being under overlords and were looking for a military son of David who would do what David did here. However, Jesus saw things as His Father saw them and recognised that the real enemy was not some Roman emperor but human sinfulness and the devil and his cohorts. He also saw failed shepherds who were not adequately or properly caring for God's sheep.

The enemy Jesus engaged was not a physically large and abusive one but a spiritual one. Jesus comes with nothing but His Word and the cross. Eventually, Jesus allows the enemies of God to take Him and is crucified. In doing so, using the language of the apostle Paul, He makes a public spectacle of them, triumphing over them in the cross (Col. 2:15).

From Text to Message

The passage before us is one so rich that there are many pitfalls to avoid as we move from exegesis to exposition and application. However, when it is read within its immediate exegetical context and the larger theological context of the book and the canon, there are significant guideposts for its explanation and application to a Christian audience in a way that is sympathetic to its original context and also its larger canonical one.

Suggestions for Preaching

Ways Into the Text

There are multiple ways in which the preacher or teacher might draw hearers into the passage. One that seems very human and therefore very contemporary, but which is also a major theme in the chapter, is to talk about the whole concept of big being better. There are no shortages of stories, anecdotes and examples that would suffice for this purpose.

An alternative way in would be to talk about the human desire for power. During the days when metropolitan phone books were part of the normal household, I opened my sermon by taking people on a tour of the phone book and noted how many company names were linked to words associated with 'power' and how few were linked to 'weak.' A similar end might be achieved by surveying advertising online or in billboards in your particular location or how nations go about demonstrating their significance in the world. The purpose would be to show how humans are fascinated with strength and power and how we Christians are captivated by such things as well (as our songs often indicate).

Moving Through the Text

If this sermon is part of a series, it is going to be helpful for your explanation of this passage to set it in its larger context. People might be reminded *briefly* about the major elements of the story so far: Hannah's story (1 Sam. 1–2), the ark narrative (1 Sam. 4–6), the request of a king (1 Sam. 8), their tall and impressive first king, Saul (1 Sam. 9–12) and his failure but Jonathan's success (1 Sam. 13–14), Saul's rejection (1 Sam. 15) and the choice of David (1 Sam. 16). You can then trade on the fact that the Goliath story is well known and therefore can be briefly summarised by retelling the stories in its sections, highlighting the interpretative elements of importance (e.g. verses 11-14 stress the impressiveness of Goliath and the fear and dismay of God's people). It is important to avoid too much detail and to give a big picture of how Saul and the people are overawed and overcome by the impressiveness of Goliath and that a contrast is offered in David who is unimpressive himself and unimpressed by the size of Goliath and his impudence.

For the purposes of explanation, it will be important to stress the links that David makes to shepherding and the blaspheming and threatening of Goliath. David comes before Goliath not with might and power but with a name, the name of the LORD of hosts, and he punishes the Philistine for his threatening behaviour toward God's sheep and his blasphemy. In recounting the victory, you might recall Hannah's prophecy of 1 Sam. 2:10. Finally, it will be important to explain Jonathan's abdication in 1 Sam. 18:1-5.

Biblical Theology and Application

In relation to biblical theology, there are a few areas to explore and explain.

First, there are the attitudes of Israel and Saul. For them, big is better. The contrast is supplied by David with whom the theology of a great God dominates, and he is willing to trust Him as Hannah had urged kings to do.

Second, there is the defiance of Goliath who mocks the LORD. Again, contrast is supplied by David who holds the LORD's reputation in the highest regard and who seeks to protect and advance God's glory.

Third, there are the references to beasts throughout the story. David sees with God's eyes and therefore sees Goliath as a threat to sheep. As God's shepherd (2 Sam. 5:2), David cares for God's sheep.

These biblical theology observations give a clear direction toward the ministry of Christ in the New Testament in the context where Israel was again overawed by power. He saw the real enemy to be sin and Satan and waged war on them in His death.

The flow through to application can be multiple. For example, the Corinthians were overawed by the wrong things in 1 Corinthians but Paul's response is to remind them that he came in weakness and was determined to know nothing among them except Christ crucified, Christ the power of God and Christ the wisdom of God (1 Cor. 2:1-5). From here you could urge people to have as models Jesus, the apostle Paul, and countless other Christians who have seen things rightly and scorned worldly power for the way of the cross in which the power of God is displayed.

Leading a Bible Study

Pray

Have one or two people pray about this Bible study, that God would use it to form you into the likeness of Jesus

Read 1 Samuel 17:1–18:5 aloud in the group

Observation (1)

In the light of the chapter, fill in the chart, noting the 'striking/key characteristics' (physical, psychological, spiritual, etc.) of each of these three people in the story. You might particularly note down any references to 'fear' in relation to each one. Highlight or draw links between any characteristics that are contrasted or similar.

Goliath	Saul and Israel	David

Interpretation

Given your research above, what do you think the main point of the passage might be?

Observation (2)

Here are some other things to observe in the passage:

- Did you notice the comments about defying or mocking in the passage? If not, see if you can find them. Who defies whom? What punishment is promised for those who defy? What punishment is given?
- Did you notice the references to beasts and animals in the passage? Where are they? What sort of beasts/animals are mentioned? How is David like a shepherd in how he sees Goliath and deals with him?

Input from Bible study group leader
Make sure that people understand that the passage emphasises seeing things as God sees them. Get them to think about what that might look like in their own lives and context.

Praying together
Get people to think about some of the ways in which our attitudes and lives as Christians are more like those of the world than like Jesus in relation to power and influence. Share the ways in which the story of Goliath has helped us to see things differently. How can we pray intelligently for ourselves, our leaders, and others?

Gather specific prayer points and pray for the things above and for each other.

17.
Saul's Alienation
(1 Samuel 18:6–19:24)

The world of 1 Samuel has now changed dramatically. In relative private, we have heard of Saul's rebuke and promised removal at the hand of the Lord's prophetic messenger (chapter 15) and then again in relative private we have heard of his replacement, David. Then, very much in public, we have seen what Israel saw – the lostness and fear of Saul and the fearlessness and confidence of his successor, David. Now a whole new world opens up for the reader of 1 Samuel. The narrator's distance is dramatically reversed as he investigates internal attitudes and dispositions, particularly Saul's. The narrator's view is expressed. Explicit comment about Saul's internal attitudes and feelings are laid bare for us to see while his external actions are portrayed and linked. Such exploration is at times painful and bewildering for the reader but nonetheless real and engaging, as it is of the other significant players (except for David) in the drama that unfolds.

It is also important to observe that the differences between the Hebrew and Greek text that we noted about chapter 17 continue here. In chapter 18 the Hebrew text is again considerably longer, and the additions are scattered throughout. Again, as with chapter 17, we will concentrate on the Hebrew text as reflected in the NIV.

Listening to the Text

Context and Structure

The context of the chapter is clear and set by the previous three chapters: the Lord's rejection of Saul (chapter 15) and choice of David (chapter 16) and David's extraordinary success by the hand of the Lord and before his people as well as the shadow that it casts over Saul and his future (chapter 17). The significant elements that structure the chapter are reflected in the headings below.

Content

Prelude/overlap/intersection (18:1-5)

In our last chapter we observed two things about verses 1-5: (a) Jonathan appears to formally give to David the signs of his rule and therefore perhaps even abdicate his future rule, and (b) they form a fitting summary to the Goliath event and, therefore, belong somewhat to that story. However, as with other passages examined previously, there may be an interlocking function of these verses whereby they have links that work in both directions, here providing a fitting introduction to general themes in this chapter and those which follow, particularly those involving a relationship with Saul and his family.

We have already noticed that wherever David goes, people seem to fall in behind him. He gathers friends everywhere. However, in the narrative that comes we will also see that there is a particular depth in the relationship with Jonathan, often accompanied with references to 'love' (see v. 3 here and also 2 Samuel 1:17-27, particularly v. 26). The context for such love should be understood in light of the word 'covenant' in verse 3, as it is connected with other covenants, such as that made between the Lord and Israel (cf. Exod. 20:6; Deut. 6:4-18).[1] Hence, while there is undoubtedly depth in the relationship between these two, there is also a bond, commitment, and allegiance. We even see later in the chapter where the men of Israel and Judah 'love' David because he joined them in the common task of battle (1 Sam. 18:16).

Finally, there is an implied contrast here between Jonathan and his father. As Samuel prophesied that kings would 'take' (1 Sam. 8:11, 13, 14, 16), so Saul 'takes' David (lit. 1 Sam. 17:31, 18:2). However, Jonathan, whose name is constructed around the Hebrew word for giving, 'gives' David his symbols of rank and inheritance.[2]

Incident 1: The song of the women (18:6-9)
The victory of chapter 17 was spectacular and undoubtedly deserved praise in song. While scholars have argued about whether there is any intentional elevation by the women of David over Saul, the fundamental point is the emphatic nature of the victory (cf. Deut. 32:30; Ps. 91:7). However, given the frailty of Saul's psyche revealed here and in the chapters which follow, it is not surprising that he hears the

---

1. Although, even if there is mutuality in the covenant here (i.e. 'Jonathan and David cut/made a covenant'), to speak of a mutual 'exchange of clothing' as Chapman does, goes beyond what the text says; Stephen B. Chapman, *1 Samuel as Christian Scripture: A Theological Commentary* (Grand Rapids, Michigan: William B. Eerdmans, 2016), p. 159.
2. Moshe Garsiel, *The Book of Samuel: Studies in History, Historiography, Theology and Poetics Combined*, Part 1: The Story and History of David and His Kingdom (Jerusalem: Rubin Mass, 2018), pp. 101-2.

comparison as insult and becomes 'very angry' and 'galled' (v. 8), and is then driven to 'keep a jealous eye on David' (v. 9). The distance between him and his people which he feels will develop as the story unfolds.

Saul's world has, therefore, drastically changed in these last three chapters. In chapter 15, he lost the kingship. At the end of chapter 16, he loses the Spirit of God to David, is tormented by a harmful spirit from the Lord but finds David, loves him greatly, and is significantly refreshed by his presence and music. Now a very different scene has emerged as a result of the Goliath incident with the result that his source of relief has also become his source of pain. David has now supplanted Saul in the affections of his troops, his son, and, from his perspective, the women of Israel. With all this background and the resultant 'jealous eye' (v. 9) the events of 'the next day' (v. 10) are not that surprising.

Incident 2: The first attack (18:10-16)

Music binds this section with the previous, as do time references ('the next day') and the internal world of Saul continues to emerge into his public life. In the past, the coming of God's Spirit had resulted in Saul being 'changed into a different person' (1 Sam. 10:6, 10; cf. 11:6). Now, an 'evil spirit' coming upon him overcomes the respite that had been supplied by David's music previously. Nevertheless, David eludes him twice (vv. 10-11). The contrast between the two men is stark in the Hebrew and epitomises the story of the rest of 1 Samuel; Saul has a spear in his *hand* (a weapon of aggression) which he will attempt to use against the Lord's chosen king, whereas David's *hand* holds a sedating instrument of peace. Later, David will be tempted to reach out his hand against Saul, but he will realise that such actions against the Lord's anointed are wrong (1 Sam. 24:5-19).

If verses 10-11 present David as innocent, verses 12-16 have him as the deliverer of Israel in the presence of the Lord. At the start of this section, we hear of Saul's fear of David (v. 12). This is matched at the end by 'all Israel and Judah' who 'loved David' (v. 16). It appears that both love and fear are related to the success that comes from the Lord being with David (v. 14) and result in Saul pushing David out of his presence and David leading the army in their campaigns. The Lord's blessing, therefore, has a double edge. It gives David success but makes him an increased threat to Saul but loved by Saul's troops.

Incident 3: Marriage (18:17-30)

The third incident in the chapter has a plot that is straightforward if not full of questions (e.g. the second marriage and the foreskin bride price). However, at its heart is the ongoing exploration of the theme of the whole chapter; the exploration of the relationship between Saul and David. Part of the arrangement in dealing with Goliath had been marriage into the royal family.

In 1 Samuel the word for love is used repeatedly in relation to David. The first person said to love him is Saul (1 Sam. 16:21) and four others join him in this chapter: Jonathan (v. 1), all Israel and Judah (v. 16), Saul's daughter Michal (v. 20), all Saul's servants (v. 22), and Michal again (v. 28). Critically, those closest to Saul are most named. However, as in the previous section, Saul reacts in fear again because of David's apparent favour in relationships (v. 29; cf. vv. 12, 15-16). In fact, the strength of relationships between David and Saul's family will only serve to exacerbate and highlight the fraught and deteriorating relationship between David and Saul and also the decreasing stability of Saul as a person.

The final few verses summarise well the chapter: 'Saul realised that *the Lord was with David* ... his *daughter loved David*, Saul *became still more afraid of him* ... David *met with more success* ... moreover, *his name became well known*.' The result was that David 'remained his enemy the rest of his life.' The rest of the book will trace the course of this enmity and its fruit.

Escapes and protection (19:1-24)

Where chapter 18 had explored relationships between Saul and key people in his life and highlighted the threat that David poses to Saul, this chapter explores three rescues that arise out of the fraught relationship with Saul.

Jonathan (19:1-7)

Again, Jonathan is the focus of the first encounter which involves mediation between Saul and David through Jonathan. It is structured around the word 'sin' (vv. 4 and 5; translated as 'wrong/wronged' in the NIV). Jonathan pleads David's innocence and the mediation is successful, involving an oath by Saul in the Lord's name (v. 6).

Michal (19:8-17)

As with the previous chapter, another child of Saul who loves David—Michal—is drawn in to defend him against their father. The background is David's success against the Philistines and then Saul being overcome again by the 'evil spirit from the Lord' with resultant failure and escape by David, aided and protected by Michal (vv. 9-17).

Psalm 59 reflects on this incident and echoes the note of innocence sounded by Jonathan previously, and sources the deliverance in God rather than humans.

Samuel (19:18-24)

With David in flight, he goes to Samuel. When pursued under Saul's command the soldiers are stopped by the most unusual defence, a prophetic trance. On the third attempt, Saul joins his men and experiences again his earlier experience, although this time it diminishes him as it apparently leaves him naked and with a reputation (v. 24). His first experience validated his kingship, where this second one validates David's, as the Spirit of the Lord protects David.

Theological Themes

The isolation of Saul

There can be little doubt that since chapter 15 the narrative focus has been on the rejection of Saul and the choice of another, that is, David. Given the explicit statements within Scripture, it cannot be denied that Saul was the object of God's choice (1 Sam. 10:24). Nevertheless, something of pallor hung over him right from the beginning, as is hinted at in various places (e.g. 1 Sam. 8:18; 12:13). Such is confirmed by his lack of hearing and obeying right from the beginning and also by the Lord's formal recognition of this and rejection of him (1 Sam. 15:10-11), accompanied by the promise of a replacement (1 Sam. 15:28). This replacement is then announced to be David (1 Sam. 16:12) and confirmed by anointing, the Spirit coming upon him (1 Sam. 16:13), and the Spirit leaving Saul (1 Sam. 16:14).

Since then we have seen the rapid deterioration of relationships in Saul's life. This could be summarised diagrammatically with solid arrows representing an antagonistic relationship and dotted arrows representing favourable or sympathetic relationships (or, in some cases, 'love').

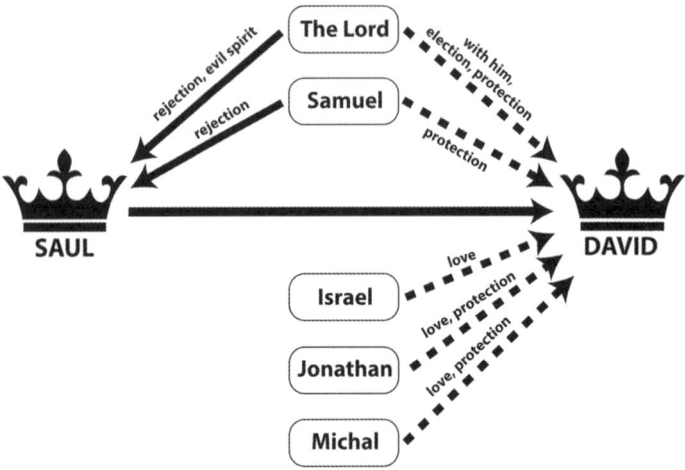

At the beginning of his story, Saul found himself in the situation of the diagram above. God, Samuel, and Israel were for him. However, by the time we reach the end of chapter 19, everything is different. A new face has appeared in Israel in the shape of David and in 1 Samuel 17–19 we have seen Saul watch David and seen Saul become jealous and aggressive against David. However, the Lord's favour has remained with David and God has protected him. Saul knows what is going on because God's prophet told him in no uncertain terms. Additionally, the Spirit of the Lord has left Saul, an evil spirit has harassed him, and the Spirit of the Lord has even driven him into a prophetic state in order to protect David.

However, there is also the relationship with Samuel. Samuel had been for him. He had been a good mentor and friend. However, now he has become distant and

Part Three: The Beginnings and End of Saul's Kingship 297

inaccessible. He sides with David and offers him protection. As for Israel, they are not negative toward Saul, but they love David and see him as a warrior who can win against their enemies. Finally, there is Saul's own family. His son Jonathan identifies with David's passion for God and the people of God, and Jonathan delights in David, defending him before his father. Saul's daughter loves David, protects him, and sets herself against her father's will for David's sake.

Saul's isolation is comprehensive, and its cause can be identified as theological. He has not sided with God's anointed or welcomed him but instead resisted him and now he is surrounded by those who see God's purposes in David and have allied with him. The end result will be horrifying and even Saul will recognise and acknowledge it in time, along with his own sinfulness. However, God appears to allow him to proceed and we will see that the results are terrifying.

Listening to the Whole of Scripture

Looking Within

As we look at Saul and what is happening to him, it is not hard to hear the words of Hannah in her prayer. Saul has had both a raising up and a bringing down. However, we have yet to see what is sure to come according to Hannah. God will give strength to His king but also, those who oppose Him will be shattered.

Looking Back

As we look back in Scripture, the things we have seen in Saul have occasionally been seen starkly in other opponents. For example, Pharaoh in Exodus 1 set himself against God's creative purposes in the descendants of Abraham to whom He had promised land, children, and blessing. He resisted far more strongly than Saul does here, and God gave him chance after chance to turn back, but he refused. In the end, he is overthrown at the sea.

Looking Forward

There are incredible links between David and Jesus. Like David, He is God's anointed and like him, He was the object of the jealousy and enmity of others. The Israelite religious leaders of His day opposed Him and Jesus spoke to them firmly, but He was also innocent as David is here. Nevertheless, eventually, He was overcome on the cross. However, God turned His apparent defeat into glorious victory, triumphing over evil through Him.

From Text to Message

If our general thrust above is correct, that is, that the main thrust of the passage has to do with siding with or resisting God's purposes in His Messiah, then there are two potential ways forward. One is to emphasise the benefits that flow from siding with God. However, that does not really appear to be the main thrust of the passage. Rather, the text seems to be exploring the impact of Saul's refusal to acknowledge and accept God's purposes in His Christ. It would therefore seem better to stick with this main theme and follow it through.

Suggestions for Preaching

Ways Into the Text

There are a variety of ways into the topic and in writing I was tempted not to tell you how I started because it sounds so overwhelmingly depressing and not a very good start for a sermon at all! However, what was done was to talk about a particular work that has had a profound influence on how Christians view the afterlife: Dante's *The Divine Comedy*. The background was given and then the content described as Dante and Virgil enter hell and Virgil guides Dante through the nine circles of hell. I observed that as the numbers of the circles grow the punishments become more awful. I then asked my people what they thought of when they thought of hell. I then said that as I'd studied the passage, I thought that Saul's existence here reminded me a little of what hell might be like. I then invited them to explore the text with me, suggesting that by the end we get a glimpse of the horror of hell and how to avoid it!

However, perhaps as you preach you may want to be a little gentler on your people. Some other ways in are to get people to think about the importance of relationships and how relating and being related to by others is at the core of our existence as humans. You might give them examples of people who have been isolated but then restored to friendship or relationship with loved ones or the like. This would then enable you to say that at the heart of this passage is the importance of relationships. God made us for relationships with each other and with Him.

Moving Through the Text

The outline of a sermon is relatively straightforward and the best way through it is simply to work through its main sections, highlighting at each point the positive reactions of people to David and Saul's negative responses. The important thing is to not emphasise the details too much but to highlight those things which help in terms of the main point. If you are a good storyteller, work through the text retelling the story in a way that explains it but makes it live. If you are not a good storyteller, make sure that you don't sterilise the story by robbing it of the drama and pathos.

Toward the end, before applying the text, you could use the diagram that I've used above or perhaps a more graphic or artistic version than mine. However, often those who are visually oriented will find this diagram helpful in summarising the main ideas.

Biblical Theology and Application

It is important that when you get toward application that you help people understand that if God is God and God is good, then He wants the best for people. That best is found in relating to Him and His Messiah, Jesus, is the only way for that to happen. This is a good sermon where two clearly different applications might be made, one for Christians and one for those who are not yet Christians.

In relation to Christians, you might explain the great blessings of being related to God for eternity and the blessings of belonging to the family of God even now. You could easily finish by reading 2 Thess. 1:5-10 and praying 2 Thess. 1:11-12.

In relation to those not yet Christians, the application might be that to set yourself against God and His purposes in His Son can only lead to isolation from God and all that is good. Explain that you become related to God by relating to His Messiah, the Lord Jesus Christ.

Leading a Bible Study

1 Samuel 18:1-19

Group leader on 1 Samuel 18:1-5

The leader might like to read and formally introduce and explain these first five verses. The most important points to make are as follows:

- We know from 1 Samuel 13 and 14 that Jonathan does not really like what he sees in his father but here we are told that he loves what he sees in David.
- Apparently, Jonathan looks at the heart as God does and sees a man with a passion for the Lord like his own and with deeds like his own.
- The covenant that is enacted here between Jonathan and David is one that is mentioned multiple times in the story that follows, and we will return to it in future Bible studies.
- Jonathan's robe is probably a symbol of his future rule. He takes it off and gives it to David, 'along with his tunic, and even his sword, bow and his belt' (18:4). By this act perhaps Jonathan conveys to David his rights as crown prince to the throne. Where David had refused the armour of Saul, he apparently accepts the armour of Jonathan. Saul, for his part, gives David authority over the army.

Back to small groups

Pray

Have one or two people pray about this Bible study, that God would use it to form you into the likeness of Jesus

Read 1 Samuel 18

Observation

1 Samuel 18:6–9

Songs are important in Samuel (remember 1 Samuel 2:1-10). If the song from 1 Samuel 2 sets the agenda up until now and this one does the same for what is to come, what might we expect for the next section of 1 and 2 Samuel?

From what you know about Saul, how do you think that he would react to the song? How *does* he react (v. 8)?

Given what Samuel says to Saul in 1 Samuel 15:28, how do you think that Saul might possibly interpret the song?

1 Samuel 18:10-16

Who does Saul fear in chapter 17? Who does he fear in these verses? Why?

1 Samuel 18:17-30

Read 1 Samuel 17:25. These verses flow from this undertaking. What do we learn about Saul's nature from them?

As an interesting added note, see if you can count the number of times in this chapter that someone is said to 'love' or 'like' David. Who are they? How are they related to Saul?

Read 1 Samuel 19
1 Samuel 18:6-30 had outlined three incidents in the relationship between Saul and David. Chapter 19 describes three deliverances or acts of protection that are exercised toward David in the face of Saul's enmity and fear, arising because of those incidents.

What are they?

What happens?

Interpretation
What do we learn from these chapters about what happens when you line yourself up with God's purposes? What do we learn about what happens when you set yourself against God's purposes?

Part Three: The Beginnings and End of Saul's Kingship 303

As those who live after Christ's coming, how do we line up with God's purposes in His Messiah?

Praying together
Gather specific prayer points and pray for the things above and for each other.

18.
Covenants, Fugitives, and Strange Bedfellows
(1 Samuel 20:1–23:28)

Perhaps you have met those people who can just find their way. They arrive in a new city, observe, sense it out, and before long make their way around almost as well as a local. They read the paper, or they listen to the local news, and before long they have worked out who people are, which ones are important and how the politics works. Perhaps as you read the previous few lines, you might even identify yourself in the description or part of it, or maybe you are like most other ordinary people and it takes you quite some time to acclimatise to new cities and new circumstances. Perhaps you find yourself geographically and/or socially disoriented when in new places or cultures. Maybe it takes a long time before you can confidently work your way around and understand the news and have some idea where the best cafes are to be found and what are the best foods to eat.

However, imagine if you then not only changed cities but changed culture, climate, terrain, and were transferred thousands of years and had to find your way around ancient cities with their people and politics, loves and hates, customs and etiquette. Well, the chapters we turn to look at now are full of all those sorts of changes. There is movement, people we have not met before, lots of them, and much journeying around in various locations with politics most of which we are unsure about.

This is the world of the chapters that face us as we near the end of the book of 1 Samuel. While our chief and primary people remain the same, their interrelationships become more complex and their locations change rapidly. That makes things difficult for us as we try to explain these passages, and it makes it hard for those listening. It is important before we dive into the passage, to think about how best to help ourselves and our hearers. A few strategies will aid us: (1) stick with the major characters and their movements; (2) avoid getting bogged down in detail, (3) regularly orient your hearers and (4) have a map that can be seen digitally or physically! All of this means that it is probably best to deal with these passages in terms of the 'big picture' rather than the details (and our analysis will do that in the pages that follow).

Listening to the Text

Context and Structure

These chapters are quite complex, and although there are a variety of approaches to their structure, the following analysis is indebted to a doctoral dissertation by Klement, subsequent interaction by Vannoy, along with a wonderfully stimulating exploration of Hebrew Narrative by Fokkelman.[1] The big decision gravitates

---

1 J. P. Fokkelman, *Narrative Art and Poetry in the Books of Samuel: Vol II: The Crossing Fates (I Sam. 13–31 and II Sam. 1)*, Studia Semitica

around whether the interactions between David, Saul and Jonathan that occur in chapters 20 and 23, begin and conclude one section or begin two separate sections. In the end, a broad chiastic structure is proposed as reflected in the following structural outline.

20:1-42	Saul, David, and Jonathan: Harasssment and Help (largely speech)
21:1-9	Encounters in Exile: Ahimelech, Priest of Nob; Doeg; Goliath's Sword
21:10–22:5	David as Fugitive
22:6-23	Revisiting Earlier Decisions: Ahimelech, Priests of Nob; Doeg; Goliath's Sword
23:1-18	Saul, David, and Jonathan: Success; Help and Harrassment (largely narrative)

Content

Saul, David, and Jonathan: Harassment and help (20:1-42)

Structure

Verses	Locations		People and Action
20:1-11a	A	At the Court	David with Jonathan: Alarm
20:11b-24a		B In the Field	Jonathan with David: Bond and Testing
20:24b-34	A′	At the Court	Saul with Jonathan: Anger
20:35–42		B′ In the Field	Jonathan with David: Bond and Parting

---

Neerlandica, p. 23 (Assen/Maastricht, The Netherlands: Van Gorcum, 1986), pp. 435-51; J. R. Vannoy, *1–2 Samuel*, CBC, 4a, p. 191; Herbert H. Klement, *II Samuel 21–24: Context, Structure, and Meaning in the Samuel Conclusion*, Europäische Hochschulschriften. Reihe 23, Theologie, Bd. 682 (Frankfurt am Main: Peter Lang, 2000), p. 139.

The broad structure of events in this chapter is outlined above. As indicated, there are four phases of interactions in two locations. While the previous chapter revealed the inner mind of Saul, this chapter focuses on the speech between the characters. The unusual strength of the conversation is reflected in the number of exclamation marks occurring in some of the standard English translations (between 11 and 14)!

David with Jonathan in the court (20:1-11a)

Although we know from preceding chapters that David is the Lord's chosen, we have also seen how Jonathan, the possible successor to the throne, is of like mind and disposition to David. Factors to be considered in their relationship with each other are:

- God has used both as deliverers from the Philistines.
- David is God's choice for the throne but is powerless to claim that throne.
- Both probably have formal obligations toward Saul: Jonathan as son and David as son-in-law and commander of Israel's army.
- The two men have formalised their relationship in a covenant (1 Sam. 18:3), which may be what causes David to go to Jonathan for help (the language used by David is language that can be used of a person coming before a superior; cf. 1 Sam. 1:22).
- In ancient society, as in many societies even today, obligations to parents do not end with adulthood and honour toward them is enjoined in Scripture in the first of the ten commandments concerned with relationships with other people (Exod. 20:12). We know Jonathan to be a godly man.

So, the question is how Jonathan as the son of Saul and covenant partner with David will act toward David as a supplicant. The first surprise, given his own previous criticism of his father (1 Sam. 14:29-30), is his response. It looks somewhat naïve, severely conflicted, or possibly a means of coping. In any case, David offers a way out by suggesting why he might not be confided in by his father (v. 3) and a way of testing whether David's assertions are correct (vv. 4-7).

The significance of David's exhortation to Jonathan in verse 8 is somewhat masked in the NIV's translation. It is not a plea for generosity but for covenant action (the word 'kindly' is the Hebrew word—*ḥsd*—often used to express God's unexpected, unmerited generosity and kindness toward those who are in helpless situations).[2] Jonathan agrees to follow the course of action suggested.

Jonathan with David in the field (20:11b-24a)

In the second half of verse 11, the reader is taken from the court to a field where they will remain until verse 24. Jonathan reaffirms his commitment to David and requests that David show him 'kindness' (vv. 14 and 15). Jonathan then requests that David not cut off his kindness from his family and together they seal their agreement in a covenant. Jonathan has asked David that he show covenant kindness to him and his household even when the Lord has 'cut' off his enemies. In verse 16, he then makes (lit. 'cuts' – the same word used in the previous verse) a covenant with David. Finally, they arrange future communication (vv. 18-23).

---

2. Translated as 'unfailing kindness' and 'kindness' in verses 14 and 15 in NIV84. For a thorough exploration of the term in Scripture, see Francis I. Andersen, 'Yahweh, the Kind and Sensitive God', in *God Who Is Rich in Mercy: Essays presented to D. B. Knox*, trans. David G. Petersen, ed. Peter T. O'Brien (Homebush West, NSW: Anzea, 1986), pp. 41-88.

Jonathan with Saul in the court (20:24b-34)

The reader is now taken back to the court. In the previous section, the relational focus was highlighted in covenant language. Here it is highlighted in the language of eating, sitting and standing. The king and Abner are sitting but Jonathan 'arose' (see NIV footnote, v. 25). Why? Perhaps his allegiances have shifted.

When David is still absent on the second day, Saul cannot ignore the absence and questions Jonathan. Saul becomes angry with Jonathan eventually hurling the same spear at him that he had hurled at David, thereby confirming the suspicions of David (v. 3) and firmly identifying Jonathan with David in Saul's mind. Jonathan's standing on the previous day is then matched by him 'getting up' (same Hebrew word used in verse 25) but also refusing to eat on this day because of 'his father's shameful treatment of David' (v. 34).

Jonathan with David in the field (20:35-42)

The fourth episode in this section occurs back in the field with an elaborate ritual involving the shooting of arrows and a boy to fetch them. The result is a reaffirmation of the bond between them after which they separate. Despite Saul's anger Jonathan will stay with his father and eventually die with him.

Encounters in exile: Ahimelech, Doeg, Goliath's sword (21:1-9)

This chapter begins David's existence as a wanderer along the lines of some of the disenfranchised and perhaps landless ones that we see in the book of Judges, such as Ehud, Gideon, Samson and the like. Two needs

Part Three: The Beginnings and End of Saul's Kingship   311

are pressing: food and weapons. However, David is not without allies and friends, nor is he aimless. In fact, given the shortage of metal and the inability in Israel to forge metal, perhaps he may even be in search of weapons as he goes to Nob. In any case, when questioned by the suspicious priest, Ahimelech, David apparently lies but ends up with food (consecrated bread) and 'the sword of Goliath the Philistine'. However, as we read, we also wonder what the significance is of the reference to, 'one of Saul's servants ... Doeg the Edomite' (v. 7). The fact is we are left hanging while David heads off to Philistine territory, to the very place the sword had come from.

David as fugitive (21:10–22:5)
In Philistine territory (21:10-15)

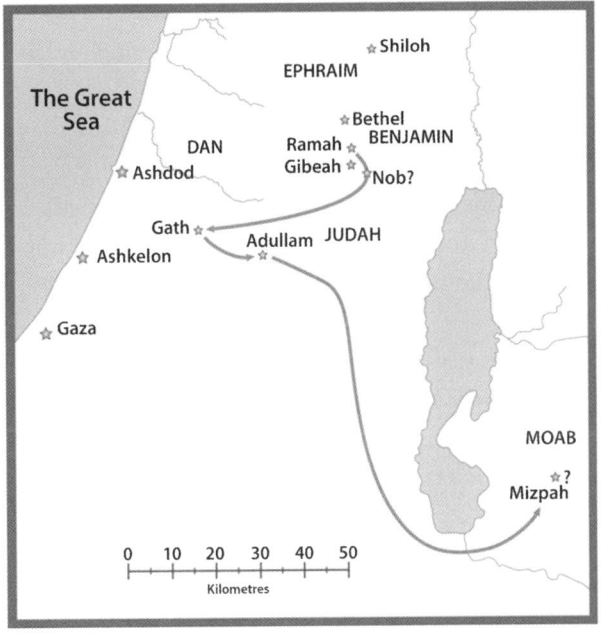

Our fear for David in Philistine territory should be assuaged by what we have already seen in 1 Samuel. After all, it was in Philistine territory that the LORD triumphed over Dagon, leaving him face down before the ark and it was also their representative, Goliath, who was left facedown before David not so long ago. Both Dagon and Goliath were decapitated.

Perhaps David is seeking some sort of alliance with Achish, king of Gath. However, any hope in this direction appears to be dashed as a result of the warning given by his servants in verse 11. David pretends to be a drooling, scratching madman who then escapes to the cave of Adullam. The Davidic acrostic Psalm 34 speaks of his encounter with Abimelech and probably refers to the events of this chapter.[3]

Refuge in the cave of Adullam (22:1-5)

Given that Saul's own family is threatened by Saul, it would not be surprising if David's were as well and they flee to him (v. 1), as do many others, with the result that their numbers grow to 'about four hundred men' (v. 2). David then moves his parents to the non-Israelite, non-Philistine territory of Moab. The Moabites were people normally shunned by the Israelites, but David has Moabite blood in his family, and so this might provide a safe place for them (see the book of Ruth, particularly chapters 1 and 4).

David is now a long way from home. He is accompanied by an odd assortment of friends, some misfits. He and his family find shelter out of the land of Israel and in the land

---

3. The psalm refers to the time David feigns madness but speaks of Abimelech rather than Achish. Possibly, 'Abimelech' was a title for Philistine kings.

of their other kin. Perhaps they are at risk of remaining there. At this point, it is helpful to remember our broad framework outlined above.

20:1-42	Saul, David, and Jonathan: Harasssment and Help (largely speech)
21:1-9	Encounters in Exile: Ahimelech, Priest of Nob; Doeg; Goliath's Sword
21:10–22:5	David as Fugitive
22:6-23	Revisiting Earlier Decisions: Ahimelech, Priests of Nob; Doeg; Goliath's Sword
23:1-18	Saul, David, and Jonathan: Success; Help and Harrassment (largely narrative)

What is it that reverses the fleeing to return and a change in fortunes? It appears to be the Word of the LORD from a prophet who counsels return and who is listened to by David, who leaves and goes to 'the forest of Hereth' in Israel (1 Sam. 22:5).

Encounters in exile: Revisiting earlier decisions (1 Samuel 22:6-23)

With our focus now back in Israel, the narrator shifts us away from David to Saul in Gibeah. Apparently David's return to Judah filters back to Saul while 'seated under the tamarisk tree on the hill at Gibeah', which is not auspicious, given the last time he was seated under a tree in chapter 14 where he also spoke against his son and was shown up by him. Not only this, he was also in the company of a priest who was the brother of the priest of Nob who helped David back in chapter 21. It was also the place that Saul acted preemptively and foolishly. It was the time when his men sided with his son whom he here accuses of conspiracy, along with his men (v. 8).

Doeg's accusations are sharp given Saul's feelings. Doeg puts the alleged treason of the priest first, even though we have no evidence of that from the earlier account. When that is added to with Ahimelech being accused of giving David provision and the sword of Goliath (vv. 9-10), it is not surprising to see the strength of Saul's response. Ahimelech is sent for, accused of treason, attempts defence but is sentenced to death. When the king's officials refuse to carry out the task, Doeg does, but Abiathar, Ahimelech's son, escapes and reports to David. We then find that David knew what Doeg would most likely do and takes responsibility for it and protects God's representative.

Saul, David and Jonathan: Success, help and harassment (23:1-29)

David and Saul compared (23:1-14)

The broad structure of the passage here falls into two parts. In the first part, David as God's chosen king interacts again with the Philistines. In the second part, Saul interacts with David and seeks to capture and thwart him. There is an implied comparison and contrast between the two as can be seen in the following structural outline of the first half of the chapter.

Part A: David versus/seeks the Philistines (23:1-6)

David *is told* of Keilah's oppression by the Philistines (v. 1)

David *inquires* of the LORD (twice), and is encouraged to engage despite resistance (vv. 2-4)

David succeeds (vv. 5-6)

Part B: Saul versus/seeks David (23:7-14)

Saul *is told* of David in Keilah and besieges David and his men (vv. 7-8)

Part Three: The Beginnings and End of Saul's Kingship   315

David *seeks* the LORD (twice), who answers favourably (vv. 9-12)

David succeeds (vv. 13-14)

These encounters show David's focus. He hears of the enemies of the people of God, seeks God, sides with Him, and is successful. Saul, for his part, is focused on opposing God's purposes for the people of God which flow through David.

Saul looks to harass the people of God and their champion – David. In contrast, David looks to protect the people of God and does so by withdrawing into the desert again. Saul is unsuccessful in his venture.

David and Jonathan (23:15-18)

We began our exploration of 1 Samuel 20-23 with a focus on three men: Saul, David and Jonathan. In that exploration, we were reminded of the LORD's choice of David and how Saul opposed that truth while Jonathan lined up with it. In verses 1-14 we have been shown that God blesses David and he is successful while Saul opposes God and fails. Verses 15-18 focus in on Jonathan. In Saul's opposition to David, Jonathan lines up with God and strengthens David in the LORD. Their covenant is renewed in verse 18.

Assault and rescue (23:19-29)

We have seen that chapters 20–23 began and ended with a focus on Saul, David, and Jonathan (i.e. 1 Sam. 20:1–23:18). Chapter 20 ended with Jonathan siding with David. However, they are bracketed by passages that involve Saul seeking David but David being rescued by God through unconventional and unusual means.

On the first occasion, it was directly at the LORD's hand. God caused Saul to be caught up into a bunch of people prophesying (1 Sam. 19:18-19). Here, Saul is pursuing David but suddenly the Philistines start attacking and he must leave his pursuit of David (vv. 26-29). Both occasions result in sayings being attached. The first results in a saying: 'Is Saul also among the prophets?' The second results in a place being named 'Sela Hammahlekoth' or 'Rock of Parting'.

Theological Themes

The passages we have looked at are long and complicated and there appears to be no coherent central themes or focus to them. However, we've seen that it appears to be a coherent whole in some way, at least as far as its central themes and its boundary markers go. It clearly belongs together. So, what is the central theme? What binds it all together?

First, it is clear that God has a definite purpose. The two brackets at either end tell us that it is bound up with David, whom God will protect using any means possible. God has a purpose in and through David as His chosen anointed king.

Second, God's choice of His king brings various and diverse reactions from different people. Some people see what God is doing and line up with it, often at significant cost. The prime example of that is Jonathan. Others set out to actively and aggressively oppose God's purpose in His king. There is a broad spectrum of people who fit this category. There is Saul, the man under threat by God's appointee and who wants to be at the centre, which means that no one else can be. Others are simply evil people who deliberately, cunningly, carefully and wickedly set themselves against God's plans. Doeg is such a person. Others simply naively and for unknown political or personal reasons want things for themselves or are out to see what benefit can be made for themselves. There is a wide cast of characters and their varying reactions to God's purposes, and His anointed David, forming the rich seam running through this long, and at first reading, complex section.

Listening to the Whole of Scripture

Looking Back

As we look back from this point in biblical revelation, this pattern has been present right from the beginning of biblical revelation. For example, in Genesis 12:1-3, God chose Abram and indicates that His purpose will flow through him. From that moment on there are detractors and devotees, people who line themselves up with that purpose and people who refuse. Some oppose God's purposes actively, aggressively and even defiantly while others are more passive and lazy. An example of the former is Pharaoh in Exodus. At first, he may not know what he is doing. However, when he is told of God's purpose through His people, he states his attitude and defiance clearly: 'Who is the Lord that I should obey him and let Israel go? I do not know the Lord and I will not let Israel go' (Exod. 5:2). Since the beginning of God's chosen people there have been those who help and those who hinder and it is exactly the same here.

Looking Forward

Scripture tells us that the centre of God's purpose for His world is not David but great David's greater Son and, sure enough, we see the same things happening when

God promotes His Son in His world. We see it in the ministry of Jesus. For example, Jonathan's clear successor is the man with the same name in the New Testament: John (the Baptist), who likens himself to the friend of the bridegroom who greets him with joy (John 3:29-30). However, there are others, such as Herod the Idumean. He lashes out with brutal and overwhelming violence resulting in the slaughter of innocent children (Matt. 2:16-18). If you read the crucifixion narrative in John's Gospel, you will see all manner of attitudes toward God's purposes in His Son. Similarly, you will see the varying responses of various groups to the proclamation of the gospel in the Acts of the Apostles. The reactions range from ready acceptance to brutal defiance.

From Text to Message

When we preach, how then should we move from text to message in a way that is faithful to the whole of the text, true to its apparent central thrust, but also that conveys what the passage is saying in itself?

The biggest problem here is that of how to preach a passage this long. The suggestion here is that you are rigorous in avoiding all those nice and interesting details that you've found in your study of the passage that are entrancing, and that you simply want to tell others. Too much detail will overwhelm if not cause people to miss the main point. For this reason, break the passage up into major sections and make sure that people grasp the main point of each section. When I did this myself, my longest explanation of a section was 530 words but most sections were between 120 and 150 words (my normal length of sermon is 20-35 minutes).

Part Three: The Beginnings and End of Saul's Kingship

Suggestions for Preaching

Ways Into the Text

As we consider the best way into the text, perhaps it is worth asking what the purpose of an introduction is. Some consider that it is to introduce the main theme or big idea of the text by way of a question or the like. To put it another way, it is to pose somehow the question that the passage will answer.

While there is much methodologically in favour of this idea, the risk is that it can be somewhat formulaic, boring, and predictable. Perhaps it might be more helpful to think that the goal is to preach the main theme of the passage and that there may be multiple ways into the passage that would enable that to be done. Hence, instead of thinking that your introduction should pose the question that the passage answers, it gives the big idea at the start to drive the rest of the sermon.

Perhaps a better way of thinking about it is that which was advocated to me when I first started preaching. A mentor at that time told me that preaching is a bit like fishing and that if you want to catch fish, you need bait. In other words, you need to entice your hearers or get them interested. Such interest might be created by asking the sorts of questions outlined above. However, there are multiple other ways as well, such as telling a story or rehearsing some history or engaging with some contemporary issue or any other variety of things. In other words, mixing and spicing things up may help and avoid predictability and boredom.

Being an English literature buff and a lover of storytelling, I remembered how Shakespeare had handled the issue in his play, *The Tempest*, and decided that I would retell the story which begins the play. There is a storm, and King Alonso and his entourage jump overboard and are washed ashore. Trinculo, the jester, seeks shelter and ends up inadvertently sharing the shelter with a deformed native and mutters to himself these words:

> *Alas, the storm is come again. My best way is to creep under the gabardine; there is no shelter hereabout: misery acquaints a man with strange bedfellows.*

From this point, I reflected on the fact that a whole host of adaptions have arisen out of this saying, particularly in the world of politics where circumstances often force enemies to become unusual friends and work together, sometimes unwittingly, toward a common objective.

This unusual introduction allowed me as the preacher to introduce this lengthy passage as one where God's appointee to the throne finds himself outside the court and is thrust into the world of ancient Israelite politics and parties where strange alliances and interactions form. Some are with good and likely suspects while others are with people unholy and ungodly, that is, strange bedfellows. I suggested to my congregation that David's experience out of the court would help us think about how our faith affects our relationships and our participation in God's purposes.

Moving Through the Text

Whatever 'hook' you use to entice your particular congregation, the structure of the sermon needs to reflect the passage. As indicated above, this is best done by working efficiently and in overview through the main sections of the passage, such as …

Part Three: The Beginnings and End of Saul's Kingship

1. Saul, David and Jonathan (1 Sam. 20:1-42)
2. The Help of a Priest (1 Sam. 21:1-9)
3. In Philistine Territory (1 Sam. 21:10-15)
4. Refuge in the Cave of Adullam (1 Sam. 22:1-5)
5. Extermination at Nob (22:6-23)
6. Saul, David and Jonathan Again (1 Sam. 23:1-29)

Biblical Theology and Application

The next section of a sermon should work through the larger biblical theological themes and work toward application along the lines indicated above. Here you might indicate that throughout the book of 1 Samuel, we have seen that God is a God of purpose and that this purpose finds its centre in His moving to appoint a king over His people. We know this purpose finds its first focus in David but its ultimate focus in Jesus.

The text of Samuel has indicated that as God works toward His purpose of a king after His own heart, there are inevitably diverse reactions, some favourable (e.g. Jonathan, Achish, the King of Moab) and others not (e.g. Saul, Doeg, the Ziphites). From here it is an easy transition to the New Testament and the equally diverse positive and negative reactions to Jesus. You might even say that such reactions were prophesied by the prophets (i.e. Mal. 4:4-6) and affirmed by Jesus (Luke 14:26-27; cf. Luke 9:57-62).

The text of Samuel also indicates to us that the presence of God's purpose in His King can, therefore, bring both pain and joy. So also it is with Jesus and those who follow Him.

This last point can easily lead to the application of the text to contemporary hearers as you indicate that aligning with Jesus will inevitably create wonderful friendships and allegiances but also strange allegiances and 'strange bedfellows'. Sometimes it will cause antagonism that will be forceful, irrational and even demonic, but at other times it will be well-conceived by intelligent and/or forceful people with whom you might normally find many commonalities.

This will allow the preacher to help the congregation with the pain that they might experience for being a Christian in some of their closest relationships and also help with the antagonism that might come about in response to their faith in Jesus. However, the final note might be that there is no better place to be than to be caught up with God's great purposes in His Son and that to be there, will eventually lead to great joy in the presence of God (Heb. 13:12-16).

Leading a Bible Study

Introduction

In this section the leader should remind people of the larger context. The book of 1 Samuel has been about introducing kinghip to Israel. We have seen Saul become the first king but God has rejected him (1 Sam. 15) and chosen David (1 Sam. 16). However, despite David being God's elect king, Saul is still actually king. That leads to inevitable problems. Explain that the main purpose of this Bible study is to explore the different reactions that result from this growing tension between the enthroned king and the chosen king.

Give people an overview of the whole of the story and introduce its main characters (being careful to not give any assessment of their character or attitudes).

Observation (in smaller groups)

Assign the following passages to the different small groups or individuals. Give them the task of analysing the key people in the passages and their attitudes to David.

Part Three: The Beginnings and End of Saul's Kingship 323

- 1 Sam. 20:1-24a, 35–42
- 1 Sam. 20:24b-34
- 1 Sam. 21:1-9; 22:6-23
- 1 Sam. 21:10–22:5
- 1 Sam. 23:1-29

Back in the large group

Draw people together as a large group. Gather the names of the various people introduced in the passages and ask the groups or individuals to analyse their attitudes toward David. At the end, see if the group can analyse the various attitudes toward David presented in the passages. What are the various responses people have to him and are there common patterns?

Application

In the larger group, read the following passages and ask them to tell you what Malachi and Jesus expected would be the reactions that people would have as God fulfilled His purposes in His world through His Son.

- Mal. 4:4-6
- Luke 14:26-27
- Luke 9:57-62

Get people to share with each other the various reactions that their friends, or they have experienced themselves as followers of Jesus. Spend time praying that God would turn the hearts of their friends toward Jesus. Pray also for those experiencing persecution and trouble because of Jesus. Pray especially for those who live in countries or localities where faith in Jesus exposes people to persecution.

19.
Encounters in the Life of a Fugitive Anointed One
(1 Samuel 24:1–26:25)

Just imagine the picture in some part of the world, of a somewhat grumpy landowner shepherd with shearing needing to be done and men gathered together to do it. In the general vicinity, another bunch of wandering, landless, hungry, some probably disenfranchised soldiers, who have been on the run, fighting skirmishes and perhaps living in caves. Add an attractive and smart shepherd's wife. Finally, add a party at the end of the day's shearing, when alcohol would undoubtedly flow. It is a formula for trouble. This is something like that which is found in the centre of the three chapters that are the focus of this section and of the passage that your Bible Study or congregation will read this coming week.

Listening to the Text

Context and Structure
In the chapter immediately before our passage, we noticed a shift in focus. At the beginning of the chapter (vv. 1-6),

David and his soldiers are engaged in offensive measures against the Philistines and are victorious. In the second incident in the chapter, Saul hears of David's movements and plans an assault on an Israelite town where David and his men are staying (vv. 7-9). David then decides that he will move on from Keilah and begins a more peripatetic existence with his men (v. 13). Saul remains in regular pursuit, forming alliances with various groups on either side, but God does not surrender David up to Saul (v. 14), and even Philistine raids deter Saul's pursuit (vv. 26-29).

Chapter 24 picks up this note of David on the run with his men, and this theme becomes something of a focus in the three chapters that we examine here. Each chapter presents incidents that happen in the life of David as Saul pursues him. In each, he has an opportunity to exact vengeance on enemies and adversaries but refuses to take advantage of the situation.

Location

Given the distance of time and the fact that most of us probably lack knowledge of even the main geographical locations of David's wanderings, it is helpful for us to refresh our minds and get a big picture of where he is and when.

Back in chapter 22, David fled to Moab with his family and, together with him, they found shelter with the king of Moab, apparently only for as long as David was present in the Moabite stronghold himself (1 Sam. 22:4). After this, David moved to the forest of Hereth in Judah (22:5), which is probably identical to that identified as Horesh in 1 Sam. 23:15. This is probably located at the modern Khirbet Khoreisa, approximately ten kilometres southeast of Hebron.

Since chapter 22, we have heard of David going north to rescue Keilah (1 Sam. 23:1-6) before returning to the hill country in the wilderness of Ziph, then to Hereth/Horesh (1 Sam. 23:15), and then to the 'strongholds of Engedi' (1 Sam. 23:29). This is where Saul is told that David is in verse 1 of chapter 24.

In the rest of our three chapters we hear of David subsequently going down to the wilderness of Paran (1 Sam. 25:1), then back to the Desert of Maon and a particular property at Carmel (1 Sam. 25:1-2), before returning to the wilderness of Ziph (1 Sam. 26:1-4).

It should be noted that 'the wilderness of Paran' is some distance away, probably near the furthest and most southern parts of Judah (Kadesh Barnea, part of Judah is said to be located there; Num. 13:26; Josh. 15:3). The distance probably explains why some LXX manuscripts have replaced the 'wilderness of Paran' with the 'wilderness of Maon' (i.e. the wilderness area around Maon). However, given that the Hebrew reading is the more difficult and therefore the one most likely to be amended, it is probably the one to be preferred. Although some scholars baulk at the distance to the wilderness of Paran, we have already seen David travelling as far as Moab for his family and their safety (1 Sam. 22:3-4) and it could be that this is a brief visit after which he returns to the region of Maon. The map that follows shows the locations of the major places mentioned in the rest of the narrative.

Content
Encounter 1: At the cave of En Gedi (24:1-22)
David, with his men, has now been on the run from Saul for some time. In our chapters, we begin with David in

the Desert of En Gedi (1 Sam. 24:1). En Gedi is an oasis midway down the western coast of the Dead Sea. It is a place of vineyards and pleasant recollections (Song. 1:14), surrounded by the Judean wilderness which can be described as a 'dry and weary land where there is no water' (Ps. 63:1). It is also a place of caves that might provide cool and safe refuge (such as it did for David and his men) or even a place to relieve oneself, which is what Saul is seeking to do in verse 3 (the literal term, 'cover his legs' is a euphemism for emptying the bowels). King Saul and David are, therefore, thrown together by an act that could clearly be considered an act of divine providence (v. 4; cf. verse 10), a point taken up by his men and applied open-endedly (lit. 'according to what is good in your eyes'; v. 4), as though right is determined by circumstances.

As it happens, David acts with some degree of hesitancy and simply cuts off the corner of Saul's robe, which could be regarded as a garment of royalty (1 Sam. 18:4; cf. 15:27). However, the act then causes him to be 'conscience-stricken' (lit. 'the heart of David struck him'; perhaps more colloquially, he had heart palpitations), by which our author appears to indicate that some value deeply ingrained in the core of David's being has been threatened. David's own explanation to his men in verse 6 is that since Saul is the LORD's anointed (repeated twice), it is the LORD, not a human like him who must control his destiny. David, therefore, protects Saul and allows him to leave and go on his way.

After following Saul out of the cave, David calls out to him. When Saul turns to look around, David openly submits by prostrating himself and explaining what has just happened and why he acted the way he did. Saul's speech compares and contrasts what he has *heard* slanderously from others (v. 10) with what he can *see* for himself in David (once in verse 11, three times in verse 12: 'see ... look ... know and see'; once in verse 16: 'May he [the LORD] see...'). Saul's dissolution is then evident in verses 16-18 as he breaks down, weeps, acknowledges David's righteousness, and admits that prior to this he has only been able to admit in anger, that David 'will be king, and that the kingdom will be established in your hands' (v. 20).

The enduring point of the chapter is not simply David's innocence in relation to Saul but how deeply his values are ingrained in him. Not only did he refuse to kill 'the Lord's Messiah' but his conscience was sensitive to the point of giving him heart palpitations (vv. 5-6). Later, David will openly leave the whole issue of Saul and himself for God to oversee (1 Sam. 26:9-11).

Encounter 2: Nabal, David, Abigail and the Lord (25:1-44)

The death of Samuel (25:1a)

With Saul's acknowledgement about David made in the previous chapter, we are told of Samuel's death in the first verse of chapter 25. Having anointed David, his death is timely. All that remains now is for the kingdom to come to David, which will be the focus for the rest of 1 Samuel and through into 2 Samuel.

Nabal, David, Abigail and the Lord (25:1b-44)

An overview of the story

There are few people in 1 Samuel who survive our writer's critical 'pen'. The man we will meet in this chapter is certainly not one of them, although his wife comes out as one of the few who does seem to escape criticism. The best way ahead in terms of understanding the thrust and purpose of the chapter is to outline it and then see if we can make sense of the details.

First, the incidents here are set between two matching stories of Saul's pursuit of David, his failures, and David's

Part Three: The Beginnings and End of Saul's Kingship 331

reactions (chapters 24 and 26). Like those incidents, there are major figures well portrayed by the writer whose storytelling clearly draws us to weigh up and assess the characters. In this chapter, David we know. The second figure is 'a certain man in Maon' whose name was Nabal (Heb: 'foolish') and who 'was very wealthy' but 'surly and mean in his doings' (vv. 2-3). He has a wife called Abigail (Heb: '[my] father was delighted') who 'was an intelligent and beautiful woman' (v. 3).

Second, the encounter between the three figures is recounted at some depth and at significant length around the matter of shearing the sheep. David ensures the good behaviour of his men and looks for something 'favourable' from Nabal at a normally festive time (vv. 7-9). Nabal's response is to shun David's request for 'favour' by shunning it and belittling his standing (vv. 10-11). That, in turn, causes David to urge his men to 'Put on your swords!' and to march forth in apparent wrath with a focus on retaliation (vv. 12-13).

Third, when Abigail hears of what has happened, she perceives the risk and intervenes to placate David (vv. 18-31), interacting with him and constantly making use of the LORD's name, reminding him of the importance of avoiding having on his conscience 'the staggering burden of needless bloodshed or of having avenged himself' (v. 31). David acknowledges that her action has resulted in her keeping him from bloodshed and vengeance (v. 31) and he accepts the gifts she has brought, acknowledging that without her intervention 'not one male belonging to Nabal would have been left alive by daybreak' (32-35).

Fourth, Abigail returns home to find her husband 'in high spirits and very drunk' but then tells him of her actions the next day, at which point he appears to have some sort of heart failure or stroke from which he dies ten days later, which is said by the narrator to have been the Lord's doing (vv. 36-38).

Finally, David rejoices in his having been kept from sin, proposes marriage, and marries Abigail. This, added to his marriage to Ahinoam of Jezreel (of Judah? Cf. Josh. 15:5-56), may have strengthened his position politically in Judah.

The purpose of the story?

For the contemporary reader, the major question is the purpose of this seeming aside in the political and marital life of David. One possibility is that this story is sandwiched between two events that herald his blamelessness (1 Sam. 24:7; 26:11) and serves to demonstrate the fragility of David's accession and how easily it might be overthrown by his humanity. Another, perhaps arising from the almost fairy-tale beginning ('[There was] a certain man in Maon…'), is that we simply have the age-old story of a hero with a problem, a villain, a beautiful and wise woman who solves the problem and the expected marriage afterwards.[1]

However, perhaps more plausible than both is the suggestion by Vannoy, building on the work of Gordon, that the account is somewhat parabolic and proleptic. Through these events 'God was speaking to David about his future and telling David that he (God) would eventually take care of Saul just as he had already taken care of Nabal.'[2] Perhaps this is particularly important for David to know

---

1 Everett Fox, *The Early Prophets: Joshua, Judges, Samuel, and Kings: A New Translation with Introductions, Commentary, and Notes*, The Schocken Bible, Volume 2 (New York: Schocken Books, 2014), p. 394.

2. J. R. Vannoy, *1–2 Samuel*, CBC, 4a, p. 225.

Part Three: The Beginnings and End of Saul's Kingship   333

given that God's prophet is not here to counsel and advise God's king. This supplies a pattern for the Lord Jesus who will journey toward the cross amidst attempts by the evil one to turn Him away from the path that He must take in His allegiance to the Father.

Encounter 3: At the camp of Saul (26:1-25)

In some sense, chapter 26 is a mirror image of chapter 24. Intelligence comes to David concerning the whereabouts of Saul. He travels there, finds him and his men in a state of deep sleep that the LORD had put them into (v. 12). Abishai does some theological reflection as had similarly happened in chapter 24. However, this time David counters with God's known, revealed will:

> *But David said to Abishai, 'Don't destroy him! Who can lay a hand on the LORD's anointed and be guiltless? As surely as the LORD lives,' he said, 'the LORD himself will strike him; either his time will come and he will die, or he will go into battle and perish. But the LORD forbid that I should lay a hand on the LORD's anointed.' (1 Sam. 26:9-11a)*

Perhaps David has learnt from both the heart palpitations in chapter 24 and also the actions and words of Abigail about not having bloodguilt on his hands when he becomes king. As a result, they simply take the spear and water-jug. The spear appears to parallel the piece of Saul's robe in chapter 24 in that it functions as yet another symbol of Saul's rule (and of threat to David). It is also an item David is familiar with, having had it thrown at him in Saul's court.

In the midst of these and other similarities between chapters 24 and this one, there are also some striking differences. Some of the most significant are:

(1) Saul admits to having 'acted foolishly' and 'made a mistake' and acknowledges that David will inevitably succeed.

(2) David sought out this encounter rather than it happening as a mere 'chance'. Why?

(3) The focus falls on Abner rather than on Saul. Again, why?

The first difference is self-explanatory and clearly highlighted by the narrator. He is affirming what the astute reader already knows but adding depth to it.

The second difference—David seeking out this encounter—possibly lies in his focus on Abner, the third difference. One cannot help but wonder if David has sought to expose Abner's ineptitude in order to compare and contrast his own innocence. Abner has yet again failed in his protection of Saul but David is guiltless (as was demonstrated in his last encounter with him in chapter 24).

Listening to the Whole of Scripture

Looking Within

As we have often done, we should return to where we began in Samuel with a needy and barren woman unable to invent her own future and her dependence upon the LORD. She asks Him to 'give' and promises that she will 'give' Him back. The chapters that we have just examined have seen Samuel's death but not before he has anointed and guided the growing David as well as overseen his election, anointing and appointment.

These chapters have shown us examples of her prayer and its advice being both overthrown and followed. David has largely eschewed exalting himself and has, at his best, thrown himself dependently upon the LORD, and the Lord has exalted him. It has not been by his strength that he has prevailed. Moreover, those who have exalted themselves and opposed the LORD and His purpose in His Messiah have been shattered. Even in exile and on the run, God has given strength to His king and exalted the horn of His anointed.

Looking Back and Forward

There are some key theological themes that run through these chapters, some of which we have already highlighted. However, it will be helpful for us to highlight them here and to give them a little focus.

The innocence of David

The summary of these three situations is best provided by the person who is the focus of two of them: Saul. In the first incident, Saul acknowledges to David that 'you are in the right and I am not' (1 Sam. 24:18a).[3] In saying this, Saul means that the argument mounted by David is correct – David is righteous in terms of his actions toward others.

In the third incident (the second involving Saul directly), the narrator records Saul saying to David, 'May you be blessed, my son David; you will do great things and surely triumph' (1 Sam. 26:25). Our author has therefore structured these events so that the reader will hear clearly and unequivocally—at least about these three incidents—that David is innocent of caprice, manipulation, or machination. If the throne comes to him, it is not because of any guilt incurred by him.

---

3. So, Fokkelman, *Samuel Vol. 2*, p. 469. Fokkelman maintains that this is the correct reading, not found in the usual translations (although, see Tanakh, JPS, published in the previous year; 1985).

That said, the story in the middle involving Nabal, Abigail and David has significant allusions to the later incident with Bathsheba where bloodguilt does affect his kingship (2 Samuel 11:1–12:25). It thereby indicates that David is constantly under the threats God had warned about in relation to kings in Deuteronomy 17 and which Samuel had reiterated in 1 Samuel 8 and 12. He was blameless in relation to Saul. However, he will not be in relation to his own house, something the writer of kings will specifically acknowledge (1 Kings 15:5).

Such reflections point us forward to the Lord Jesus. As God's true Messiah, He is blameless where David is not. David may be a shadow, but Jesus is the reality.

Intimacy

From the beginning of our exposure to Saul, we have noticed the distance between him and the LORD and his reliance upon others in terms of relationship with the LORD (e.g. 1 Sam. 15:24-30). In contrast, David's relationship with the LORD seems intimate and not reliant on priests and priestly paraphernalia. David feels pangs of conscience over possible wrongdoing, thinks theologically and is protected from bloodguilt. He is a man who appears to know God, something reinforced by the psalms that are associated with his name in the Psalter and that refer to various incidents related to his time outside the court.

Again, these reflections provide a shadow of which Jesus is the reality. His intimacy with the Father is deep, direct and without flaw.

Threat and temptation

In these chapters, we have seen David under threat and temptation. This can be illustrated in at least two places.

The first involves a third party, is full of circumstantial logic, and even significant theological truth. In chapter 24 at En-Gedi, he is not searching for Saul and is given plausible theological reasons for thinking that he would be justified in dealing with Saul.

The second involves Nabal. Given Nabal's ingratitude, he could retaliate and be like Saul and exert his power as king. In this sense, he is under temptation constantly. However, while our narrator demonstrates this temptation, he also is at pains to indicate David's righteousness in his coming to the throne.

Jesus is Himself under temptation. However, He does not need to be rescued from sin by a wise woman. He is dependent upon His Father. He does war with Satan by living in submission to the Word of God and by following the path laid out for Him in Scripture. He is the true faithful human and the true and totally dependent Christ.

Protection

The humanity of David is shown in the middle story of our passage. He is capable of anger and would have exercised it if not for the intervention of Abigail or the Lord's intervention in sending a deep sleep upon Saul's army. As we will later see, without such interventions, he is entirely capable of sin and misuse of power. Perhaps by such mechanisms, our narrator is implicitly urging us even at this early stage to look for another who will succeed where David fails. Such a one will need to be without sin. In this way, the narrative of Samuel points us forward to Him who is without sin, the true anointed One before whom all heaven and earth will bow.

From Text to Message

As you can see from the above analysis, this passage opens up so many opportunities for preaching and it is hard to make decisions about which direction to take (and, to be very frank, I have taken a variety of approaches over years of preaching on it!).

Perhaps the best way forward might be to go with the notion of the blamelessness of David (despite his human failings). This passage as a whole seems to lay stress on that and on God's protection of him as he comes to the throne. A sermon based on this notion might pursue this throughout the passage and note that although David is not perfect in these chapters, he gets the right things right and in this manner is a type of the Lord Jesus.

Ways Into the Text

One way into the text might be to explore the question of the abuse of power. Some consider that the abuse of power or authority may be *the* prime source and true essence of moral evil. Why? Because it refuses to accept responsibility for the welfare of others, especially those under the abuser's direct care. You might point out that even if this thesis is an overstatement, the abuse of power is a significant evil in our society.

It would be good to give good, solid, and contemporary examples of the abuse of power and define what it looks like. You might then say that it exists at every level of social life in our world: international relationships, politics, families, the church, and wherever else human power exists. This would then lead you to say that our passages will help us understand how to think about and respond to the abuse of power.

Part Three: The Beginnings and End of Saul's Kingship 339

Moving Through the Text and Biblical Theology

Once you have introduced the topic, you would then work through chapters 24–26 using the major chapter divisions that we have noted (i.e. three chapters: 1 Samuel 24:1-22; 25:1-44; and 26:1-25). This would then allow you to use the more topical headings we have observed and used here as a means of summarising the main things learnt from the passages as well as pointing toward Jesus as the superior King. These are

- Innocence
- Intimacy
- Threat and temptation
- Protection

At the end of this section, you might add an additional biblical theological heading along the lines of 'A Theological Footnote'. Here you might emphasise what you hope people have already grasped, which is that even if this passage throws a good light on David as innocent, the rest of the books of Samuel will indicate that he is far from perfect. Two prime incidents bundled into one show this: (a) David's taking of Uriah's wife and (b) his abuse of power by having his army kill Uriah. These are not the only examples of David's shortcomings, but they are the best known and most easily demonstrated ones. This would then open the door to indicate that we need to look beyond David to another who will succeed where David fails. Jesus is the only human with these credentials. He is the true Messiah: Jesus *the* Christ.

Application

Often, preachers think that their job is done once they have pointed toward Jesus as the Christ. However, the text itself points us forward to other points of application, that is, other places where we can learn from the less than perfect behaviour of the people in these three chapters. One way to do this would be to return to the idea with which the sermon was begun, that is the abuse of power. You could then observe the places where abuse of power is evident in the passage just examined (e.g. David's men, David seeking to kill first and worry about God's concerns later, Saul's admitting of failures in this area, etc.).

This exploration might lead back to how each of these abuses of power are critiqued by Hannah's prayer in 1 Samuel 2. God seeks people who will not gain advantage by wielding and abusing power but by depending upon God. Jesus is like this. He does not rule with a fetish for power but on a cross, making Him a true human. This would then lead into urging people in whatever station of life they are in, to be like their Lord and to follow Him in the way of the cross, which has nothing to do with abusing power but empowering by service. This can then be applied to the major categories of people in your congregation (perhaps beginning with your own leadership!).

Leading a Bible Study

Introduction

As usual, remind people of the larger context of the book and the point we have reached. The critical things are that David is now on the run from Saul with his followers. We know that he will be king one day and so the emphasis is on what sort of king he will be.

Because of the various movements within the text, it may be helpful to show them a map with the main places on it. This will help those who are more visually oriented. You might also highlight the death of Samuel and its significance.

Observation (in smaller groups)

Assign the three major passages to different individuals or small groups and give them the task of assessing the main characters of their passage (it may be helpful for you to identify who they are and perhaps give some biodata about them). What is good about what they do? How does the author show us what is good? Who are they contrasted and compared with?

- 1 Sam. 24:1-22
- 1 Sam. 25:1-44
- 1 Sam. 26:1-25

Back together again

When you have people back together, ask them to identify the main characters in their passage. Where do they get things right? Where do they get things wrong? How do you know that they get things wrong? Are there any clues within the text that help evaluate the characters?

Pool the results. Since David is the common figure in all, it will be helpful to emphasise him. When doing so, particularly note where he gets things right and where he gets things wrong. Explore whether people think he is blameless or not.

[This next section could be done either as a large group or back in smaller groups.]

Take people back to Hannah's song. Read it through again and get participants to identify what is commended and what is not. Then get them to put the various characters through the grid of commended/not commended things. How do they measure up?

Application

This section could be done in a larger group or back in small groups. Give people the task of reading through Philippians 2:1-11 and identifying what attitudes are being commended here by the apostle Paul. What is their theological basis? How is the leadership of Jesus exemplary? How does it compare and contrast with the people that have been examined in 1 Samuel?

Spend time praying …

- Thanking God for Jesus, His willing service of others, His sacrificial death.
- That our lives might be characterised not by the failures we've seen in the characters in 1 Samuel but by those exemplified by Jesus.
- For the needs of each other and for our sacrificial support and encouragement of each other.

20.
David in Philistia
(1 Samuel 27:1–31:13)

Up until this point, the most chapters that we have tackled in one sermon or Bible study has been four chapters. However, the suggestion here is that five chapters be done together. The reason is that they contain much information and cover many incidents and are probably better understood from a 'big picture' perspective. They do cover some incidents that might need some more significant focus (e.g. Saul and the necromancer). However, such things are probably better addressed in separate sermons or Bible studies rather than in a series of expository sermons. If you consider five chapters to be too long, you might also consider dividing it into two or more (I have done it both as one and as two sermons at different times for different reasons).

Listening to the Text
Context and Structure
The context for these passages is clear and straightforward. Kingship has been on view from before Samuel. However, the first two chapters of 1 Samuel set the scene with a woman (Hannah) wanting children and requesting a child from the

LORD. Her attitude toward God and her prayer set the theological backdrop for the kingship that would follow, and which would be overseen by her child, Samuel. The first king was Saul, but he failed to be a king who lived under God's Word and dependent upon God, and as a result, was rejected as king by the LORD (chapter 15) and David was chosen to succeed him (chapter 16). However, that choosing of David is now ten chapters ago. In the chapters since, David has grown in age and stature. He is a king in the making and Saul is a king in decline. In the first chapter of our previous section, Saul acknowledges that David was more righteous than he (1 Sam. 24:17) and that he would replace him as king (1 Sam. 24:20). In the immediately preceding chapter to ours, he added that David 'will do great things and surely triumph' (1 Sam. 26:25).

Location

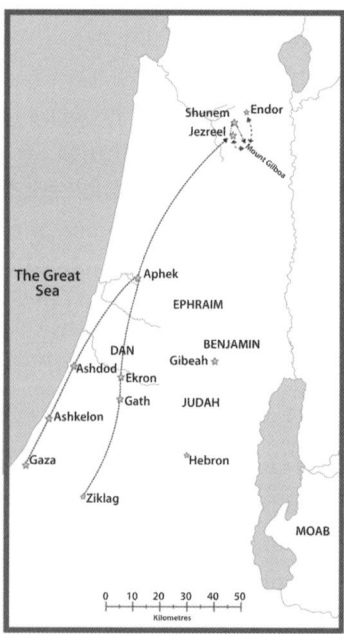

Part Three: The Beginnings and End of Saul's Kingship 345

Content
The notes below are necessarily brief. However, they are designed to highlight the key interpretative elements within the story that would need to be conveyed to hearers. They also assume that you have at least read the whole text in full and, hopefully, at least one secondary source that might help with interpretative matters.

David among the Philistines (27:1–28:2)

Chapter 27 speaks of the growing retinue, including David's household, his men (maybe as many as 600), and their families. Perhaps the sheer bulk of people made him consider a safe haven in Philistine territory with Achish, the son of Maoch, king of the Philistine city of Gath. The impact was as desired. Saul, upon hearing of his defection, 'no longer searched for him' (v. 4). David is then given the southern town of Ziklag, from which he and his men raid some traditional enemies of Israel in that area. It was a cunning move as it would undoubtedly have enhanced his reputation in his home tribe. However, while David was conducting raids on the *enemies* of Israel, he was telling Achish a different story: that he was conducting raids on *Israel herself* (v. 10). In order for the deception to work, David had to make sure that no one was left alive and the result was that Achish develops a significant trust in his vassal/servant (v. 12). However, the day inevitably came when David is invited to join a battle against his own people. His ploy had been so successful that Achish promises to make God's anointed one his bodyguard for life (1 Sam. 28:1-2). The scheming of David now threatens to capture him, at which point the narrator does not tell us David's response but holds us in suspense and switches the point of view back to Israel.

The 'necromancer' at Endor (28:3-25)

In verse 3, our narrator reminds us that Samuel the prophet is dead and that Saul had expelled the mediums and spiritists from the land. In other words, Saul is bereft of someone who might put him in touch with the supernatural (and we have had no hint that he was on familiar terms with spiritual things himself but rather, sought to rely on others; e.g. 1 Sam. 15:30-32). So, Saul turns to seek alternatives that he had set laws concerning (v. 7). The contrast with David is profound. Although God provides David readily with godly advisors and guides him by a variety of means, Saul is reduced to disguising himself, going to a necromancer, and requesting her to bring up Samuel (v. 11).[1] In any case, he has success, and Saul falls to the ground before Samuel (vv. 8-15).

When you are preaching on this passage, questions will abound in people's minds and perhaps will make their way to their mouths later. Whatever else is said, the following must be affirmed: (1) the narrator wants us to know that it is Samuel himself who speaks here – the clothing, manner, language and style are unmistakeable; and (2) there will be no relief for Saul since the Lord will hand both him and Israel to the Philistines on the coming day. The news devastates Saul, and in the apparent absence of any religious functionaries, he is looked after by this illegal outsider.

---

1 There is significant debate about what the phrase used here means (lit. 'a woman of a possessor/owner of a spirit/ghost'). Given that the words used not only have connotations of spirits and also of Baal, we might assume that none of it is good and it breaches a number of relevant laws for Israelites, not least the ones Saul himself has set. Hereafter she is broadly referred to as the 'necromancer'.

Part Three: The Beginnings and End of Saul's Kingship 347

David dismissed by the Philistines (29:1-11) [2]

Previously, the narrator left us hanging while we wondered about David and the Philistines. Now, after promising Saul's end, he takes us back to David again, where we remember his dilemma and delicate situation brought upon him because of his deception. As a result, he is at the beck and call of a Philistine commander and unable to help his people. David has clearly decided to continue the façade. He and his men march at the rear of the Philistine troops (v. 2). However, the rest of the Philistines raise the issue with Achish, referring to David and his men using the derogatory term 'Hebrews'. Achish defends him but the Philistine commanders reject any involvement by David, lest he 'turn against us during the fighting' and by fighting against the Philistines 'regain his master's favour' (v. 4). When the news is conveyed to David by Achish, he appears to feign disappointment and then return home.

Ziklag and the Amalekites (1 Samuel 30:1-31)
Amalek

The Amalekites are notorious in biblical history. They were the first to attack Israel after they had left Egypt (Deut. 25:17-19) and their behaviour caused the Lord to declare that he would blot out the remembrance of Amalek from under heaven and not forget. Saul was meant to deal with them in chapter 15 but failed.

---

2. It should be noted that it is possible that the author has, for thematic reasons, put events in other than chronological order in this chapter and the next. We will follow the order in which they are presented.

Distress (30:1-6)

In 1 Sam. 27:8, we were told that David had earlier raided the Amalekites and left none alive. It is possible that the actions described here by the Amalekites on David's Philistine town are retaliatory for that assault. However, where David left none alive, the Amalekites took captives here. The distress of David and his men is deep and long (v. 4), and talk begins about stoning David, which drives David to 'find strength in the LORD his God' (v. 6).

Dependence and success (30:7-20)

David's dependence upon God—in marked contrast to Saul—finds its focus in seeking God's will and Word through His priest, Abiathar. Such seeking of the LORD has been part of David's life in his banishment (e.g. 1 Sam. 23:2, 4) and, as we have seen, is tried by Saul but without success (v. 6). Moreover, it stays part of his life until he is entrenched as king (e.g. 1 Sam. 30:8; 2 Sam. 2:1; 5:19, 23), after which we do not hear of its use by David.

Once he has sought the LORD's advice, it is followed, and the result is as God indicates; they are successful. Everything is recovered and there is significant extra spoil (vv. 16-20).

The weak, taking, and giving (30:21-31)

On their rush to recover their families and goods, a third of David's band had been too weary to continue (vv. 9-10). On the return of the other two-thirds, David came forward and greeted them but some of his men, named by the narrator as 'evil men and troublemakers (v. 22), suggested that they be given their wives and children but not share in the plunder. As one with his men, David names them as 'brothers' but urges them to respond to God's generosity with their own toward their own; 'All will share alike.'

Moreover, he made it 'a statute and ordinance for Israel from that day to this' (v. 25). Here is a man growing into a king who does not 'take' (1 Sam. 8:11-17) but is 'one ... among ... brothers' (Deut. 17:14-20).

One cannot but wonder if our author has deliberately contrasted David and Saul in these chapters. On the one hand, there is the isolation of Saul from people and the LORD in 1 Sam. 28. On the other, there is David's consultation of God, the defeat of the enemies of God, and his presence among the people as a brother and one who makes laws that have the good of God's people in mind. In other words, the David we meet here is no longer a lad with enthusiasm, a sling and stone. He is a true shepherd of God's people, ready to take on the leadership of God's people in place of Saul. He has been forged by the wilderness, and as if to strengthen his claim, David sends gifts to the elders of Judah (v. 26) and those where he and his men had roamed (vv. 27-31).

These verses then present David as a type of our Lord, Jesus the Christ. Jesus strengthens Himself in weakness by turning to God, is concerned for the weak and poor, defeats the spiritual enemies of God and makes a public display of them on the cross (Col. 2:15) and scatters abroad His gifts to the poor (Ps. 112:9; Eph. 4:8).

The death of Saul and Jonathan (31:1-13)
Reflecting on a death
The contrasts between Saul and David in the previous chapters made it clear that it is only a matter of time before Saul will die and the kingdom will be given to David, his neighbour. The report, however, is short, simple, and solemn in its presentation:

> *Now the Philistines fought against Israel; the Israelites fled before them, and many fell slain on Mount Gilboa. The Philistines pressed hard after Saul and his sons, and they killed his sons Jonathan, Abinadab and Malki-Shua.*
> (1 Sam. 31:1-2)

Kings had been requested as a potent weapon against foreign aggression, particularly that posed by the Philistines. However, Saul finally dies at their hands. The only ones successful against the Philistines have proved to be those who allow God to fight for them and who are humbly dependent upon Him, as Hannah had suggested they should be.

We have seen Saul's isolation grow throughout his reign. It is now complete in his death as not even his armour bearer is willing to help him avoid the ignominy of abuse at the hand of the Philistines. In isolation, he takes his own life by falling on his sword. In the following verses, recognising what has happened, the Israelite army flees and the Philistine army occupies their houses. They desecrate the body of Saul, proclaim the good news to their people, and put Saul's armour in the temple of their gods. For readers of Samuel, this final note may provide a faint glimmer of hope. After all, they know that this is not the first time that such a thing has happened and that the last time it did, God fought for His glory and humbled His enemies.

Some echoes of Saul's life

The final chapter of 1 Samuel is full of pathos. It is also full of hints about his life. The first hint is the presence of the Philistines. 1 Samuel 8 clearly hinted that kingship was wanted in order to deal with the problems of such external enemies. They wanted a king like the other nations. He was, in many ways, a portrait of what they wanted. However, the larger, more powerful enemy they feared has been successful. His progeny lie dead as well. The Philistines look to have been victorious despite their king.

The second hint is the men of Jabesh Gilead. They recall for us the story of a foreign aggressor threatening to gouge out the eyes of their warriors. However, Saul empathised with their weakness, he was filled with the Spirit of God, burned with anger, marshalled the people and led them in a spectacular victory as God's anointed one. He was a man so full of potential and promise rightly remembered by these men.

Listening to the Whole of Scripture

As we contemplate the death of the first king of God's chosen people, it will be helpful for us to remember what we have done quite often, that is, the secret to kingship as laid out in Hannah's prophetic prayer. There could not be a clearer presentation of what is looked for: no arrogance, self-exaltation or pride; no glorying in strength but rather humility and dependence. It is, after all, not by strength that one prevails but it is the needy and humble that He seats with princes and causes to inherit a throne of honour.

With that in mind, we can read the Chronicler's assessment of Saul's kingship. In 1 Chronicles 10:13-14 he gives this assessment of Saul's death.

> *Saul died because he was unfaithful to the Lord; he did not keep the word of the Lord and even consulted a medium for guidance, and did not inquire of the Lord. So the Lord put him to death and turned the kingdom over to David son of Jesse. (1 Chron. 10:13-14)*

In the end, Saul's death was the result of his failure to be humble before God. He was unfaithful, did not heed the Word of God and sought other advice. He did not inquire of the Lord. Therefore, the Lord put him to death.

The rest of the books of Chronicles make clear that Saul was not alone. There were occasional kings who although not perfect *did* fear the Lord. David was one of those and Josiah another. However, they were very rare. The vast bulk followed in the footsteps of Saul. They did not fear the Lord and 2 Chronicles tells us where that ended up – with Israel in exile without a king (see 2 Chron. 36:15-21).

The New Testament points us to One better than David and Josiah. Quoting Psalm 40:6-8, the writer of the book of Hebrews says:

> *Therefore, when Christ came into the world, he said:*
> *'Sacrifice and offering you did not desire,*
> *but a body you prepared for me;*
> *with burnt offerings and sin offerings*
> *you were not pleased.*
> *Then I said, "Here I am—it is written about me in the scroll—*
> *I have come to do your will, O God."'*
> *(Heb. 10:5-7)*

From Text to Message

There are a number of ways that the preacher or teacher might go in terms of explaining or proclaiming this lengthy passage. At the heart of this passage is the comparison and contrast that develops between Saul and David. This comparison and contrast is focused on two key moments in the life of each man. For Saul, it is his desperation in seeking the advice of a necromancer in the absence of Samuel. He has lived without the Word of God or dependence upon God and so has nowhere to go but to the netherworld in an attempt to drag up the word of a prophet. For David, there is his marked dependence upon God which finds its focus in seeking God's will and Word and then reflecting God's grace to others in his rule and care for God's people.

Both men, therefore, give options for God's king but also for God's people in general. Godly kings will consistently do as David does at his best. Ungodly kings will be like Saul. In the end, however, what makes a godly or ungodly human is also true. This enables the message to be both full of Christ (the perfect King and Christ) but also full of advice on how to live rightly before God even as Jesus did, perfectly.

Suggestions for Preaching

Ways Into the Text

Funerals are sobering functions for most of us if we are thinking people. They help us to think about what is most valuable in life and because this passage focuses on the last days of King Saul it draws us in, to think of our own approach to life. For this reason, it seems entirely appropriate and probably quite helpful for the preacher or teacher to use the concept of thinking about the end of our lives.

One way into this might be to introduce the sermon or Bible study by getting people to come with you in their imagination to some indeterminate time in the future to their funeral. There are people from all walks of life there and you wonder what is going to be said.

If this is done well, and people are given time to think, then it will help them reflect on what is important to them and what they want to be known for in life. The value of this exercise can be reinforced with your hearers by noting that the writer of Ecclesiastes says that visiting funerals can be a wise thing to do. It's wise because it gives you a sober perspective from which to view life.

Such an introduction would lead well into introducing the passage as the climactic one in the story of Saul and would give hearers an opportunity to contemplate his life and therefore their own. Moreover, it may very well help us to consider how we ourselves might live in the light of our own impending death. Such introductions can't be done regularly but a passage such as ours lends itself to such usage.

Moving Through the Text

Moving through the text should be relatively straightforward, although the preacher would need to be efficient and try not to focus on the detail but on the major ideas of each major section of the passage, as have been demarcated above. If you are a person who likes using visual aids for people, then this passage can be helped by data projector slides that have well-presented maps of the major locations that are referred to within the text. Many commentaries or websites provide some good maps for such purposes, but it is best to go for the more minimalist versions of them rather than those which are full of distractions such as too many names, too many terrain details, and the like. Less is best in such maps. You are welcome to reproduce the one supplied with this chapter.

Part Three: The Beginnings and End of Saul's Kingship 355

Biblical Theology and Application

Under the heading of 'Listening to the Whole of Scripture,' there is a way ahead suggested for biblical theology and application. In the end, being a good king is all about being a good human. The same principles apply, that is, living humbly and obediently under the Word of God. Jesus is the ideal human and also the ideal king. No matter which direction you take, it is important to realise that good biblical theology does not end with 'the Jesus bit'. This tends to stress that Jesus is the 'yes and amen' to all the promises of God but does not tell people what difference this makes to the way that they live. Preachers need to help people do that in the same way that Scripture itself does. A good example can be found in most of the New Testament epistles which not only teach theology and biblical theology but also press on to explain what difference that theology makes to how people act.

Leading a Bible Study

Introduction

Before beginning the study, it will be good to ensure (again!) that people are familiar with the people and background. David was anointed king while Saul was still acting as king. David won the great victory over Goliath and ever since then just about everyone has come to love David, except for Saul and his men. He's even made friends with some of the Philistines and because of danger from Saul is now living in a place called Ziklag in Philistine territory to the south.

Give an overview of the five passages using the major themes. Tell them that there's been a lot of activity and so you have broken them into groups and want them to pretend that they are the ancient equivalent of newspaper reporters. You've been asked to give a report on exactly what has happened where and what the key people (and even ordinary people) are feeling about the key people and events. Identify the people you spoke to and what their feelings were. You should do so on the basis of information supplied in the text itself.

Observation (in smaller groups)

The major passages for investigation are as follows:

Passage	Possible people to speak to
1 Sam. 27:1–28:2	David, one of his wives, Achish, an imagined, mysteriously escaped Amalekite
1 Sam. 28:3-25	Saul, the 'necromancer' at Endor (about her business and what Samuel said)
1 Sam. 29:1-11	Achish, a Philistine commander, David, one of David's men
1 Sam. 30:1-31	Abiathar the priest, one of David's wives, David, one of the two hundred tired men, one of the others who went on to the village, one of the Amalekites.
1 Sam. 31:1-13	A Philistine warrior involved in the battle, an Israelite survivor, a Philistine soldier sent to strip the dead, one of the people of Jabesh Gilead.

Back together again

When you have people back together, go to each group of 'news reporters' and ask them to give a report on what they learnt, including things like what happened, who the 'good guys/girls' or 'bad guys/girls' were and what made you think that.

Ask the participants to particularly pool what they learnt about David and Saul from the people that they spoke to. What is commendable about each? What is not commendable? Who are the heroes?

If you are the leader, summarise findings and perhaps write them up on a whiteboard or the like. Particularly emphasise the things that the author of the book has highlighted in terms of what is good or bad about David or Saul.

Application

This section should probably be done back in small groups.

Invite people to discuss and report back on the whole of 1 Samuel and...

- Two or three ways in which David IS a model of Jesus who is to come
- Two or three ways in which David is NOT a model of Jesus
- What can we learn as Christians from these passages in terms of how to live rightly before God as people who follow Jesus and want to please Him and the Father?

Spend time in groups of two or three praying for each other about these things.

Further Reading

Helpful reading for Preachers and Teachers of 1 Samuel.

While specific commentaries and other helpful books are mentioned in footnotes throughout, the following books are useful for preachers and teachers (with a particular focus on 1 Samuel).

Introductory Books on Expository Preaching

Adam, Peter, *Speaking God's Words: A Practical Theology of Expository Preaching*. Vancouver: Regent, 2004.

Millar, J. Gary, and Campbell, Phil., *Saving Eutychus: How to Preach God's Word and Keep People Awake*. Kingsford, Australia: Matthias Media, 2013.

Commentaries for Preachers and Teachers

Baldwin, Joyce G., and Wiseman, D. J., *1 and 2 Samuel: An Introduction and Commentary*. TOTC, v. 8. Nottingham, England, Downers Grove, Ill.: InterVarsity Press, 2008.

Bergen, Robert D., *1, 2 Samuel*. NAC, v. 7. Nashville, Tenn: Broadman & Holman, 2002.

Chisholm, Robert B., *1 and 2 Samuel: Teach the text commentary*. Eds. Mark L. Strauss, John H. Walton, and Rosalie D. Rosset. TTCS. Grand Rapids, Michigan: Baker Books, 2013.

Davis, Dale R., *1 Samuel: Looking on the heart*. Focus on the Bible. Fearn, Ross-shire, Scotland: Christian Focus, 2007.

Leithart, Peter J., *A Son to Me: An Exposition of 1 & 2 Samuel*. Moscow, ID: Canon, 2003.

Reid, Andrew, *1 and 2 Samuel: Hope for the Helpless*. Reading the Bible today. Sydney South: Aquila Press, 2008.

Tsumura, David T., *The First Book of Samuel*. NICOT. Grand Rapids, Mich.: Eerdmans, 2009.

Vannoy, J. R., *1–2 Samuel*. CBC, Carol Stream, IL, 2009.

Woodhouse, John, *1 Samuel: Looking for a Leader*. Ed. R. K. Hughes. Preaching the Word. Wheaton, Illinois: Crossway Books, 2008.

About The Proclamation Trust

The Proclamation Trust is all about unashamedly preaching and teaching God's Word the Bible. Our firm conviction is that when God's Word is taught, God's voice is heard, and therefore our entire work is about helping people engage in this life-transforming work.

We have three strands to our ministry:

Firstly we run the Cornhill Training Course which is a three-year, part-time course to train people to handle and communicate God's Word rightly.

Secondly we have a wide portfolio of conferences we run to equip, enthuse and energise senior pastors, assistant pastors, students, ministry wives, women in ministry and church members in the work God has called them to. We also run the Evangelical Ministry Assembly each summer in London which is a gathering of over a thousand church leaders from across the UK and from around the world.

Thirdly we produce an array of resources, of which this book in your hand is one, to assist people in preaching, teaching and understanding the Bible.

For more information please go to www.proctrust.org.uk

978-1-5271-0533-1

Teaching Mark

Robin Sydserff

Mark's gospel is a book that we think we know. It appears straight forward, fast paced and simple. However anyone who has spent any time engrossed in its pages will be aware that under the surface there is great depth and profundity. Robin has written *Teaching Mark* to help the preacher and teacher in the study to not just skim the surface of this life changing account but to go deep and see what is really there.

Robin Sydserff has preached through Mark three times in the last 10 years and taught this material in a variety of other contexts – it shows! He not only has a deep knowledge and love of the text but an infectious passion for the Lord Jesus Christ Himself. Mark's gospel is familiar to many but Teaching Mark *will help any bible study leader or preacher to hear God's voice more clearly and to teach His word more faithfully. It will inspire many to preach Christ and Him crucified from this great gospel!*

Paul Clarke
Senior Minister, St Andrews Free Church, Scotland

978-1-5271-0157-9

Teaching 2 Kings

Bob Fyall

2 Kings begins with the succession of Elijah by Elisha and flows largely downward right up to the exile of Judah in Babylon. Amidst the numerous kings and serious failings there are always the vital signs that the true God is still on the throne and working out his purposes in his people and beyond.

Like many other books containing Old Testament narrative, 1 and 2 Kings are both well–known and obscure. Certain stories are very familiar, others seldom preached or taught. It is our hope that this book will greatly help many people dig deeply into this epic narrative and serve people well by teaching it faithfully, relevantly and thoroughly.

Here Bob Fyall takes you into his workshop, or better, clinic, and teaches you to feel the pulse (or is it electric current?) of the narratives in 2 Kings. Telling applications often jump out from his observations, and, even if you miss those, the leading questions are lasered in on all the essential matters that will open up the text. Timid souls who, either from fear or lethargy have avoided preaching from 2 Kings, are now 'without excuse.'

Dale Ralph Davis
Respected Author and Old Testament Scholar

978-1-5271-0563-8

Teaching 2 Peter & Jude

Angus MacLeay

The books of 2 Peter and Jude are some of the least preached in the New Testament. However, these dynamic little books have an important message to be declared to the church in the 21st century. The need to 'contend for the faith' is vital in a confusing church landscape of compromise, pragmatism and drift. These books are dense and brimming with truth and so our hope is that this book helps you see all that is contained within their pages.

Teaching 2 Peter and Jude is a great addition to the growing 'Teaching the Bible' series. It will be a great aid to those who have the privilege and joy of teaching or preaching these particular books. Whether you are a small group leader, preacher, youth worker or someone who simply want help with their personal Bible study, this book will help you to comprehend and communicate the messages of 2 Peter and Jude.

The study embodies exactly the qualities it seeks to enable: humble listening to God's Word, wrestling with the literary structure, big idea, aim, illustration and application, a willingness to contend for the faith, a contending that is biblical in shape, tone and purpose, a fresh focus on the Lord Jesus Christ, a sustained determination to grow in knowledge of Christ, seasoned with wholesome realism about the ever present danger from false teaching. Every preacher will appreciate such prayerful wisdom, and the fruit from decades of preaching that lie behind a book of this quality.

Johnny Juckes
President, Oak Hill College, London

Christian Focus Publications

Our mission statement —

STAYING FAITHFUL

In dependence upon God we seek to impact the world through literature faithful to His infallible Word, the Bible. Our aim is to ensure that the Lord Jesus Christ is presented as the only hope to obtain forgiveness of sin, live a useful life and look forward to heaven with Him.

Our books are published in four imprints:

CHRISTIAN FOCUS

Popular works including biographies, commentaries, basic doctrine and Christian living.

CHRISTIAN HERITAGE

Books representing some of the best material from the rich heritage of the church.

MENTOR

Books written at a level suitable for Bible College and seminary students, pastors, and other serious readers. The imprint includes commentaries, doctrinal studies, examination of current issues and church history.

CF4•K

Children's books for quality Bible teaching and for all age groups: Sunday school curriculum, puzzle and activity books; personal and family devotional titles, biographies and inspirational stories — because you are never too young to know Jesus!

Christian Focus Publications Ltd,
Geanies House, Fearn, Ross-shire,
IV20 1TW, Scotland, United Kingdom.
www.christianfocus.com